GOOD NEWS
for the millions of followers
of low-carbohydrate diets

Nearly a million readers of *The All-in-One Carbohydrate Gram Counter* can attest to the advantages
of having such a valuable source at their fingertips.
Now, well-known nutrition expert, Jean Carper has
completely revised and updated this book with the
latest information available from food manufacturers and the U.S. Department of Agriculture.
This convenient and important handbook contains
over 5,500 entries on just about every kind of food
imaginable—including the food served in top res-
taurant chains.

AN INVALUABLE BOOK
IF YOU ARE CONCERNED
ABOUT YOUR WEIGHT.

The
All-In-One
Carbohydrate
Gram Counter

Revised Edition

By Jean Carper

BANTAM BOOKS
TORONTO · NEW YORK · LONDON · SYDNEY

THE ALL-IN-ONE CARBOHYDRATE GRAM COUNTER
*A Bantam Book | published by arrangement with
Workman Publishing Co., Inc.*

PRINTING HISTORY
Bantam edition | November 1973

2nd printing	.... April 1974	6th printing	.... June 1976
3rd printing	.. December 1974	7th printing	.... January 1977
4th printing	.... May 1975	8th printing	.. September 1977
5th printing	.... March 1976	9th printing	...... January 1978
	10th printing	.... January 1979	

Revised Bantam edition | August 1980

ISBN 0–553–13977–0

Published simultaneously in the United States and Canada

PRINTED IN THE UNITED STATES OF AMERICA

0 9 8 7 6 5

Contents

Introduction

There are any number of reasons why you might want to know how much carbohydrate you're consuming. There are two types of carbohydrates: simple carbohydrates or sugars and complex carbohydrates or starches found in such foods as grains and vegetables.

It's been known for years that sugar rots the teeth, and there has been some evidence—by no means conclusive—that sugar might be implicated in chronic diseases such as heart trouble. Some persons have an inborn metabolic intolerance to sugar; some develop diabetes. And even perfectly normal people can experience attacks of trembling and headaches after eating too much sugar. It seems medically certain that people vary in their response to sugar. As Dr. Jesse Roth of the National Institute of Arthritis and Metabolic Diseases has said, a person should learn his or her individual capacity for simple carbohydrates just as a person learns his capacity for alcohol. Some people can simply tolerate sugar better than others.

On the other hand, some people want to know which foods have complex carbohydrates because they want to eat *more* of them, to get the vitamins, minerals and fiber found in so-called starchy foods.

But all that aside, there's another whopping reason that most people want to know the carbohydrate counts of food. That's so they can *restrict* carbohydrates to *lose weight*. Some persons who never seem to lose weight by counting calories achieve amazing success on one of the several low-carbohydrate diets that have sprung up lately—although such diets are not really new (the first one appeared in the 1880s). As explained in books and magazines, there are many variations on the low-carbohydrate diet theme: the Drinking Man's Diet, Dr. Stillman's Quick Weight Loss Diet, and of course the sensational best seller, *Dr. Atkins' Diet Revolution*. Undeniably, some dieters simply find low-carbohydrate diets in which they can eat certain calorie-laden foods with impunity pleasanter and more effective than counting calories. You may be one of these.

Presumably, if you are following a low-carbohydrate diet you already know the rules of your specific diet and are committed to losing weight. So there is no use wasting your time by telling you all the reasons you should lose weight or the horrible things that will happen to you if you don't. If you're embarked on or are contemplating a low-carbohydrate diet, all you need to know now is what foods you can safely eat so as not to exceed the carbohydrate limit you have set for yourself. And that's where this book will help you.

In it you'll find the latest information on how many grams of carbohydrate there are in all kinds of foods —both fresh and processed (the latter by brand name, of course). We have included not only the usual brands but also the "house-brand" names of the A & P and Safeway Supermarkets, such as Ann Page from A & P and Lucerne from Safeway. (Other supermarkets contacted did not have such information or did not wish to publicize it.)

And there's a whole special section on fast-foods— everything from Big Mac's to Dairy Queen sundaes— valuable information not found in any other popular book, to my knowledge.

A word about the figures in the book: This book was first published in 1973, and has been an enormous success. Dozens of people have written to say how much it helped them to lose weight. It has sold over half a million copies. Since the original publication, some of the carbohydrate counts have changed due to new analyses or reformulation of products, and new products have been introduced. Thus, new figures were gathered in 1979 for this complete revision. Of course, some of the carbohydrate counts are the same or similar, since the carbohydrate grams in many basic foods such as milk, cheese, bread, as well as alcoholic drinks, don't change much. And a few companies did not have any new information. But I would estimate that two-thirds to three-fourths of the figures are brand new. For example, the baby food companies have eliminated most or all of the sugar in their fruits and vegetables, in some cases reducing the carbohydrate count in a jar of baby foods by 100 per cent. Many companies now have their products analyzed in a laboratory instead of "calculating" the carbohydrates from the food's recipe as they did in the past. That means in some cases slightly altered figures.

All of the figures bearing brand names in this book were provided by food companies and are the latest the company had available. If some of your favorite products are missing, it is because the company does not have the information or did not provide it.

In some cases the information from the company has been translated from 100 gram units or other serving sizes (for example, to one slice of bacon or one slice of bread) to make it easier for you. This translation may account for some minor variations in figures.

Within the last few years many more companies have started putting nutritional information on their products, although they are not required by the federal government to do so, unless they make specific nutritional claims for the food. However, if they do label, they must provide the information in a standardized form. Still, it is difficult to make comparisons among various brand name foods without running all around the supermarket. Thus, another benefit of this book: you can pick out the lower carbohydrate items *before* you go shopping.

Most carbohydrate counts should remain exceedingly stable over the years. However, occasionally a food-maker will change the composition of a product, severely changing the carbohydrate count. For example, during the lifetime of this book, some soft drink companies came out with saccharin-sweetened soft drinks that slashed the sugar and thus the carbohydrate count to virtually nothing. Diet Rite, for example, instead of having 12 grams per 8 fluid ounces, as listed in the book, had none—and advertised this fact. Many readers wrote in to ask which was correct.

This happens only rarely, but in such cases of conflict, you can believe the carbohydrate information on the food label. The accuracy of a food company's labeling is regulated by the federal Food and Drug Administration, and a company would be subject to severe penalties for putting out a label that is grossly inaccurate.

Also some manufacturers have asked me to point out that their figures are the best average calculations or analyses they have on specific products, but because of normal variations beyond their control, there may be ever-so-slight variations from batch to batch from the same manufacturer. Even such factors as seasonal conditions or soil composition may influence final food nutritional values.

All of the gram counts without any brand name or company attribution are from the U. S. Department of Agriculture. And here, too, some calculations were done to make sure the figures were in the most convenient form.

To sum up, the new revised All-In-One Carbohydrate Gram Counter will provide you with the latest, most accurate data available about fresh foods, processed foods, and fast-foods.

Jean Carper
January, 1980

How To Use
This Book

The most important organizational fact about the *All-in-One Carbohydrate Gram Counter,* as you will quickly see, is that it is alphabetized for easy use according to food categories. That is, you don't have to look in the front of the book under B for bean soup and then flip to the T's to find out if tomato soup is lower in carbohydrate count. It runs through the alphabet, starting with appetizers and ending with yogurt. All the breads are listed together in the B section, all the fruits are grouped together under F, the vegetables under V, and so on. Simply by looking at the Table of Contents in the front of the book, you can quickly spot which category a food is in and turn directly to that section. You'll then find the foods alphabetized within the sections. Some foods, to be sure, just don't fit easily into categories, and rather than force them into some artificial grouping, we've listed them alphabetically too, even though there may be only one or two of a kind; for example, baking powder and cornstarch have listings of their own. And for the first time we've included a special Fast Foods section at the end of the book.

In other words, the book is akin to a dictionary—with headings at the top of each page, too, to help you out. If you get stuck and can't decide where a food might be, just consult the index.

We have tried to standardize the language and food serving sizes as much as possible to make them useful, but here again we haven't strained the point. We have tried to be realistic. For example, under cereals, you won't find all of them in either 1-cup or ½-cup portions. The reason: simply because they are not really comparable. A person may easily sit down to a full cup of puffed rice, but rarely to a full cup of the heavier All-bran. A more realistic portion for bran is ⅓ of a cup. Therefore, we have followed the manufacturers' recommendations and provided single serving sizes they believe appropriate.

For some items, for example, frozen pies, we've given the carbohydrate content for the entire pie. Often the producer provides the information in portions of ⅛ of a pie. But it seemed to us that a person who wanted to eat only ⅛ of a pie when we had given figures for only a ⅛ wedge would have to go through the laborious procedure of first figuring out the total carbohydrate content of the whole pie and then dividing by eight. Consequently we've stated the gram count of the entire pie. A person can then cut it anyway he wants and figure accordingly; he's not tied down to a single serving size arbitrarily decided by us.

Whenever you see the word "prepared" the figures are based on the assumption that the food has been prepared according to the manufacturer's directions. If you alter the preparation, for example, by adding meat drippings instead of water to a gravy mix or using milk when water is called for on the package or adding other embellishments of your own, you must figure these extras in. Whenever milk is called for in a preparation, we assume it is whole milk—not skim or nonfat or condensed milk. If you use any of the latter —either raising or lowering the carbohydrate content in the finished product—you will have to make provision for it.

In most cases companies prefer to tell you how many carbohydrate grams are in the finished prepared product—for example, a cup of pudding from pudding mixes, because it's rare that the powder would be used in any other way. But in some instances you will find the gram count for the dry mix only—*before* preparation. That way, if you want to add another ingredient to your mix, you're free to do so and add up the extra carbohydrates. Also on this note: whenever you merely add water to a mix, you're not adding carbohydrates—for example, when you make a Lipton's soup. If you use the dry soup mix in any other fashion, say as a dip mix, you have the same carbohydrate count in the dry mix as in the cup of prepared soup.

In keeping with our determination to make this book easy to use, we've taken due note of the power of identity of brand names. Whenever possible, without interfering with the organization, we've used brand names for quick identification. Thus, when you look up a certain cookie, cracker or cereal, you don't have to peruse the whole list searching for a description of your cookie. We don't have Cheez-Its listed under "crackers, cheese"; we have it simply alphabetized under Cheez-Its. And we have Oreo cookies under O and not under "chocolate creme sandwich." The same goes for Frankenberry cereal (under F in the cereal section). Of course, it was not always possible to do this without creating a chaotic organization, and in many cases the only identifying factor is a description of the product (chocolate chip cookies, for example) and the name of the manufacturer.

Within the listings, we repeat the measurements frequently, even though they are the same, rather than place the portion size at the head of a section which may be a page or two back. However, on items like cookies and crackers and frozen "TV" dinners, where the portion size is not confusing—one cookie or cracker or a complete dinner—we've simply noted the portion at the head of the section. This has also been done on fairly short listings.

To avoid confusion, whenever possible, we have stated the measurement in the most easily used terms: cups and tablespoons and fluid ounces for liquids and items such as canned fruits and vegetables; and weight ounces for items like cheese and frozen fish fillets. In the latter case, by noting the number of weight ounces on the package and the number of ounces for the gram count in the book, you can figure out how many carbohydrate grams there are in the portion you have chosen to eat. That is, if a package of frozen eggplant Parmesan weighs 5½ ounces and contains 21 carbohydrate grams and you eat half the package, you have eaten 10.5 grams of carbohydrate.

Despite our best efforts, there's no way we can save you from doing some figuring on your own, simply because no one, including yourself, wants to eat the same amount of a certain food at every sitting. And, of course, when you use your own recipes, there's no way possible that we could give figures on the finished product, because home recipes vary greatly just as do recipes for commercially prepared foods. If you're whipping up your own tapioca pudding, we can tell you how many carbohydrate grams are in the dry tapioca, in the eggs, milk and sugar, and you'll have to take it from there. Only you know how much of an ingredient you really use.

For doing your own conversions, here's an equivalency table that may be of help:

1 tablespoon = 3 teaspoons
2 tablespoons = 1 fluid ounce
4 tablespoons = ¼ cup
5⅓ tablespoons = ⅓ cup
16 tablespoons = 1 cup
1 cup = 8 fluid ounces
     = ½ pint
2 cups = 1 pint
2 pints = 1 quart
1 pound = 16 ounces

Happy gram counting!

Abbreviations

art	artificial
diam	diameter
fl	fluid
in	inch
lb	pound
med	medium
oz	ounce
pkg	package
swt	sweetened
tbsp	tablespoon
tsp	teaspoon
unswt	unsweetened
w	with
wo	without

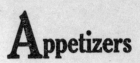Appetizers

	GRAMS
Frozen	
Cheese straws: 1 piece / **Durkee**	1
Frankfurter: 1 piece / **Durkee** Franks-n-Blankets	1
Puff pastry: 1 piece	
Beef puffs / **Durkee**	3
Cheese puffs / **Durkee**	3
Chicken puffs / **Durkee**	3
Chicken liver puffs / **Durkee**	3
Shrimp puffs / **Durkee**	3

Baby Food

BAKED GOODS

	GRAMS
Biscuits, teething: 1 piece / **Gerber**	9
Cookies, animal shaped: 1 cookie / **Gerber**	4
Cookies, arrowroot: 1 cookie / **Gerber**	4
Pretzels: 1 pretzel / **Gerber**	5
Toast, zwieback: 1 piece / **Gerber**	5

STRAINED BABY FOODS

Cereal: 1 jar

High protein w apples and bananas / **Heinz**	26
High protein w applesauce and bananas / **Gerber**	20
Mixed w apples and bananas / **Heinz**	20
Mixed w applesauce and bananas / **Beech-Nut**	19.2
Mixed w applesauce and bananas / **Gerber**	24
Mixed w fruit / **Beech-Nut**	26
Oatmeal w apples and bananas / **Heinz**	22
Oatmeal w applesauce and bananas / **Gerber**	20
Oatmeal w fruit / **Beech-Nut**	17.6
Rice w apples and bananas / **Beech-Nut**	19.4
Rice w apples and bananas / **Heinz**	24
Rice w applesauce and bananas / **Gerber**	26

3

Cereal, dry: ½ oz

Barley / **Gerber**	11
Barley / **Heinz**	11
High protein / **Gerber**	6
High protein / **Heinz**	7
High protein w apple and orange / **Gerber**	8
Mixed / **Gerber**	10
Mixed / **Heinz**	10
Mixed w banana / **Gerber**	11
Oatmeal / **Gerber**	10
Oatmeal / **Heinz**	10
Oatmeal w banana / **Gerber**	10
Rice / **Gerber**	11
Rice / **Heinz**	11
Rice w banana / **Gerber**	11

Formula, meat base: 2 tbsp / **Gerber**
Infant Formula   4

Fruits and Desserts: 1 jar

Apple betty / **Beech-Nut**	16.9
Apple blueberry / **Gerber**	21
Apple raspberry / **Gerber** Strained Fruits	21
Apples and apricots / **Beech-Nut**	14
Apples and cranberries w tapioca / **Heinz**	31
Apples and pears / **Heinz**	17
Applesauce	
Beech-Nut	15.2
Gerber	14
Heinz	16
and apricots / **Gerber**	28
and apricots / **Heinz**	25
and cherries / **Beech-Nut**	17.6
w pineapple / **Gerber**	13
and raspberries / **Beech-Nut**	14.5
Apricots w tapioca / **Beech-Nut**	15.7
Apricots w tapioca / **Gerber**	23
Apricots w tapioca / **Heinz**	18

GRAMS

Bananas
    w pineapple / **Beech-Nut** — 17.1
    w pineapple and tapioca / **Gerber** — 24
    w pineapple and tapioca / **Heinz** — 21
    w tapioca / **Beech-Nut** — 15.9
    w tapioca / **Gerber** — 22
    w tapioca / **Heinz** — 23
Cottage cheese w pineapple / **Gerber** — 22
Dutch apple dessert / **Gerber** — 24
Fruit dessert / **Gerber** — 23
Fruit dessert / **Heinz** — 21
Fruit dessert w tapioca / **Beech-Nut** — 15.9
Hawaiian delight / **Gerber** — 26
Orange-pineapple dessert / **Beech-Nut** — 15.6
Peach cobbler / **Gerber** — 25
Peach cobbler / **Heinz** — 25
Peach melba / **Beech-Nut** — 14.2
Peaches / **Beech-Nut** — 13.5
Peaches / **Gerber** — 26
Peaches / **Heinz** — 30
Pears
    Beech-Nut — 15.7
    Gerber — 15
    Heinz — 18
    and pineapple / **Beech-Nut** — 18.5
    and pineapple / **Gerber** — 14
    and pineapple / **Heinz** — 18
Pineapple dessert / **Beech-Nut** — 16.1
Pineapple-orange dessert / **Heinz** — 21
Plums w tapioca / **Beech-Nut** — 18.5
Plums w tapioca / **Gerber** — 28
Plums w tapioca / **Heinz** — 18
Prunes w tapioca / **Beech-Nut** — 26.2
Prunes w tapioca / **Gerber** — 25
Prunes w tapioca / **Heinz** — 27
Pudding
    Cherry vanilla / **Gerber** — .24

	GRAMS
Custard / **Heinz**	18
Custard, apple / **Beech-Nut**	17.1
Custard, chocolate / **Gerber**	23
Custard, vanilla / **Gerber**	21
Orange / **Gerber**	26
Tutti-frutti / **Heinz**	24

Juices: 1 can

Apple / **Beech-Nut**	12.8
Apple / **Gerber**	16
Apple / **Heinz**	15
Apple-cherry / **Beech-Nut**	11.6
Apple-cherry / **Gerber**	15
Apple-cherry / **Heinz**	15
Apple-grape / **Beech-Nut**	13.3
Apple-grape / **Gerber**	16
Apple-grape / **Heinz**	19
Apple-peach / **Gerber**	15
Apple-plum / **Gerber**	16
Apple-prune / **Heinz**	16
Mixed fruit / **Beech-Nut**	14
Mixed fruit / **Gerber**	15
Orange / **Beech-Nut**	12.7
Orange / **Gerber**	14
Orange / **Heinz**	15
Orange-apple / **Beech-Nut**	12.8
Orange-apple / **Gerber**	16
Orange-apple-banana / **Gerber**	15
Orange-apple-banana / **Heinz**	17
Orange-apricot / **Gerber**	15
Orange-banana / **Beech-Nut**	13.4
Orange-pineapple / **Beech-Nut**	13
Orange-pineapple / **Gerber**	16
Prune-orange / **Beech-Nut**	15.1
Prune-orange / **Gerber**	21

GRAMS

Main Dishes: 1 jar

Beef	
Beech-Nut	.2
Beech-Nut High Meat Dinner	7.4
Gerber	0
w beef hearts / **Gerber**	1
and noodles / **Beech-Nut**	9.7
and noodles w vegetables / **Gerber**	9
w vegetables / **Gerber**	
High Meat Dinner	7
Cereal and egg yolks / **Gerber**	9
Cereal, egg yolks and bacon / **Beech-Nut**	8.5
Cereal and eggs / **Heinz**	11
Chicken	
Beech-Nut	.4
Beech-Nut High Meat Dinner	9
Gerber	0
Noodle / **Beech-Nut**	10
Noodle / **Gerber**	9
w vegetables / **Beech-Nut**	9.7
w vegetables / **Gerber**	
High Meat Dinner	7
Cottage cheese w bananas / **Heinz**	19
Cottage cheese w pineapple / **Gerber**	
High Meat Dinner	28
Egg yolks / **Beech-Nut**	.6
Egg yolks / **Gerber**	1
Egg yolks / **Heinz**	1
Grits w egg yolks / **Gerber**	10
Ham	
Beech-Nut	.2
Beech-Nut High Meat Dinner	7.4
Gerber	1
w vegetables / **Gerber**	
High Meat Dinner	8
Lamb / **Beech-Nut**	.2

GRAMS

Lamb / **Gerber**	0
Liver, beef / **Gerber**	2
Macaroni and cheese / **Gerber**	10
Macaroni, tomato sauce, beef / **Beech-Nut**	10.6
Macaroni w tomatoes and beef / **Gerber**	11
Pork / **Gerber**	0
Soup, chicken, cream of / **Gerber**	11
Turkey	
Beech-Nut	.2
Beech-Nut High Meat Dinner	8.1
Gerber	0
and rice / **Beech-Nut**	11.6
and rice w vegetables / **Gerber**	9
w vegetables / **Gerber**	
High Meat Dinner	8
Veal	
Beech-Nut	.2
Beech-Nut High Meat Dinner	7.2
Gerber	0
w vegetables / **Gerber**	
High Meat Dinner	8
Vegetables	
and bacon / **Beech-Nut**	9.2
and bacon / **Gerber**	12
and beef / **Beech-Nut**	11
and beef / **Gerber**	8
and chicken / **Gerber**	8
and ham / **Beech-Nut**	10.7
and ham / **Gerber**	9
and lamb / **Beech-Nut**	9.6
and lamb / **Gerber**	9
and liver / **Beech-Nut**	9.5
and liver / **Gerber**	9
and turkey / **Gerber**	9

Vegetables: 1 jar

Beans, green / **Beech-Nut**	7.4

GRAMS

Beans, green / **Gerber**	7
Beans, green / **Heinz**	6
Beets / **Gerber**	10
Beets / **Heinz**	9
Carrots / **Beech-Nut**	7
Carrots / **Gerber**	7
Carrots / **Heinz**	12
Corn, creamed / **Beech-Nut**	18.9
Corn, creamed / **Gerber**	15
Corn, creamed / **Heinz**	19
Garden vegetables / **Beech-Nut**	10.9
Garden vegetables / **Gerber**	7
Mixed / **Gerber**	10
Mixed / **Heinz**	10
Peas / **Beech-Nut**	12.4
Peas / **Gerber**	8
Peas, creamed / **Heinz**	10
Spinach, creamed / **Gerber**	7
Squash / **Beech-Nut**	6.7
Squash / **Gerber**	8
Squash / **Heinz**	12
Sweet potatoes / **Beech-Nut**	16.5
Sweet potatoes / **Gerber**	21
Sweet potatoes / **Heinz**	19

Yogurt: 1 jar

w mixed fruit / **Beech-Nut**	17.1
w peach-apple / **Beech-Nut**	15.3
w pineapple / **Beech-Nut**	18

JUNIOR BABY FOODS

Cereal: 1 jar

Mixed cereal w applesauce and bananas / **Gerber**	40
Oatmeal w applesauce and bananas / **Gerber**	35
Rice cereal w mixed fruit / **Gerber**	40

GRAMS

Fruits and Desserts: 1 jar

Apple betty / **Beech-Nut**	28.1
Apple blueberry / **Gerber**	37
Apple raspberry / **Gerber**	34
Apples and apricots / **Beech-Nut**	22.9
Apples and cranberries / **Heinz**	31
Apples and pears / **Heinz**	30
Applesauce	
Beech-Nut	25.3
Gerber	22
Heinz	26
and apricots / **Gerber**	46
and apricots / **Heinz**	41
and cherries / **Beech-Nut**	29.4
w pineapple / **Gerber**	23
and raspberries / **Beech-Nut**	24
Apricots w tapioca / **Beech-Nut**	26.2
Apricots w tapioca / **Gerber**	38
Apricots w tapioca / **Heinz**	33
Banana dessert / **Beech-Nut**	33.8
Bananas w pineapple and tapioca / **Beech-Nut**	28.5
Bananas w pineapple and tapioca / **Gerber**	40
Bananas w tapioca / **Gerber**	36
Cottage cheese w pineapple / **Gerber**	40
Dutch apple dessert / **Gerber**	40
Fruit dessert / **Gerber**	38
Fruit dessert / **Heinz**	34
Fruit dessert w tapioca / **Beech-Nut**	26.4
Hawaiian delight / **Gerber**	45
Peach cobbler / **Gerber**	40
Peach melba / **Beech-Nut**	24
Peaches / **Beech-Nut**	22.6
Peaches / **Gerber**	40
Peaches / **Heinz**	50

GRAMS

Pears
Beech-Nut	26.1
Gerber	25
Heinz	30
and pineapple / **Beech-Nut**	30.8
and pineapple / **Gerber**	25
and pineapple / **Heinz**	32

Pineapple-orange dessert / **Heinz**	37
Plums w tapioca / **Beech-Nut**	30.8
Plums w tapioca / **Gerber**	47
Prunes w tapioca / **Beech-Nut**	43.7
Prunes w tapioca / **Gerber**	42

Pudding
Cherry vanilla / **Gerber**	40
Custard / **Heinz**	30
Custard, apple / **Beech-Nut**	28.5
Custard, chocolate / **Gerber**	39
Custard, vanilla / **Gerber**	37

Tropical fruit dessert / **Beech-Nut**	26.4
Tutti-frutti / **Heinz**	36

Main Dishes: 1 jar

Beef
Beech-Nut	.2
Beech-Nut High Meat Dinner	7.4
Gerber	0
and noodles / **Beech-Nut**	16
and noodles w vegetables / **Gerber**	16
and rice w tomato sauce / **Gerber** Toddler Meals	17
Stew / **Gerber** Toddler Meals	11
w vegetables / **Gerber** High Meat Dinner	6

Cereal and egg yolk / **Gerber**	15
Cereal, egg yolks and bacon / **Beech-Nut**	14.9
Cereal and eggs / **Heinz**	17

Chicken

Beech-Nut	0
Beech-Nut High Meat Dinner	9
Gerber	0
Noodle / **Beech-Nut**	15.9
and noodles / **Gerber**	17
Stew / **Gerber** Toddler Meals	10
Sticks / **Gerber**	1
w vegetables / **Beech-Nut**	15.9
w vegetables / **Gerber**	4
Cottage cheese w bananas / **Heinz**	32
Ham / **Beech-Nut** High Meat Dinner	.2
Ham / **Gerber**	0
Ham casserole w green beans and potatoes / **Gerber** Toddler Meals	14
Ham w vegetables / **Gerber** High Meat Dinner	8
Lamb / **Beech-Nut**	.2
Lamb / **Gerber**	0
Lasagna, beef / **Gerber** Toddler Meals	17
Macaroni and beef / **Beech-Nut**	17.4
Macaroni and cheese / **Gerber**	17
Macaroni, tomato, beef / **Gerber**	17
Meat sticks / **Gerber**	1
Peas, split w ham / **Gerber**	24
Peas, split w vegetables and ham / **Beech-Nut**	22.1
Spaghetti, tomato sauce / **Beech-Nut**	18.5
Spaghetti w tomato sauce and beef / **Gerber**	23
Spaghetti and meatballs / **Gerber** Toddler Meals	20

Turkey

Beech-Nut	.2
Beech-Nut High Meat Dinner	8.1
Gerber	0
and rice w vegetables / **Beech-Nut**	16
and rice w vegetables / **Gerber**	14

GRAMS

Sticks / **Gerber**   1
w vegetables / **Gerber**   7
Veal
   Beech-Nut   .2
   Beech-Nut High Meat Dinner   7.2
   Gerber   0
   w vegetables / **Gerber**   8
Vegetables
   and bacon / **Beech-Nut**   17.4
   and bacon / **Gerber**   15
   and beef / **Beech-Nut**   16
   and beef / **Gerber**   15
   and chicken / **Gerber**   18
   and ham / **Gerber**   18
   and lamb / **Beech-Nut**   17
   and lamb / **Gerber**   14
   and liver / **Beech-Nut**   15.7
   and liver / **Gerber**   17
   and turkey / **Gerber**   17
   and turkey casserole / **Gerber**
      Toddler Meals   14

Vegetables: 1 jar

Beans, green / **Beech-Nut**   12.3
Beans, green creamed / **Gerber**   16
Carrots / **Beech-Nut**   13.4
Carrots / **Gerber**   13
Carrots / **Heinz**   12
Corn, creamed / **Gerber**   24
Corn, creamed / **Heinz**   32
Mixed / **Gerber**   17
Peas, creamed / **Heinz**   19
Spinach, creamed / **Gerber**   14
Squash / **Beech-Nut**   6.7
Squash / **Gerber**   11
Sweet potatoes / **Beech-Nut**   27.4

	GRAMS
Sweet potatoes / **Gerber**	31
Sweet potatoes / **Heinz**	30

Yogurt: 1 jar

w mixed fruit / **Beech-Nut**	28.5
w peach-apple / **Beech-Nut**	25.6
w pineapple / **Beech-Nut**	30

Baking Powder

	GRAMS
Canned, 1 tsp / **Royal**	1.3

Beer, Ale, Malt Liquor

	GRAMS
12 fluid ounces	
Ale / **Red Cap**	12
Beer	
Andeker	15
Black Label	12
Budweiser	12.8
Busch	12.4
Coors	12
Goebel	13.4
Grenzquell	11
Hamms	12
Heidelberg	11

	GRAMS
Michelob	14.9
Michelob Light	12
Miller's	14
Miller's Lite	2.8
Natural Light	6
Old Milwaukee	13.5
Olympia	13
Olympia Gold Light	2
Pabst Blue Ribbon	13
Pabst Extra Light	3
Pabst Light	4
Rheingold	15
Schlitz (Regular)	13.4
Schlitz (Repeal)	10.6
Schlitz Light	5
Stag	12
Stroh Bock	14.1
Stroh Bohemian	13.6
Stroh Bohemian 3.2	11.6
Stroh Light	7.1
Stroh Light 3.2	8.8
Tuborg USA	13
Malt Liquor / **Budweiser**	14.4
Malt Liquor / **Schlitz**	13.5

Biscuits

	GRAMS
Refrigerator: 1 biscuit	
Ballard Oven Ready	10
Hungry Jack Butter Tastin	12

	GRAMS
Hungry Jack Flaky	11.5
Merico	10.5
Merico Butter-Me-Not	10
Merico Texas Style	14.5
1869 Brand	13
Pillsbury Country Style	10
Pillsbury Prize	9.5
Baking powder / **1869 Brand**	13
Baking powder, prebaked / **1869 Brand**	11.5
Baking powder / **Tenderflake** Dinner	8
Buttermilk	
Hungry Jack Extra Rich	9
Hungry Jack Flaky	13
Hungry Jack Fluffy	12
1869 Brand	13.5
Prebaked / **1869 Brand**	11.5
Pillsbury	10
Pillsbury Big Country	15
Pillsbury Extra Lights	10.5
Tenderflake Dinner	7.8
Corn bread / **Pillsbury**	12.5

Bread

	GRAMS
1 slice unless noted: an average slice weighs about one ounce	
Bran / **Brownberry**	15
Brown, plain, canned: ½-in slice / **B & M**	17.1
Brown, raisin, canned: ½-in slice / **B & M**	16.6

	GRAMS
Cinnamon raisin / **Thomas'**	12
Corn and molasses / **Pepperidge Farm**	14
English muffin style / **Mrs. Wright's**	10.5
French	
Earth Grains / 1 oz	13.5
Mrs. Wright's	12
Pepperidge Farm	14
Wonder	13.5
Sourdough: 1 oz / **Earth Grains**	14.5
Garlic, frozen / **Stouffer's**	9
Gluten / **Thomas'** Glutogen	6
Gluten, frozen / **Thomas'** Glutogen	6
Grecian style w sesame seeds / **Mrs. Wright's**	17.5
Hollywood Light	13
Hollywood Dark	12.5
Honey bran / **Pepperidge Farm**	11
Honey Wheatberry / **Arnold**	16
Honey Wheatberry / **Pepperidge Farm**	12
Italian: 1 oz / **Pepperidge Farm**	14
Italian / **Mrs. Wright's**	18
Meal	
Colonial Country / 2 oz	28
Kilpatrick's Country / 2 oz	28
Manor Country / 2 oz	28
Rainbo Country / 2 oz	28
Roman Meal	13.5
Naturél / **Arnold**	12
Nut / **Brownberry**	15
Oatmeal / **Brownberry**	15
Oatmeal / **Pepperidge Farm**	12
Profile Dark	12.5
Profile Light	13
Protein / **Thomas'** Protogen	8
Protein, frozen / **Thomas'** Protogen	10
Pumpernickel	
Arnold	14

	GRAMS
Earth Grains / 2 oz	26
Pepperidge Farm Family	14
Pepperidge Farm Party	4
Raisin / **Arnold** Tea	14
Raisin / **Pepperidge Farm**	13
Raisin cinnamon / **Brownberry**	16.5
Raisin nut / **Brownberry**	14.5
Rye	
Arnold Melba Thin	9.5
Arnold Soft	15
Brownberry Extra Thin	12
Earth Grains Light / 2 oz	27
Earth Grains Party / 2 oz	26
Pepperidge Farm Family	15
Pepperidge Farm Party	3
Wonder	13.5
Jewish / **Pepperidge Farm**	16
Jewish, seeded / **Arnold**	14
Jewish, unseeded / **Arnold**	14
Seedless / **Pepperidge Farm**	15
Sourdough / **DiCarlo**	13.5
Vienna w poppy seeds / **Mrs. Wright's**	11
Wheat	
Arnold American Granary	12.5
Arnold Bran'nola	15.5
Arnold Brick Oven Whole Wheat	
(small family)	9.5
Arnold Brick Oven Whole Wheat 16 oz	9.5
Arnold Brick Oven Whole Wheat 32 oz	13
Arnold Melba Thin Whole Wheat	6.5
Brownberry	17.5
Brownberry Great Grains	13
Brownberry Sandwich Dark	14.5
Buckwheat	12.5
Colonial / 1 oz	14
Colonial Honey Grain / 1 oz	13.5
Earth Grains Berry / 1 oz	13.5

GRAMS

Earth Grains Earth / 1 oz 13
Earth Grains 100% Whole Wheat / 1 oz 13.5
Earth Grains Very Thin / 1 oz 15
Fresh Horizons 9.5
Home Pride Butter Top Wheat 13
Home Pride Wheatberry 13.5
Kilpatrick's / 1 oz 14
Kilpatrick's Honey Grain / 1 oz 13.5
Light Wheat Fiber 10.5
Manor / 1 oz 14
Manor Honey Grain / 1 oz 13.5
Mrs. Wright's Grain Belt 14
Pepperidge Farm 1½ lb 17
Pepperidge Farm Very Thin Whole Wheat .. 7
Pepperidge Farm Whole Wheat 1 lb 12
Pritikin 100% Whole Wheat 12.5
Rainbo / 1 oz 14
Rainbo Honey Grain / 1 oz 13.5
Thomas' Whole Wheat 10
Wonder 13.5
Wonder Whole Wheat 12
Cracked wheat: 1 oz / **Earth Grains** 14.5
Cracked wheat / **Pepperidge Farm** 13
Cracked wheat / **Wonder** 13.5
Dark style / **Mrs. Wright's** Special Formula .. 9
Granola bran / **Mrs. Wright's** 13
Honey bran / **Mrs. Wright's** 16
Light style / **Mrs. Wright's** Special Formula .. 9
Sprouted wheat / **Pepperidge Farm** 12
Wheat germ / **Pepperidge Farm** 11
White
Arnold Brick Oven 16 oz 11
Arnold Brick Oven 32 oz 14.5
Arnold Brick Oven (small family) 11
Arnold Country 17
Arnold Hearthstone Country 12.5
Arnold Melba Thin 7

	GRAMS
Brownberry Extra Thin	13.5
Brownberry Sandwich	15.5
Butternut	14
Colonial / 1 oz	14.5
Colonial Butter / 1 oz	14.5
Colonial Contour / 1 oz	13
Earth Grains Very Thin / 1 oz	14
Fresh Horizons	9.5
Hart's	14
Hearthstone	15
Hillbilly	12.5
Home Pride Butter Top White	13
Homestyle	14
Kilpatrick's / 1 oz	13.5
Kilpatrick's Butter / 1 oz	14.5
Kilpatrick's Contour / 1 oz	13
Light White Fiber	11
Manor / 1 oz	14.5
Manor Butter / 1 oz	14.5
Manor Contour / 1 oz	13
Millbrook	14
Mrs. Karl's	14
Mrs. Wright's	15
Mrs. Wright's Butter and Egg	12.5
Mrs. Wright's Low Sodium	9.5
Mrs. Wright's Sandwich Bread Country Style (thin sliced)	10.5
Ovenjoy 16 oz	12
Ovenjoy 22 oz	14
Ovenjoy 24 oz	15
Ovenjoy Sandwich Bread 22 oz	11.5
Ovenjoy Sandwich Bread (thin sliced) 24 oz	11.5
Pepperidge Farm Family	14
Pepperidge Farm Sandwich	12
Pepperidge Farm Thin Sliced	13
Pepperidge Farm Toasting	16

GRAMS

Pepperidge Farm Unsliced / 1 oz	14.5
Pepperidge Farm Very Thin	8
Rainbo / 1 oz	14.5
Rainbo Butter / 1 oz	14.5
Rainbo Contour / 1 oz	13
Safeway 16 oz	13
Safeway (thin sliced) 16 oz	12
Safeway (thin sliced) 24 oz	13
Sweetheart	14
Weber's	14
Weight Watchers	6.5
Wonder	13.5
Wonder Low Sodium	13.5
w buttermilk / **Mrs. Wright's**	15
w buttermilk / **Mrs. Wright's** Sandwich Bread (thin sliced)	11.5
w buttermilk / **Wonder**	13.5
Refrigerator, to bake / **Pillsbury** Hotloaf	17

BREAD CRUMBS

Bread crumbs: 1 cup / **Contadina**	79.9

BREAD MIXES

Prepared: 1 loaf unless noted

Applesauce spice / **Pillsbury**	336
Apricot nut / **Pillsbury**	352
Banana / **Pillsbury**	336
Blueberry nut / **Pillsbury**	352
Cherry nut / **Pillsbury**	352
Corn: 1 pkg / **Aunt Jemima** Easy Mix	204
Corn: 1 pkg / **Pillsbury**	208
Cranberry / **Pillsbury**	352
Date / **Pillsbury**	460
Nut / **Pillsbury**	320
Oatmeal raisin / **Pillsbury**	352

BREADSTICKS

GRAMS

1 stick

Stella D'Oro	6.6
Stella D'Oro Dietetic	6.7
Onion / **Stella D'Oro**	6.5
Sesame / **Stella D'Oro**	6.6
Sesame / **Stella D'Oro** Dietetic	7

STUFFING MIXES

Chicken & Herb: 1 oz / **Pepperidge Farm** Pan Style	20
Chicken-flavored, prepared w butter: ½ cup / **Stove Top**	21
Chicken-flavored, prepared: ½ cup cooked w butter / **Uncle Ben's** Stuff'n Such	24.8
Chicken-flavored, prepared: ½ cup cooked wo butter / **Uncle Ben's** Stuff'n Such	24.8
Corn bread: 1 oz / **Pepperidge Farm**	21
Corn bread, prepared w butter: ½ cup / **Stove Top**	20
Corn bread, prepared: ½ cup cooked w butter / **Uncle Ben's** Stuff'n Such	26.9
Corn bread, prepared: ½ cup cooked wo butter / **Uncle Ben's** Stuff'n Such	26.9
Cube: 1 oz / **Pepperidge Farm**	21
Pork-flavored, mix, prepared w butter: ½ cup / **Stove Top**	20
Sage, prepared: ½ cup cooked w butter / **Uncle Ben's** Stuff'n Such	24.9
Sage, prepared: ½ cup cooked wo butter / **Uncle Ben's** Stuff'n Such	24.9
Seasoned: 1 oz / **Pepperidge Farm**	23
Seasoned: 1 oz / **Pepperidge Farm** Pan Style	21
Seasoned white bread: 1 oz / **Mrs. Cubbinson's**	20
w rice, prepared w butter: ½ cup / **Stove Top**	23

CROUTONS

	GRAMS
¼ cup unless noted	
Artificial bacon / **Bel Air**	6
Caesar Salad / **Brownberry**	6
Cheddar cheese: 1 oz / **Pepperidge Farm**	19
Cheese / **Brownberry**	6
Cheese and garlic / **Bel Air**	6
Cheese-garlic: 1 oz / **Pepperidge Farm**	17
Croutettes: .7 oz dry mix / **Kellogg's**	15
Garlic / **Bel Air**	6
Italian cheese / **Bel Air**	6
Onion and garlic / **Brownberry**	6
Onion-garlic: 1 oz / **Pepperidge Farm**	19
Plain / **Bel Air**	7
Plain: 1 oz / **Pepperidge Farm**	20
Seasoned / **Bel Air**	6
Seasoned / **Brownberry**	6
Seasoned: 1 oz / **Pepperidge Farm**	19
Toasted / **Brownberry** "Buttery"	6

Butter and Margarine

	GRAMS
Butter	
Regular: ½ cup (¼ lb stick)	trace
1 tbsp	trace
Whipped: ½ cup	trace
1 tbsp	trace
Margarine	
Imitation: 1 tbsp	
Mazola diet	0

	GRAMS
Mrs. Filbert's diet soft	0
Parkay diet	0
Weight Watchers	0
Regular and Soft: 1 tbsp	
Blue Bonnet	0
Blue Bonnet Diet	0
Blue Bonnet Soft	0
Chiffon	0
Chiffon Soft	0
Coldbrook	0
Coldbrook Soft	0
Dalewood	0
Empress	0
Empress Soft	0
Fleischmann's	0
Fleischmann's Diet	0
Fleischmann's Parve	0
Fleischmann's Soft	0
Holiday	0
Mazola	0
Meadowlake	0
Mrs. Filbert's	0
Mrs. Filbert's Soft	0
Nucoa	0
Nucoa Soft	0
Parkay	0
Swift Allsweet	0
Spread: 1 tbsp	
Blue Bonnet	0
Coldbrook	0
Fleischmann's	0
Mrs. Filbert's Spread	0
Parkay light	0
Whipped: 1 tbsp	
Blue Bonnet Whipped stick and Soft	0
Chiffon Soft	0
Fleischmann's Soft	0
Mrs. Filbert's Soft	0

Cakes

FROZEN DESSERT CAKES

1 whole cake unless noted

	GRAMS
Banana / **Pepperidge Farm**	160
Banana / **Sara Lee**	214
Banana nut, layer / **Sara Lee**	212
Black Forest / **Sara Lee**	223
Boston Creme / **Pepperidge Farm**	172
Cheesecake	
Mrs. Smith's	138
Cream cheese, small / **Sara Lee**	84
Cream cheese, large / **Sara Lee**	142
Cream cheese, cherry / **Sara Lee**	181
Cream cheese, French / **Sara Lee**	199
Cream cheese, French, strawberry /	
Sara Lee	220
Cream Cheese, strawberry / **Sara Lee**	180
Chocolate / **Pepperidge Farm**	172
Chocolate / **Sara Lee**	194
Chocolate Bavarian / **Sara Lee**	180
Chocolate 'n Cream / **Sara Lee**	190
Chocolate fudge / **Pepperidge Farm**	250
Chocolate fudge / **Pepperidge Farm** Half Cakes	125
Chocolate, German / **Pepperidge Farm**	240
Chocolate, German / **Sara Lee**	138
Coconut / **Pepperidge Farm**	260
Coconut / **Pepperidge Farm** Half Cakes	130

GRAMS

	GRAMS
Crumbcake, blueberry / **Stouffer's**	32
Crumbcake, chocolate chip / **Stouffer's**	27
Crumbcake, French / **Stouffer's**	30
Cupcake, cream-filled / **Stouffer's**	36
Cupcake, yellow / **Stouffer's**	30
Devil's food / **Pepperidge Farm**	260
Devil's food / **Sara Lee**	200
Double chocolate, layer / **Sara Lee**	192
Golden / **Pepperidge Farm** Half Cakes	125
Golden / **Sara Lee**	219
Golden, layer / **Pepperidge Farm**	250
Lemon Bavarian / **Sara Lee**	178
Lemon coconut / **Pepperidge Farm**	168
Mandarin orange / **Sara Lee**	207
Orange / **Sara Lee**	202
Pound cake	
Plain / **Sara Lee**	144
Plain: 1 oz / **Stouffer's**	14
Apple nut / **Pepperidge Farm** Old Fashioned	200
Banana nut / **Sara Lee**	151
Butter / **Pepperidge Farm** Old Fashioned	150
Carrot / **Pepperidge Farm** Old Fashioned	200
Chocolate / **Pepperidge Farm** Old Fashioned	150
Chocolate / **Sara Lee**	130
Chocolate Swirl / **Sara Lee**	179
Family size / **Sara Lee**	222
Home style / **Sara Lee**	127
Raisin / **Sara Lee**	193
Cherry shortcake / **Mrs. Smith's**	330
Strawberry 'n Cream / **Sara Lee**	219
Strawberry shortcake / **Mrs. Smith's**	312
Strawberry shortcake / **Sara Lee**	207
Vanilla / **Pepperidge Farm**	270
Walnut / **Sara Lee**	178

MIXES

GRAMS

Prepared according to package directions:
1 whole cake

Angel food	
Betty Crocker	360
Betty Crocker One-Step	384
Duncan Hines	360
Pillsbury	396
Chocolate / **Betty Crocker**	384
Confetti / **Betty Crocker**	404
Lemon custard / **Betty Crocker**	384
Raspberry / **Pillsbury**	396
Strawberry / **Betty Crocker**	404
Apple raisin / **Duncan Hines**	396
Apple raisin, spicy / **Duncan Hines** Moist and Easy	297
Applesauce raisin / **Betty Crocker** Snackin' Cake	306
Banana / **Betty Crocker**	408
Banana / **Duncan Hines** Supreme	420
Banana / **Pillsbury Plus**	408
Banana nut / **Duncan Hines** Moist and Easy	279
Banana walnut / **Betty Crocker** Snackin' Cake	297
Bundt cake	
Chocolate macaroon / **Pillsbury**	564
Fudge nut crown / **Pillsbury**	492
Lemon blueberry / **Pillsbury**	504
Marble / **Pillsbury**	612
Pound / **Pillsbury**	540
Triple fudge / **Pillsbury**	504
Butter / **Duncan Hines**	432
Butter / **Pillsbury Plus**	396
Butter brickle / **Betty Crocker**	420
Butter fudge / **Duncan Hines**	408
Butter pecan / **Betty Crocker**	384

	GRAMS
Cheesecake / **Pillsbury** No Bake	328
Cheesecake / **Jell-O**	264
Cheesecake / **Royal**	248
Cherry / **Duncan Hines**	408
Cherry chip / **Betty Crocker**	408
Chocolate / **Betty Crocker** Pudding Cake	270
Chocolate / **Duncan Hines**	396
Chocolate almond / **Betty Crocker** Snackin' Cake	297
Chocolate chip / **Betty Crocker** Snackin' Cake	315
Chocolate chip / **Duncan Hines**	288
Chocolate chip, double / **Duncan Hines**	288
Chocolate, dark / **Pillsbury Plus**	420
Chocolate fudge / **Betty Crocker**	384
Chocolate fudge / **Betty Crocker** Snackin' Cake	306
Chocolate, German / **Betty Crocker**	408
Chocolate, German / **Pillsbury Plus**	420
Chocolate, milk / **Betty Crocker**	408
Chocolate, sour cream / **Betty Crocker**	384
Chocolate, sour cream / **Duncan Hines**	408
Chocolate, Swiss / **Duncan Hines**	396
Chocolate w chocolate frosting / **Betty Crocker** Stir n' Frost	264
Coconut pecan / **Betty Crocker** Snackin' Cake	288
Cupcake / **Flako**	25
Date nut / **Betty Crocker** Snackin' Cake	297
Devil's food / **Betty Crocker**	396
Devil's food / **Duncan Hines**	396
Devil's food / **Pillsbury Plus**	420
Fudge marble / **Duncan Hines**	420
Fudge marble / **Pillsbury Plus**	432
Gingerbread / **Betty Crocker**	324
Gingerbread: 3-in square / **Pillsbury**	36
Lemon	
Betty Crocker	408
Betty Crocker Pudding Cake	270
Duncan Hines	420

	GRAMS
Pillsbury Plus	444
w lemon frosting / **Betty Crocker**	
Stir n' Frost	228
Lemon chiffon / **Betty Crocker**	420
Marble / **Betty Crocker**	444
Orange / **Betty Crocker**	408
Orange / **Duncan Hines**	420
Pineapple / **Duncan Hines**	420
Pineapple upside-down w topping /	
Betty Crocker	378
Pound / **Betty Crocker**	324
Spice / **Betty Crocker**	396
Spice / **Duncan Hines**	420
Spice w vanilla frosting / **Betty Crocker**	
Stir n' Frost	282
Spice raisin / **Betty Crocker** Snackin' Cake	306
Strawberry / **Betty Crocker**	408
Strawberry / **Duncan Hines**	420
Strawberry / **Pillsbury**	432
Streusel cake	
Cinnamon / **Pillsbury**	600
Devil's food / **Pillsbury**	600
Fudge marble / **Pillsbury**	600
German chocolate / **Pillsbury**	576
Lemon / **Pillsbury**	600
White	
Betty Crocker	396
Duncan Hines	408
Pillsbury Plus	432
Sour cream / **Betty Crocker**	396
Yellow	
Betty Crocker	408
Betty Crocker Butter Recipe	396
Duncan Hines	420
Pillsbury Plus	420
w chocolate frosting / **Betty Crocker**	
Stir n' Frost	222

COFFEE CAKE

1 whole cake	GRAMS
Almond, frozen / **Sara Lee**	154.4
Almond, frozen / **Sara Lee** Coffee Ring	145.2
Apple, frozen / **Sara Lee** Danish	150.4
Apple cinnamon, mix, prepared / **Pillsbury**	320
Blueberry, frozen / **Sara Lee** Coffee Ring	140
Blueberry, frozen / **Sara Lee** Danish	144
Butter pecan, mix, prepared / **Pillsbury**	312
Butter streusel, frozen / **Sara Lee**	132
Cherry, frozen / **Sara Lee** Danish	147
Cinnamon streusel, mix, prepared / **Pillsbury**	328
Cinnamon streusel, frozen / **Sara Lee**	144
Coffee cake, mix, prepared / **Aunt Jemima** Easy Mix	232
Maple crunch, frozen / **Sara Lee** Coffee Ring	124
Pecan, small, frozen / **Sara Lee**	83
Pecan, large, frozen / **Sara Lee**	144
Raspberry, frozen / **Sara Lee** Coffee Ring	145
Sour cream, mix, prepared / **Pillsbury**	280

SNACK CAKES

Big Wheels: 1 cake / **Hostess**	21
Brownie, small / **Hostess**	24
Brownie, large / **Hostess**	39
Choco-Diles: 1 cake / **Hostess**	37
Crumb cake: 1 cake / **Hostess**	22
Cupcakes	
Chocolate: 1 cake / **Hostess**	30
Chocolate: 3½ oz / **Rainbo**	62
Orange: 1 cake / **Hostess**	27
Devil Dog's: 1 piece / **Drake's**	24.1
Ding Dongs: 1 cake / **Hostess**	21
Donuts: 1 donut unless noted	
Hostess plain / 1 donut	12
Hostess Crunch / 1 donut	16

	GRAMS
Hostess Enrobed / 1 donut	14
Cinnamon: 1 donut / **Hostess**	15
Powdered: 1 donut / **Hostess**	15
Sugar: 2½ oz / **Rainbo** Gem	38
Filled Twins: 3 oz / **Rainbo**	56
Funny Bones: 1¼ oz cake / **Drake's** Family Pkg	19.5
Ho Ho's: 1 cake / **Hostess**	16.5
Macaroon, fudge: 1 cake / **Hostess**	33
Oatmeal cake, creme filled: 2 oz / **Frito-Lay**	36
Pound, marble: 1 cake / **Drake's**	31.2
Pound, plain: 1 cake / **Drake's**	40
Pound, raisin: 1 cake / **Drake's**	40.2
Ring Ding: 1 piece / **Drake's**	47.3
Ring Ding Jr: 1⅓ oz cake / **Drake's** Family Pkg	21.7
Sno Balls: 1 cake / **Hostess**	25
Suzy Q / **Hostess**	38
Suzy Q, chocolate: 1 cake / **Hostess**	36
Tiger Tails: 1 cake / **Hostess**	76
Twinkies: 1 cake / **Hostess**	26
Twinkies, devil's food: 1 cake / **Hostess**	25
Yankee Doodles: 1 cake / **Drake's**	18
Yodels: ⅞ oz cake / **Drake's**	15.9

Candy

	GRAMS
Breath candy: 1 piece	
Breath Savers, sugar free / **Life Savers**	1.8
Certs Clear	2
Certs Pressed	1.5
Chewels	2.4

Clorets Mints	1.6
Dentyne Dynamints	.3
Trident Mints	2
Butter mints: 1 piece / **Kraft**	2
Butterscotch: 1 piece / **Rothchilds**	4
Caramels: 1 piece / **Kraft**	6
Caramel Nip: 1¾ oz / **Pearson**	43

Chocolate and chocolate-covered bars:
  1 oz unless noted

Ghirardelli	16.4
w almonds / **Ghirardelli**	15.7
Hershey's	17
w almonds / **Hershey's**	15
Nestlé's	17
w almonds / **Nestlé's**	17
Baby Ruth: 1 bar	31
Butterfinger: 1 bar	28
Choco'Lite / **Nestlé's**	18
Choc-O-Roon: 2 oz / **Frito-Lay**	35
Chunky, regular	10.8
Chunky, pecan	15.1
Crisp / **Ghirardelli**	16.4
Crunch / **Nestlé's**	18
Forever Yours	21.5
Golden Almond / **Hershey's**	12
Kit Kat: 1.1 oz	19
Krackel	18
Marathon	19.4
Mars Almond	17.7
Milky Way	19.5
Mint / **Ghirardelli**	16.7
Mr. Goodbar: 1.3 oz	18
$100,000 / **Nestlé's**	19
Rally: 1.5 oz	22
Reggie: 1 bar	29
Snickers	18.2

GRAMS

Special Dark Bar: 1.2 oz / **Hershey's**	22
3 Musketeers	21.7
Tootsie Roll	21.5
Chocolate and chocolate-covered bits	
Hershey-ets: 1.1 oz	21
Kisses: 1 oz / **Hershey's**	15
M & M's, plain: 1 oz	19.4
M & M's, peanut: 1 oz	16.4
Raisinets: 1 oz	19
Rolo: 1 piece	3.8
Chocolate Parfait: 1¾ oz / **Pearson**	40
Chocolate Toffee: 1 piece / **Rothchilds**	3.3
Coffee Nip: 1¾ oz / **Pearson**	43
Coffioca: 1¾ oz / **Pearson**	40
Cough drops: 1 drop / **Beech-Nut**	2.5
Cough drops: 1 drop / **Pine Bros.**	2
Good and Plenty: 1 box	34
Good 'n Fruity: 1 box	34
Hard candies	
Life Savers, all flavors: 1 drop	2.2
Life Savers Sugar Nothings, all flavors:	
1 tablet	2
Licorice Nip: 1¾ oz / **Pearson**	43
Lollipops: 1 lollipop	
Fruit: .5 oz size / **Life Savers**	16
Swirled: .5 oz size / **Life Savers**	16
Vanilla: .5 oz size / **Life Savers**	16
Marshmallow: 1 piece / **JETS**	6
Marshmallows, miniature: 12 pieces / **Kraft**	6
Mint: 1 drop / **Life Savers**	1.7
Mint Parfait: 1¾ oz / **Pearson**	40
Peanut Bar: 1 oz / **Munch**	13.8
Peanut Butter Bar: 1¾ oz / **Frito-Lay**	27
Peanut Butter Cup: 1 piece / **Reese's**	9
Peanut candy, canned: 1 oz / **Planters**	
Old Fashioned	15

	GRAMS
Sour Bites: 1 tablet / **Life Savers**	1
Starburst Fruit Chews: 1 oz	26.8
Toffee: 1 piece / **Rothchilds** Creamy	3.3

DIETETIC CANDY

Chocolate bars	
Almond: ¾ oz bar / **Estee**	9.6
Almond: 1 section of 3 oz bar / **Estee**	3.1
Bittersweet: 1 section of 3 oz bar / **Estee**	3.3
Crunch: ⅝ oz bar / **Estee**	8.8
Crunch: 1 section of 2½ oz bar / **Estee**	2.9
Fruit and nut: 1 section of 3 oz pkg / **Estee**	3.2
Milk: ¾ oz bar / **Estee**	10.2
Milk: 1 section of 3 oz pkg / **Estee**	3.4
Chocolates, boxed: 1 piece	
Peanut butter cups / **Estee**	2.9
Raisins, chocolate covered / **Estee**	.1
T.V. Mix / **Estee**	.6
Estee-Ets, plain / 1 piece	.6
Estee-Ets, peanut / 1 piece	6
Gum drops, fruit: 1 piece / **Estee**	.8
Gum drops, licorice: 1 piece / **Estee**	.8
Hard candies: 1 piece	
Assorted / **Estee**	3
Cough / **Estee**	3
Creme / **Estee**	3
Peppermint / **Estee**	3
Mint candies: 1 piece	
Assorted / **Estee** 5 Pak	1
Assorted fruit / **Estee** 5 Pak	1
Peppermint / **Estee**	1
Sour cherry / **Estee**	1
Sour lemon / **Estee**	1
Sour orange / **Estee**	1
Spearmint / **Estee**	1

Cereals

DRY READY-TO-SERVE

GRAMS

Measurements vary according to what companies consider appropriate one-serving sizes. The servings generally are one ounce in weight.

	GRAMS
All-bran: ⅓ cup / **Kellogg's**	22
Alpha-Bits: 1 cup / **Post**	24
Apple Jacks: 1 cup / **Kellogg's**	26
Boo Berry: 1 cup / **General Mills**	24
Bran, plain, added sugar, defatted wheat germ: 1 cup	59.1
Bran, plain, added sugar, malt extract: 1 cup	44.6
Bran Buds: ⅓ cup / **Kellogg's**	23
Bran Chex: ⅔ cup / **Ralston Purina**	20
Bran Flakes 40%: ⅔ cup / **Kellogg's**	23
Bran Flakes 40%: ⅔ cup / **Post**	22
Buc Wheats: ¾ cup / **General Mills**	23
Cap'n Crunch: ¾ cup	22.9
Cap'n Crunch's Crunchberries: ¾ cup	22.9
Cap'n Crunch's Peanut Butter: ¾ cup	20.9
Cheerios: 1¼ cup / **General Mills**	20
Chocolate Crazy Cow: 1 cup / **General Mills**	24
Cocoa Krispies: ¾ cup / **Kellogg's**	26
Cocoa Pebbles: ⅞ cup / **Post**	25
Cocoa Puffs: 1 cup / **General Mills**	25
Concentrate: ⅓ cup / **Kellogg's**	15
Cookie Crisp, chocolate chip: 1 cup / **Ralston Purina**	25
Cookie Crisp, vanilla wafer: 1 cup / **Ralston Purina**	25
Corn Chex: 1 cup / **Ralston Purina**	25
Corn flakes: 1 cup / **General Mills** Country	24

GRAMS

Corn flakes: 1 cup / **Kellogg's**	25
Corn flakes: 1¼ cup / **Post** Toasties	24
Corn flakes: 1 cup / **Ralston Purina**	24
Corn flakes: 1 cup / **Safeway**	24
Corn flakes, sugar-coated: ⅔ cup /	
Kellogg's Frosted	26
Corn Total: 1 cup / **General Mills**	24
Corny-Snaps: 1 cup / **Kellogg's**	24
Count Chocula: 1 cup / **General Mills**	24
Country Morning: ⅓ cup / **Kellogg's**	18
Country Morning w raisins and dates:	
⅓ cup / **Kellogg's**	19
Cracklin' Bran: ⅓ cup / **Kellogg's**	19
Crispy Rice: 1 cup / **Ralston Purina**	25
Family Style: ½ cup / **C.W. Post**	19
Family Style w raisins: ½ cup / **C.W. Post**	19
Franken Berry: 1 cup / **General Mills**	24
Froot Loops: 1 cup / **Kellogg's**	25
Frosty O's: 1 cup / **General Mills**	24
Fruit Brute: 1 cup / **General Mills**	24
Fruity Pebbles: ⅞ cup / **Post**	25
Golden Grahams: 1 cup / **General Mills**	24
Grape-Nuts: ¼ cup / **Post**	22
Granola: 1 oz / **Nature Valley**	19
Granola w cinnamon and raisins:	
1 oz / **Nature Valley**	19
Granola w coconut and honey:	
1 oz / **Nature Valley**	18
Granola w fruit and nuts: 1 oz / **Nature Valley**	20
Grape-Nut Flakes: ⅞ cup / **Post**	23
Heartland, plain: 1 oz	18
Heartland, coconut: 1 oz	18
Heartland, raisin: 1 oz	18
Honeycomb: 1⅓ cup / **Post**	25
Kaboom: 1 cup / **General Mills**	24
King Vitamin: ¾ cup	23.3
Kix: 1½ cup / **General Mills**	24

	GRAMS
Life: ⅔ cup	19.7
Lucky Charms: 1 cup / **General Mills**	24
Mini-Wheats: about 5 biscuits / **Kellogg's**	22
Mini-Wheats, frosted: about 4 biscuits / **Kellogg's**	24
Oat flakes, fortified: ⅔ cup / **Post**	20
Pep: ¾ cup / **Kellogg's**	24
Product 19: ¾ cup / **Kellogg's**	24
Quaker 100% Natural: ¼ cup	17
Quaker 100% Natural w apples and cinnamon: ¼ cup	18
Quaker 100% Natural w raisins and dates: ¼ cup	17.8
Quisp: 1⅙ cup	23.1
Raisin bran: ¾ cup / **Kellogg's**	29
Raisin bran: ½ cup / **Post**	22
Raisin bran: ½ cup / **Ralston Purina**	22
Raisin bran: ½ cup / **Safeway**	22
Rice: 1 cup / **Safeway** Crispy Rice	25
Rice, frosted: 1 cup / **Kellogg's**	26
Rice, puffed: ½ oz / **Malt-O-Meal**	12
Rice, puffed: 1 cup / **Quaker**	12.7
Rice Chex: 1⅛ cup / **Ralston Purina**	25
Rice Krinkles, frosted: ⅞ cup / **Post**	26
Rice Krispies: 1 cup / **Kellogg's**	25
Safeway Tasteeos: 1¼ cup	22
Special K: 1¼ cup / **Kellogg's**	21
Strawberry Crazy Cow: 1 cup / **General Mills**	25
Sugar Corn Pops: 1 cup / **Kellogg's**	26
Sugar Frosted Flakes: ¾ cup / **Ralston Purina**	25
Sugar Smacks: ¾ cup / **Kellogg's**	25
Super Sugar Crisp: ⅞ cup / **Post**	25
Toasty O's: 1 oz	20
Total: 1 cup / **General Mills**	23
Trix: 1 cup / **General Mills**	25
Wheat, puffed: ½ oz / **Malt-O-Meal**	10
Wheat, puffed: 1 cup / **Quaker**	10.8

GRAMS

Wheat, shredded: 1 biscuit / **Quaker**	11
Wheat Chex: ⅔ cup / **Ralston Purina**	23
Wheaties: 1 cup / **General Mills**	23

TO BE COOKED

Measurements vary

Barley, pearled: ¼ cup uncooked (1 cup cooked) / **Quaker** Scotch Brand	36.3
Barley, pearled: ¼ cup uncooked (¾ cup cooked) / **Quaker** Scotch Brand Quick	36.3
Farina: 1 cup cooked / **H-O** Cream Enriched	26
Farina: ⅔ cup / **Pillsbury**	17
Farina: ⅔ cup prepared w milk and salt / **Pillsbury**	26
Farina: ⅙ cup uncooked / **Quaker** Hot 'n Creamy	21.7
Grits: ¼ cup uncooked / **Albers**	33
Grits: 1 packet / **Quaker** Instant Grits Product	17.7
Grits: ⅙ cup uncooked / **3-Minute Brand** Quick	22
Grits, hominy, white: 3 tbsp / **Aunt Jemima** Quick Enriched	22.4
Grits, hominy, white: 3 tbsp / **Aunt Jemima** Regular	22.4
Grits, hominy, white: 3 tbsp / **Quaker** Quick	22.4
Grits, hominy, white: 3 tbsp / **Quaker** Regular	22.4
Grits w artificial cheese flavor: 1 packet / **Quaker** Instant Grits Product	21.6
Grits w imitation bacon bits: 1 packet / **Quaker** Instant Grits Product	21.6
Grits w imitation ham bits: 1 packet / **Quaker** Instant Grits Product	21.3
Malt-O-Meal Chocolate: 1 oz uncooked (about ¾ cup cooked)	21

GRAMS

Malt-O-Meal Quick: 1 oz uncooked
(about ¾ cup cooked)   22
Oats and oatmeal
    H-O Old Fashioned: ¾ cup cooked   24
    H-O Quick: ¾ cup cooked   23
    Harvest Quick: 1 oz uncooked   18
    Quaker Old Fashioned: ⅓ cup uncooked   18.4
    Quaker Quick: ⅓ cup uncooked   18.4
    Ralston Purina: 1 oz uncooked   19
    Ralston Purina Quick: 1 oz uncooked   19
    Safeway Quick: ⅓ cup uncooked   18
    3-Minute Brand Quick: 1 oz uncooked   18
    Instant: 1 packet / **H-O**   18.3
    Instant: ½ cup uncooked / **H-O**   22
    Instant: ¾ cup cooked / **H-O** Regular   22
    Instant: 1 packet / **H-O** Sweet and Mellow   28.8
    Instant: 1 packet / **Quaker** Regular   18.1
    Instant: 1 packet / **3-Minute Brand**
    Stir 'n Eat   18
    Instant w apple and brown sugar:
    1 packet / **3-Minute Brand** Stir 'n Eat   24
    Instant w apples and cinnamon:
    1 packet / **Quaker**   26
    Instant w bran and raisins:
    1 packet / **Quaker**   29.2
    Instant w cinnamon and spice:
    1 packet / **Quaker**   34.8
    Instant w maple and brown sugar:
    1 packet / **H-O**   31.7
    Instant w maple and brown sugar:
    1 packet / **Quaker**   31.9
    Instant w raisins and spice: 1 packet / **H-O**   32.9
    Instant w raisins and spice: 1 packet /
    Quaker   31.4
Ralston: 1 oz uncooked / **Ralston Purina**   20
Ralston: 1 oz uncooked / **Ralston Purina** Instant   20
Rye: ¼ cup uncooked / **Con Agra** Cream of Rye   19

Whole wheat: ⅓ cup uncooked
  (⅔ cup cooked) / **Quaker** Pettijohns   20.6

Cheese

1 oz unless noted   GRAMS

American
  Pimento / **Borden**   .5
  Processed / **Borden**   .5
  Processed / **Borden** Made In Wisconsin   .6
  Processed: 1 slice / **Borden** Single Slices   1.5
  Processed / **Kraft** Singles   2
  Sliced: 1 slice / **Lucerne** 24 Single Slices   1.4
  Sliced: 1 slice / **Safeway**   .6
American-flavored, processed, single wrap slices /
  Kraft Light 'n Lively   2
Blue / **Borden Bleu**   1
Blue / **Casino**   1
Brick / **Casino**   1
Brick, slices / **Kraft**   0
Brie, Danish / **Tiny Dane**   0
Camembert / **Borden**   .5
Cheddar / **Borden** Longhorn   .6
Cheddar / **Borden** Wisconsin Old Fashioned   .6
Cheddar / **Kraft** Cracker Barrel   1
Colby / **Borden**   .6
Colby, low sodium / **Swift Pauly**   1
Farmer's
  Dutch Garden   1

GRAMS

Friendship	.8
Wispride	1
Salt free / **Friendship**	.8
Bulk: ½ cup / **Breakstone**	1
Midget: ½ cup / **Breakstone**	2
Fondue / **Swiss Knight**	1
Gouda / **Borden** Dutch Maid	.5
Gruyere / **Borden**	.5
Gruyere, plain / **Swiss Knight**	less than 1
Liederkranz / **Borden**	.4
Limburger / **Borden** Dutch Maid	.6
Limburger / **Mohawk Valley**	0
Monterey Jack / **Borden**	.6
Monterey Jack / **Casino**	1
Monterey Jack / **Kraft**	1
Mozzarella / **Borden**	.8
Muenster, slices / **Kraft**	0
Pimento / **Borden** Made In Wisconsin	.5
Pizza / **Borden**	.8
Provolone / **Borden**	1
Provolone, sharp / **Casino**	1
Provolone, slices / **Kraft**	1
Ricotta / **Borden**	1
Romano / **Casino**	1
Roquefort / **Borden**	.5
Scamorze / **Kraft**	1
Skim milk cheese, low fat / **Swift Pauly** Slim Line	2
Swiss	
Natural / **Borden**	.5
Natural / **Borden** Imported Switzerland	.5
Natural / **Borden** Imported Finland	.5
Natural / **Kraft**	0
Processed / **Borden**	.5
Processed / **Borden** Made In Wisconsin	.5

COTTAGE CHEESE

GRAMS

½ cup unless noted

Creamed
Borden	3.3
Friendship / 4 oz	4
Lucerne	4
Meadow Gold	4
w chives / **Borden**	3.3
w chives / **Lucerne**	4
w fruit salad: 4 oz / **Friendship** Calorie Meter	13
w fruit salad / **Lucerne**	15
w pineapple / **Borden**	8.4
w pineapple: 4 oz / **Friendship**	15
w pineapple / **Lucerne**	15
w vegetable salad / **Borden**	4.7
w vegetable salad: 4 oz / **Friendship** Garden Salad	4

Dry cottage cheese
Borden	3.1
Lucerne	3
Pot style / **Breakstone**	3

Low-fat
Borden Lite Line	4
Breakstone	4
Friendship Calorie Meter / 4 oz	4
Friendship Pot Style / 4 oz	4
Lucerne Lowfat	4
Viva Lowfat	4
Weight Watchers Lowfat	4
wo salt: 4 oz / **Friendship** Calorie Meter	4
Skim milk, large curd / **Breakstone**	4

CREAM AND NEUFCHATEL CHEESE

GRAMS

1 oz

Cream cheese
Borden	1
Philadelphia Brand	1
Lucerne	1
w chives / **Borden**	.6
w pimento / **Borden**	.6
Imitation / **Philadelphia** Brand	2

Cream cheese, whipped
Philadelphia Brand	1
w bacon and horseradish / **Philadelphia** Brand	1
w blue cheese / **Philadelphia** Brand	2
w chives / **Philadelphia** Brand	1
w onion / **Philadelphia** Brand	2
w pimento / **Philadelphia** Brand	2
w smoked salmon / **Philadelphia** Brand	1

Neufchatel cheese
Calorie-wise	1
w bacon and horseradish / **Kraft**	1
w blue cheese / **Kraft**	2
w clams / **Kraft**	2
w dill pickles / **Kraft**	2
w garlic and onions / **Kraft**	2
w olive and pimento / **Borden**	2.7
w onions / **Kraft**	3
w pimento / **Borden**	2.9
w pineapple / **Kraft**	3
w relish / **Borden**	3.5

GRATED AND SHREDDED CHEESE

1 oz (= about ⅓ cup or about 5½ tbsp)

American, grated / **Borden**	2.6
Parmesan, grated / **Borden**	1

GRAMS

Parmesan, grated / **Kraft**	1
Parmesan, grated / **Lucerne**	1
Parmesan and Romano, grated / **Borden**	.9
Romano / **Kraft**	1

CHEESE FOODS

1 oz unless noted

American	
Borden	2
Lucerne / 1 slice	1.4
Lucerne 10 Single Slices / 1 slice	.8
Safeway / 1 slice	1
Swift Pauly	2
Blue / **Borden** Blue Brand	2.3
Blue / **Borden** Vera Blue	.6
Blue / **Wispride** Cold Pack	2
Cheddar flavor / **Wispride** Cold Pack	7
Pimento	
Borden	2
Lucerne / 1 slice	1.4
Safeway / 1 slice	1.5
Swift Pauly	1
Sweet Munchee / **Swift Pauly**	2
Swiss	
Borden	2
Lucerne 10 Single Slices / 1 slice	1.6
Swift Pauly	2
Wispride Cold Pack	7

CHEESE SPREADS

1 oz

American / **Borden**	2.3
American w bacon / **Borden** Cheese 'N Bacon	1.2
Blue / **Roka**	1
Cheddar flavor, processed / **Wispride**	2

	GRAMS
Cheez Whiz	2
w garlic / **Borden**	2.3
Limburger / **Borden**	2.3
Smoke-flavored / **Borden**	1.3
Smoke-flavored / **Squeez-A-Snak**	.5
Velveeta, processed / **Kraft**	2

WELSH RAREBIT

	GRAMS
Canned: 1 cup / **Snow's**	16.8
Frozen: 5 oz / **Green Giant** Boil-in-Bag	
Toast Toppers	12
w sherry, canned: 1 cup / **Snow's**	16.8

Chewing Gum

1 stick or piece	GRAMS
Adams Sour	2.3
Beech-Nut	2.2
Beechies	1.5
Bubble	
Bubble Yum	7
Bubblicious	6.2
Care Free, all flavors	2
Orbit	trace
Trident Stick	2.1
Dietetic / **Estee**	.9
Chiclets	1.5
Clorets	1.5
Dentyne	1.3
Freshen-Up	2.4
Fruit, dietetic / **Estee**	.9

GRAMS

Fruit Stripe	2.2
Orbit, all flavors	trace
Peppermint, dietetic / **Estee**	.9
Spearmint, dietetic / **Estee**	.9
Trident	1.2
Wrigley's, all flavors	2.3

Chinese Foods

GRAMS

Apple-cinnamon roll, frozen: 1 roll / **La Choy**	6
Bamboo shoots, canned: 8½ oz / **Chun King**	7.3
Bamboo shoots, canned: 8 oz / **La Choy**	4
Bean sprouts, canned: 16 oz / **Chun King**	11.8
Bean sprouts, canned: 1 cup / **La Choy**	2
Chop suey	
Beef, frozen: 32 oz / **Banquet** Buffet Supper	39.1
Beef, frozen: 7 oz / **Banquet** Cookin' Bag	9.5
Vegetables, canned: 1 cup / **La Choy**	10
Chow mein, canned: 1 cup unless noted	
Beef / **La Choy**	6
Beef / **La Choy** Bi-Pack	10
Chicken / **La Choy**	5
Chicken / **La Choy** Bi-Pack	9
Chicken / **La Choy** 50 oz	9
Meatless / **La Choy**	6
Meatless / **La Choy** 50 oz	9
Mushroom / **La Choy** Bi-Pack	11
Pepper oriental / **La Choy**	10
Pepper oriental / **La Choy** Bi-Pack	11
Pork / **La Choy** Bi-Pack	11

GRAMS

Shrimp / **La Choy**	6
Shrimp / **La Choy** Bi-Pack	10
Vegetables: 16 oz can / **Chun King**	14.6
Chow mein, frozen	
Beef: 1 cup / **La Choy**	12
Chicken: 32 oz / **Banquet** Buffet Supper	36.4
Chicken: 7 oz / **Banquet** Cookin' Bag	9.7
Chicken: 1 cup / **La Choy**	9
Chicken wo noodles: 9 oz / **Green Giant** Boil-in-Bag	15
Shrimp: 1 cup / **La Choy**	11
Egg rolls, chicken, frozen: 1 roll / **La Choy**	4
Egg rolls, lobster, frozen: 1 roll / **La Choy**	4
Fried rice, chicken, canned: 1 cup / **La Choy**	80
Fried rice, Chinese style, canned: 1 cup / **La Choy**	86
Fried rice and pork, frozen: 1 cup / **La Choy**	34
Noodles, canned: 1 cup	
Chow mein / **La Choy**	32
Ramen-beef / **La Choy**	33
Ramen-chicken / **La Choy**	29
Ramen-oriental / **La Choy**	31
Rice / **La Choy**	40
Wide chow mein / **La Choy**	32
Pea pods, frozen: 1 pkg / **La Choy**	20
Pepper oriental, frozen: 1 cup / **La Choy**	12
Sweet and sour pork, frozen: 1 cup / **La Choy**	48
Vegetables, mixed Chinese, canned: 1 cup / **La Choy**	2
Water chestnuts, canned: 8½ oz / **Chun King**	27
Won ton, frozen: 1 cup / **La Choy**	12

Chips, Crisps and Similar Snacks

	GRAMS
1 oz unless noted	
Cheddar Bitz / Frito-Lay	19
Cheese Doodles / **Old London**	17.3
Cheese Pixies / **Wise**	14.5
Chee.tos / Frito-Lay	15
Cheez Balls / **Planters**	15
Cheez Curls / **Planters**	15
Corn chips	
Fritos	15
Granny Goose	14.9
Old London	14.6
Old London Dipsy Doodles	14.6
Planters	15
Wise	14.8
Barbecue-flavored / **Fritos**	5
Barbecue-flavored / **Wise**	15.3
Corn Nuggets, toasted: 1⅜ oz / **Frito-Lay**	29
Fiesta chips / **Granny Goose**	16.8
Funyuns	19
Jalapeno Corn Toots / **Granny Goose**	14.9
Munchos / Frito-Lay	15
Onion-flavored rings / **Old London**	21.2
Onion-flavored rings / **Wise**	22.2
Potato chips	
Frito-Lay	14
Frito-Lay Natural Style	15
Frito-Lay Ruffles	15
Granny Goose	13.4
Planters Stackable	17
Pringles	15

	GRAMS
Pringles Country Style	14
Pringles Extra Rippled	15
Wise	14.2
Wise Ridgies	14.2
Barbecue-flavored / **Granny Goose**	13.2
Barbecue-flavored / **Frito-Lay**	14
Barbecue-flavored / **Wise**	14.2
Green onion-flavored / **Granny Goose**	13.4
Onion-garlic-flavored / **Wise**	14.2
Sour cream-and-onion-flavored / **Frito-Lay**	15
Potato sticks, canned: 1½ oz / **O & C**	22
Potato sticks / **Wise Julienne**	15
Puffs-Crunchy, cheese-flavored / **Chee.tos**	15
Rinds, fried	
Bacon / **Wise Bakon Delites**	0
Bacon, barbecue-flavored /	
Wise Bakon Delites	0
Pork / Baken-Ets	.5
Pork / **Granny Goose**	0
Snack Sticks	
Lightly salted / **Pepperidge Farm**	18
Pumpernickel / **Pepperidge Farm**	17
Sesame / **Pepperidge Farm**	16
Whole wheat / **Pepperidge Farm**	17
Taco chips / **Old London**	16.3
Tortilla chips	
Doritos	19
Granny Goose	18.7
Planters Nacho	14
Planters Taco	14
Nacho cheese flavor / **Doritos**	18
Taco flavor / **Doritos**	18
Wheat chips, imitation bacon-flavored /	
Bakon-snacks	14

Chocolate and Chips

	GRAMS
For Baking: 1 oz unless noted	
Chips	
Butterscotch-flavored / **Nestlé's** Morsels	19
Chocolate: ¼ cup / **Hershey's**	24
Chocolate / **Nestlé's** Morsels	17
Chocolate-flavored / **Baker's**	20
Chocolate, semi-sweet / **Ghirardelli**	17.8
Chocolate, semi-sweet: 1½ oz / **Hershey's**	26
Chocolate, semi-sweet: 1½ oz / **Hershey's** Mini	26
Chocolate, semi-sweet / **Nestlé's** Morsels	18
Peanut butter-flavored / **Reese's**	13
Choco-bake / **Nestlé's**	12
Chocolate / **Ghirardelli** Eagle Bar	16.7
Chocolate, ground / **Ghirardelli**	30.4
Chocolate, solid	
Ghirardelli Milk Chocolate Blocks	16.4
Hershey's	7
German's sweet / **Baker's**	17
Semi-sweet / **Baker's**	17
Unswt / **Baker's**	9

Cocktails

ALCOHOLIC

	GRAMS
Canned: 2 fl oz	
Apricot Sour / **Party Tyme**	6
Banana Daiquiri / **Party Tyme**	6
Daiquiri / **Party Tyme**	5
Gimlet / **Party Tyme**	5
Gin and Tonic / **Party Tyme**	5
Mai Tai / **Party Tyme**	6
Manhattan / **Party Tyme**	2
Margarita / **Party Tyme**	6
Martini / **Party Tyme**	0
Pina Colada / **Party Tyme**	5
Rum and Cola / **Party Tyme**	5
Scotch Sour / **Party Tyme**	6
Screwdriver / **Party Tyme**	6
Tom Collins / **Party Tyme**	6
Vodka Martini / **Party Tyme**	0
Vodka Tonic / **Party Tyme**	5

NONALCOHOLIC MIXES

Dry: 1 packet	
Alexander / **Holland House**	16
Banana Daiquiri / **Holland House**	16
Bloody Mary / **Holland House**	14
Daiquiri / **Holland House**	17
Gimlet / **Holland House**	17
Grasshopper / **Holland House**	17
Mai Tai / **Holland House**	17
Margarita / **Holland House**	17
Mint Julep / **Holland House**	17

GRAMS

Pina Colada / **Holland House**	16
Pink Squirrel / **Holland House**	17
Screwdriver / **Holland House**	17
Strawberry Margarita / **Holland House**	15
Strawberry Sting / **Holland House**	18
Tequilla Sunrise / **Holland House**	15
Tom Collins / **Holland House**	17
Vodka Sour / **Holland House**	16
Wallbanger / **Holland House**	16
Whiskey Sour / **Holland House**	17

Liquid: 1 fl oz unless noted

Amaretto / **Holland House**	16
Apricot Sour / **Holland House**	12
Black Russian / **Holland House**	23
Blackberry Sour / **Holland House**	12
Bloody Mary / **Holland House** Regular	2
Bloody Mary / **Holland House** Extra Tangy	2
Bloody Mary / **Holland House** Smooth 'n Spicy	1
Cocktail Host / **Holland House**	12
Collins Mixer: 8 fl oz / **Canada Dry**	20
Cream of Coconut / **Holland House** Coco Casa	22
Daiquiri / **Holland House**	13
Dry Martini / **Holland House**	2
Gimlet / **Holland House**	10
Mai Tai / **Holland House**	8
Manhattan / **Holland House**	7
Margarita / **Holland House**	9
Old Fashioned / **Holland House**	9
Pina Colada / **Holland House**	15
Strawberry Sting / **Holland House**	8
Tom Collins / **Holland House**	16
Whiskey Sour: 8 fl oz / **Canada Dry**	22
Whiskey Sour / **Holland House**	13
Whiskey Sour / **Holland House** Low Calorie	2

Cocoa

	GRAMS
Cocoa: 1 oz / **Hershey's**	14
Cocoa: 1 tbsp / **Marvel**	4
Cocoa, chocolate flavor: ¾ oz / **Nestlé's**	19
Cocoa	
Mix: 1 oz / **Hershey's**	20
Mix: 3 tbsp / **Hershey's** Instant	17
Mix: 3 tbsp, prepared w 8 oz milk /	
Hershey's Instant	29
Mix: 1 oz / **Nestlé's**	22
Mix: 1 oz / **Ovaltine**	22
Mix: .69 oz / **Ovaltine** Reduced Calorie	15
Mix, all flavors, instant: 1 oz / **Carnation**	22

Coconut

	GRAMS
Fresh	
In shell: 1 coconut	37.3
Meat: 1 piece (2 x 2 x ½ in)	4.2
Meat, shredded or grated: 1 cup	7.5
Cream, (liquid from grated meat):	
1 cup	20.2
Milk, (liquid from mixture of grated meat	
and water): 1 cup	12.5
Water, (liquid from coconuts): 1 cup	11.3
Canned or packaged: ¼ cup	
Plain / **Baker's** Angel Flake	1

	GRAMS
Plain / **Baker's** Premium Shred	9
Plain / **Baker's** Southern Style	8
Plain, shredded / **Durkee**	2
Cookie-coconut / **Baker's**	12

Coffee

	GRAMS
Chase & Sanborn: 1 cup	0
Decaf Instant: 1 tsp	1
General Foods International: 6 fl oz	
Cafe Francais, swtd, prepared	7
Cafe Vienna, swtd, prepared	11
Orange Cappuccino, swtd, prepared	10
Suisse Mocha, swtd, prepared	7
Nescafé Instant: 1 tsp	1
Nescafé Instant, freeze-dried, decaffeinated: 1 tsp	1
Postum (cereal beverage), instant: 6 fl oz	2
Taster's Choice Instant, freeze-dried: 1 tsp	1
Taster's Choice Instant, freeze-dried, decaffeinated: 1 tsp	1

Condiments

	GRAMS
A.1 Sauce / 1 tbsp	2.8
Catsup: 1 tbsp / **Del Monte**	4

	GRAMS
Catsup: 1 tbsp / **Tillie Lewis**	6
Chili sauce: 1 tbsp / **Heinz**	3.8
Chutney: 1 tbsp / **Major Grey's**	13.1
Horseradish: 1 tbsp	.2
Cream style	.4
Oil style	.2
Horseradish, raw: 1 lb	89.4
Hot sauce: 1 tsp / **Frank's**	2
Mustard, prepared	
Brown: 1 tbsp / **French's** Brown 'n Spicy	1
Brown: 1 tsp / **Mr. Mustard**	.4
Cream salad: 1 tbsp / **French's**	1
Dijon: 1 tsp / **Grey Poupon**	.2
w horseradish: 1 tbsp / **French's**	1
w onion: 1 tbsp / **French's**	5
Yellow: 1 tbsp / **French's** Medford	1
Sauce Diable: 1 tbsp / **Escoffier**	4.2
Sauce Robert: 1 tbsp / **Escoffier**	4.5
Seafood cocktail: ¼ cup / **Del Monte**	17
Seafood cocktail: 2 oz / **Pfeiffer**	12
Soy sauce: 1 tbsp / **La Choy**	1
Steak sauce: 1 tbsp / **Steak Supreme**	4.7
Taco sauce: 1 tbsp / **Ortega**	4.8
Tartar sauce: 1 tbsp	
Best Foods	.2
Hellmann's	.2
Seven Seas	1
Tartar sauce, mix: 1 pkg / **Lawry's**	10
Vinegar: 1 fl oz	
Champagne / **Regina**	.1
Red wine / **Regina**	.1
Red wine w garlic / **Regina**	.1
Wine, cooking	
Marsala: 1 fl oz / **Holland House**	2
Red: 1 fl oz / **Holland House**	1
Sauterne: ¼ cup / **Regina**	4.8
Sherry: 1 fl oz / **Holland House**	2

	GRAMS
Sherry: ¼ cup / **Regina**	4.7
White: 1 fl oz / **Holland House**	1
Worcestershire: 1 tbsp / **French's**	2
Worcestershire, hickory smoke-flavored: 1 tbsp / **French's** Smoky	2

See also Sauces, Seasonings

Cookies

	GRAMS
1 piece as packaged unless noted	
Adelaide / **Pepperidge Farm**	7
Angel Puffs / **Stella D'Oro** Dietetic	1.5
Angelica Goodies / **Stella D'Oro**	14.2
Anginetti / **Stella D'Oro**	4
Animal crackers	
Keebler	1.8
Sunshine	1.7
Iced / **Sunshine**	3.7
Barnum's Animal's / **Nabisco**	1.9
Anisette sponge / **Stella D'Oro**	9.6
Anisette toast / **Stella D'Oro**	9.3
Applesauce / **Sunshine**	11.9
Applesauce, iced / **Sunshine**	11.9
Arrowroot / **Sunshine**	3
Assortment	
Stella D'Oro Hostess with the Mostest	5.4
Stella D'Oro Lady Stella	5.5
Aunt Sally, iced / **Sunshine**	19.7
Big Treat / **Sunshine**	26.6
Biscos / **Nabisco**	6

GRAMS

Bordeaux / **Pepperidge Farm**	5
Breakfast Treats / **Stella D'Oro**	15.8
Brown sugar / **Pepperidge Farm**	7
Brussels / **Pepperidge Farm**	6
Butter-flavored / **Nabisco**	3.6
Butter-flavored / **Sunshine**	3.5
Buttercup / **Keebler**	3.6
Cameo creme sandwich / **Nabisco**	9.5
Capri / **Pepperidge Farm**	10
Chessman / **Pepperidge Farm**	6
Chinese dessert cookies / **Stella D'Oro**	20.7
Chip-A-Roos / **Sunshine**	7.7
Chocolate brownie / **Pepperidge Farm**	6
Chocolate chip	
Estee Dietetic	4
Keebler Old Fashioned	11
Keebler Rich 'n Chips	8.9
Pepperidge Farm	6
Chocolate chip coconut / **Sunshine**	9.7
Chocolate fudge sandwich / **Sunshine**	9.4
Chocolate-strawberry wafers, dietetic, single	
serving pkg: 1 pkg / **Estee**	10.5
Cinnamon sugar / **Pepperidge Farm**	7
Cinnamon toast / **Sunshine**	2.3
Coconut Bar / **Keebler**	9.4
Coconut Bar / **Sunshine**	6.2
Coconut cookies / **Stella D'Oro** Dietetic	6.3
Coconut Chocolate Drop / **Keebler**	8.5
Coconut macaroons / **Nabisco**	12.1
Como Delight / **Stella D'Oro**	18.4
Cream Lunch / **Sunshine**	7.3
Crescents, almond-flavored / **Nabisco**	5
Cup Custard, chocolate / **Sunshine**	9.3
Cup Custard, vanilla / **Sunshine**	9.3
Danish Wedding / **Keebler**	5
Date-Nut Granola / **Pepperidge Farm**	7
Devilsfood / **Keebler**	13.9

GRAMS

Dixie Vanilla / **Sunshine**	13.1
Egg biscuits	
Stella D'Oro	6.5
Stella D'Oro Dietetic	6.5
Anise / **Stella D'Oro** Roman	18.5
Rum and brandy / **Stella D'Oro** Roman	18.5
Sugared / **Stella D'Oro**	12
Vanilla / **Stella D'Oro** Roman	18.5
Egg Jumbo / **Stella D'Oro**	9.1
Big bar: 2 oz / **Frito-Lay**	38
Fig bar / **Keebler**	14.3
Fig bar / **Sunshine**	9.2
French vanilla creme / **Keebler**	13.2
Fudge Chip / **Pepperidge Farm**	7
Fudge Stick / **Keebler**	5.1
Fudge Stripes / **Keebler**	7.5
German chocolate / **Keebler**	9.4
Ginger snap	
Keebler	4.3
Nabisco	5.4
Sunshine	4.4
Gingerman / **Pepperidge Farm**	5
Golden bars / **Stella D'Oro**	15.9
Golden Fruit / **Sunshine**	14.4
Graham crackers	
Sunshine Sweet-Tooth	6.4
Chocolate-covered / **Keebler** Deluxe	5.6
Cinnamon: smallest piece when broken	
on score line / **Keebler** Crisp	2.7
Crumbs: 1 bag / **Sunshine**	77.9
Honey: smallest piece when broken on	
score line / **Keebler**	2.8
Honey / **Nabisco** Honey Maid	5.3
Hydrox / **Sunshine**	7.1
Hydrox, mint / **Sunshine**	7.1
Hydrox, vanilla / **Sunshine**	7.1
Irish oatmeal / **Pepperidge Farm**	7

	GRAMS
Keebies / **Keebler**	7.1
Kichel / **Stella D'Oro** Dietetic	.6
Krisp Kreem, chocolate / **Keebler**	3.4
Krisp Kreem, strawberry / **Keebler**	3.7
Krisp Kreem, vanilla / **Keebler**	3.7
Lady Joan / **Sunshine**	6.1
Lady Joan, iced / **Sunshine**	5.8
LaLanne Sesame / **Sunshine**	1.8
LaLanne Soya / **Sunshine**	1.9
Lemon / **Sunshine**	9.8
Lemon Coolers / **Sunshine**	4.5
Lemon nut crunch / **Pepperidge Farm**	7
Lemon Thins, dietetic / **Estee**	4
Lido / **Pepperidge Farm**	10
Love Cookies / **Stella D'Oro** Dietetic	14
Mallopuffs / **Sunshine**	12.2
Mandel toast / **Stella D'Oro**	9.9
Margherite combination / **Stella D'Oro**	10.5
Margherite, vanilla / **Stella D'Oro**	10.7
Marigold sandwich / **Keebler**	12.9
Milano / **Pepperidge Farm**	7
Mint Milano / **Pepperidge Farm**	8
Molasses crisps / **Pepperidge Farm**	4
Molasses and spice / **Sunshine**	11.9
Nassau / **Pepperidge Farm**	8
'Nilla wafers / **Nabisco**	2.9
Nutter Butter / **Nabisco**	9.2
Oatmeal	
Sunshine	8.9
Almond / **Pepperidge Farm**	6
Iced / **Keebler** Old Fashioned	12.7
Iced / **Sunshine**	11.6
Marmalade / **Pepperidge Farm**	7
Peanut butter / **Sunshine**	10.5
Raisin / **Nabisco**	11.5
Raisin / **Pepperidge Farm**	8
Raisin, dietetic / **Estee**	4

Opera Creme Sandwich / **Keebler**	11.6
Orbit Creme Sandwich / **Sunshine**	7
Oreo / **Nabisco**	7.3
Orleans / **Pepperidge Farm**	4
Peanut / **Pepperidge Farm**	5
Peanut butter / **Keebler** Old Fashioned	10.4
Peanut butter wafers / **Sunshine**	4.2
Peanut creme patties / **Nabisco**	3.8
Pecan Sandies / **Keebler**	9.2
Penguin / **Keebler**	11.8
Penguin, peanut butter / **Keebler**	11.3
Pfeffernusse / **Stella D'Oro** Spice Drops	6.8
Pirouette / **Pepperidge Farm**	5
Pirouette, chocolate-laced / **Pepperidge Farm**	5
Pitter Patter / **Keebler**	10.9
Raisin bar, iced / **Keebler**	10.5
Raisin Bran / **Pepperidge Farm**	7
Raisin fruit biscuit / **Nabisco**	12.1
Royal Nuggets / **Stella D'Oro** Dietetic	.1
St. Moritz / **Pepperidge Farm**	6
Sandwich	
Estee Dietetic	8
Assortment / **Nabisco** Pride	7.3
Creme, Swiss / **Nabisco**	6.6
Creme, chocolate fudge / **Keebler**	13
Creme, lemon / **Keebler**	13.8
Creme, vanilla / **Keebler**	11.1
Lemon / **Estee** Dietetic	8
Scotties / **Sunshine**	5
Sesame cookies / **Stella D'Oro** Regina	5.9
Sesame cookies / **Stella D'Oro** Regina Dietetic	5.6
Shortbread / **Pepperidge Farm**	7.5
Shortbread, almond / **Keebler** Spiced Windmill	9.2
Shortbread, pecan / **Nabisco**	8.9
Social Tea Biscuit / **Nabisco**	3.6
Social Tea Sandwich / **Nabisco**	7.2

GRAMS

Sorrento cookies / **Stella D'Oro**	7.8
Sprinkles / **Sunshine**	11.4
Sugar / **Keebler** Old Fashioned	12.4
Sugar / **Pepperidge Farm**	7
Sugar / **Sunshine**	11.9
Sugar Rings / **Nabisco**	10.6
Sunflower Raisin / **Pepperidge Farm**	6
Swedish Kremes / **Keebler**	12.2
Swiss Fudge / **Stella D'Oro**	7.7
Tahiti / **Pepperidge Farm**	9
Taste of Vienna / **Stella D'Oro**	10.2
Toy cookies / **Sunshine**	2.1
Vanilla snaps / **Nabisco**	2.3
Vanilla Thins, dietetic / **Estee**	4
Vienna Finger sandwich / **Sunshine**	10.5
Wafers	
Assorted, dietetic / **Estee**	4.1
Brown edge / **Nabisco**	4.1
Chocolate, dietetic / **Estee**	3
Peanut butter-chocolate, dietetic / **Estee**	9.6
Spiced / **Nabisco**	7.4
Sugar / **Biscos**	2.5
Sugar / **Sunshine**	6.6
Sugar, lemon / **Sunshine**	6.5
Vanilla / **Keebler**	2.6
Vanilla / **Sunshine**	2.2
Vanilla, dietetic / **Estee**	3
Yum Yums / **Sunshine**	10.4
Zanzibar / **Pepperidge Farm**	4
Zuzu Ginger Snaps / **Nabisco**	3

COOKIE MIXES AND DOUGH

Bar, date, mix, prepared:	
1/32 pkg / **Betty Crocker**	9
Bar, Vienna, mix, prepared:	
1/24 pkg / **Betty Crocker**	10

Brownies
    Chocolate chip butterscotch, mix, prepared:
        1/16 pkg / **Betty Crocker**   20
    Fudge, mix, prepared:
        1/24 pkg / **Betty Crocker** Family Size   21
    Fudge, mix, prepared:
        1/16 pkg / **Betty Crocker** Regular Size   21
    Fudge, mix, prepared:
        1/24 pkg / **Betty Crocker** Supreme   20
    Fudge, mix, prepared:
        1 brownie / **Duncan Hines** Double Fudge   21
    Fudge, mix, prepared:
        1½-in square / **Pillsbury**   10
    Fudge, mix, prepared:
        1½-in square / **Pillsbury** Family Size   10.5
    Fudge, refrigerator, to bake:
        1/16 pkg / **Pillsbury**   17
    German chocolate, mix, prepared:
        1/16 pkg / **Betty Crocker**   26
    Walnut, mix, prepared:
        1/16 pkg / **Betty Crocker**   21
    Walnut, mix, prepared:
        1/24 pkg / **Betty Crocker** Family Size   21
    Walnut, mix, prepared:
        1½-in square / **Pillsbury**   10
    Walnut, mix, prepared:
        1½-in square / **Pillsbury** Family Size   10.5
Butterscotch nut, refrigerator, to bake:
  1/36 pkg / **Pillsbury**   7
Chocolate chip, mix, prepared:
  1/36 pkg / **Betty Crocker** Big Batch   9
Chocolate chip, refrigerated: 1 cookie / **Merico**   8
Chocolate chip, refrigerator, to bake:
  1/36 pkg / **Pillsbury**   7.3
Fudge, refrigerator, to bake: 1/30 pkg / **Pillsbury**   8.5
Fudge chip, mix, prepared: 1 cookie / **Quaker**   9.5

GRAMS

Ginger, refrigerator, to bake: 1/36 pkg /
   Pillsbury Spicy   7.3
Macaroon, coconut, mix, prepared:
   1/24 pkg / **Betty Crocker**   10
Oatmeal, mix, prepared:
   1/36 pkg / **Betty Crocker** Big Batch   9
Oatmeal, mix, prepared: 1 cookie / **Quaker**   9.5
Oatmeal chocolate chip, refrigerator, to bake:
   1/36 pkg / **Pillsbury**   7.3
Oatmeal raisin, refrigerator, to bake:
   1/36 pkg / **Pillsbury**   8
Peanut butter, mix, prepared:
   1/36 pkg / **Betty Crocker** Big Batch   8
Peanut butter, mix, prepared: 1 cookie / **Quaker** 8
Peanut butter, refrigerator: 1 cookie / **Merico** 7
Peanut butter, refrigerator, to bake:
   1/36 pkg / **Pillsbury**   6.3
Sugar, mix, prepared:
   1/36 pkg / **Betty Crocker** Big Batch   9
Sugar, mix, prepared: 1 cookie / **Quaker**   9.5
Sugar, refrigerator: 1 cookie / **Merico**   8
Sugar, refrigerator, to bake:
   1/36 pkg / **Pillsbury**   8.3

Corn Starch

GRAMS

1 tbsp

Argo   8.3
Duryea's   8.3
Kingsford's   8.3

Crackers

GRAMS

1 cracker unless noted

Butter-Flavor Thins / **Keebler**	2.8
Cheese filled: 1½ oz / **Frito-Lay**	25
Cheese Peanut Butter Snax / **Keebler**	1.1
Cheez-Its: 1 piece / **Sunshine**	.6
Che-zo / **Keebler**	.6
Club: smallest piece when broken on score line / **Keebler**	2
Flings Curls / **Nabisco**	.8
Gold Fish	
Cheddar cheese: 1 oz / **Pepperidge Farm**	17
Lightly salted: 1 oz / **Pepperidge Farm**	18
Parmesan cheese: 1 oz / **Pepperidge Farm**	17
Pizza: 1 oz / **Pepperidge Farm**	18
Pretzel: 1 oz / **Pepperidge Farm**	21
Sesame-garlic: 1 oz / **Pepperidge Farm**	17
Taco: 1 oz / **Pepperidge Farm**	18
Thins, cheddar cheese: 4 thins / **Pepperidge Farm**	9
Thins, lightly salted: 4 thins / **Pepperidge Farm**	9
Thins, rye: 4 thins / **Pepperidge Farm**	9
Thins, wheat: 4 thins / **Pepperidge Farm**	9
Hi-Ho / **Sunshine**	2.1
Kavli Flatbread: 1 wafer	7.5
Matzos: 1 sheet or 1 cracker	
American / **Manischewitz**	23
Diet-Thins / **Manischewitz**	24.2
Egg Matzo / **Manischewitz**	26.5
Egg 'n' Onion / **Manischewitz**	24.1
Onion Tams / **Manischewitz**	1.8
Regular Matzo / **Manischewitz**	24.1

GRAMS

Tam Tams / **Manischewitz**	1.7
Tasteas / **Manischewitz**	23.7
Thin Tea / **Manischewitz**	24.4
Whole Wheat / **Manischewitz**	24.2
Melba Toast: 1 piece	
Garlic rounds / **Old London**	1.6
Onion rounds / **Old London**	1.5
Pumpernickel / **Old London**	3.2
Rye, salted / **Old London**	3.3
Rye, unsalted / **Old London**	3.3
Sesame, rounds / **Old London**	1.3
Wheat, salted / **Old London**	3.3
Wheat, unsalted / **Old London**	3.3
White / **Old London**	3.3
White, unsalted / **Old London**	3.3
White rounds, salted / **Old London**	1.6
Mixed Suites, green onion: 1 oz / **Pepperidge Farm**	21
Mixed Suites, pretzel-cheese: 1 oz / **Pepperidge Farm**	22
Mixed Suites, sesame-cheese: 1 oz / **Pepperidge Farm**	19
Oyster / **Keebler** Crax	.4
Oyster / **Keebler** Zesta Crax	.2
Oyster / **Sunshine**	.6
Peanut butter: 1½ oz / **Frito-Lay**	24
Ritz / **Nabisco**	2.1
Ritz Cheese / **Nabisco**	1.9
Ry Krisp: 1 triple cracker	5
Ry Krisp, seasoned: 1 triple cracker	5
Saltines and soda crackers	
Export soda: smallest piece when broken on score line / **Keebler**	4.3
Krispy / **Sunshine**	2
Milk Lunch Biscuit / **Keebler**	4.5
Premium / **Nabisco**	2
Premium, unsalted tops / **Nabisco**	2

GRAMS

Royal Lunch / **Nabisco**	7.8
Sea toast / **Keebler**	11.1
Sunshine	3.3
Uneeda, unsalted / **Nabisco**	3.7
Waldorf, low sodium / **Keebler**	2.4
Zesta / **Keebler**	2
Zesta, unsalted / **Keebler**	2.3
Shapies, cheese-flavored / **Nabisco**	.8
Shapies, cheese-flavored shells / **Nabisco**	.9
Sip 'N Chips, cheese-flavored / **Nabisco**	1
Sociables / **Nabisco**	1.3
Toast	
Bacon / **Keebler**	2
Cheese / **Keebler**	1.9
Onion / **Keebler**	2.1
Rye: smallest piece when broken on	
score line / **Keebler**	2.2
Sesame / **Keebler**	2
Wheat / **Keebler**	2
Town House / **Keebler**	2
Triangle Thins / **Nabisco**	1.1
Triscuit / **Nabisco**	3
Twigs / **Nabisco**	1.6
Waverly Wafers / **Nabisco**	2.6
Wheat Thins / **Nabisco**	1.2
Zwieback / **Nabisco**	5.4

Cream

GRAMS

Half and Half: 1 tbsp	
10.5% fat / **Borden**	.6
10.5% fat / **Sealtest**	.6

GRAMS

11.5% fat / **Borden** .5
12% fat / **Lucerne** .6
12% fat / **Meadow Gold** .6
12% fat / **Sealtest** .6
Light: 1 tbsp
16% fat / **Sealtest** .6
18% fat / **Borden** .6
18% fat / **Sealtest** .6
25% fat / **Sealtest** .5
Whipping, heavy
Borden / 1 tbsp .5
Lucerne / 1 tbsp .5
Lucerne Sterilized / 1 tbsp .5
Meadow Gold / 1 tbsp .5
Sealtest / 1 tbsp .5
In aerosol can:
1 fl oz / **Lucerne** Real Cream Topping 5.1
Whipping, medium: 1 tbsp / **Borden** .5
Whipping, medium: 1 tbsp / **Sealtest** .5

NON-DAIRY CREAMERS

Dry
Carnation Coffee-Mate / 1 packet 1.7
Coffee Tone / 1 tsp 1
Cremora / 1 tsp 1
Liquid
Coffee Tone Freezer Pack / 1 tbsp 2
Lucerne Cereal Blend / ½ cup 12
Powdered: 1 tsp / **Pet** 1

SOUR CREAM

Borden / 2 tbsp 1
1 cup 7.7
Friendship / 2 tbsp 1
1 cup 8

	GRAMS
Lucerne / 2 tbsp	1.2
1 cup	10
Lucerne, half and half / 2 tbsp	1.7
1 cup	13.4
Sealtest / 2 tbsp	1
1 cup	8
Sealtest, half and half / 2 tbsp	1
1 cup	8
Imitation sour cream / **Borden's Zest** 2 tbsp	1.8
1 cup	14
Imitation sour cream / **Pet** 1 tbsp	1

Dessert Mixes

GRAMS

Apple cinnamon, prepared: ⅔ cup /
   Pillsbury Appleasy   44
Apple caramel, prepared: ½ cup /
   Pillsbury Appleasy   35
Apple raisin, prepared: ⅔ cup /
   Pillsbury Appleasy   46

Diet Bars

GRAMS

All flavors: 1 bar / **Pillsbury** Figurines	10.5
All flavors: 1 stick / **Pillsbury** Food Sticks	6.7
Cinnamon: 1 bar / **Carnation** Slender Bars	12
Chocolate: 1 bar / **Carnation** Slender Bars	11.5
Vanilla: 1 bar / **Carnation** Slender Bars	12

Dinners

FROZEN DINNERS

GRAMS

1 dinner

Beans and beef patties: 11 oz / **Swanson "TV"**	73
Beans w franks: 10¾ oz / **Banquet**	63.1
Beans w franks: 10¾ oz / **Morton**	79
Beans w franks: 11¼ oz / **Swanson "TV"**	75
Beef	
Banquet / 11 oz	20.9
La Choy	56
Morton / 10 oz	20
Swanson 3 Course / 15 oz	58
Swanson "TV" / 11½ oz	34
Beef, chopped: 11 oz / **Banquet**	32.8
Beef, chopped: 11 oz / **Morton**	18
Beef, sirloin, chopped: 10 oz / **Swanson "TV"**	37
Beef, sliced: 14 oz / **Morton** Country Table	64
Beef, sliced: 17 oz / **Swanson** Hungry-Man	51
Beef steak, chopped: 18 oz / **Swanson** Hungry-Man	70
Beef tenderloin: 9½ oz / **Morton** Steak House Dinner	47
Chicken / **La Choy**	55
Chicken, boneless: 10 oz / **Morton**	22
Chicken, boneless: 19 oz / **Swanson** Hungry-Man	74
Chicken breast: 15 oz / **Weight Watchers**	30
Chicken croquette: 10¼ oz / **Morton**	46
Chicken, fried	
Banquet / 11 oz	48.4
Banquet Man Pleaser / 17 oz	89.2
Morton / 11 oz	49

GRAMS

Morton Country Table / 15 oz	96
Swanson Hungry-Man / 12 oz	37
Swanson Hungry-Man / 15¾ oz	78
Swanson Hungry-Man Barbecue-flavored / 16½ oz	72
Swanson 3 Course / 15 oz	64
Swanson "TV" / 11½ oz	48
Barbecue-flavored: 12 oz / **Swanson** Hungry-Man	43
Barbecue-flavored: 11¼ oz / **Swanson** "TV"	47
Crispy fried: 10¾ oz / **Swanson** "TV"	51
w whipped potatoes: 7 oz / **Swanson** "TV"	25
Chicken w dumplings: 12 oz / **Banquet**	36.4
Chicken w dumplings: 11 oz / **Morton**	30
Chicken w noodles: 12 oz / **Banquet**	50.7
Chicken w noodles: 10¼ oz / **Morton**	40
Chicken oriental style: 16 oz / **Weight Watchers**	31
Chop suey, beef: 12 oz / **Banquet**	38.8
Chow mein, chicken: 12 oz / **Banquet**	38.8
Enchilada / **El Chico**	67
Enchilada, beef: 12 oz / **Banquet**	63.6
Enchilada, beef: 15 oz / **Swanson** "TV"	72
Enchilada, cheese: 12 oz / **Banquet**	58.8
Fish: 8¾ oz / **Banquet**	43.6
Fish: 9 oz / **Morton**	21
Fish 'n' Chips: 15¾ oz / **Swanson** Hungry-Man	68
Fish 'n' Chips: 10¼ oz / **Swanson** "TV"	40
Flounder: 16 oz / **Weight Watchers**	16
German style: 11¾ oz / **Swanson** "TV"	40
Haddock: 8¾ oz / **Banquet**	45.4
Haddock: 16 oz / **Weight Watchers**	15
Ham: 10 oz / **Banquet**	47.7
Ham: 10 oz / **Morton**	56
Ham: 10¼ oz / **Swanson** "TV"	47
Hash, corned beef: 10 oz / **Banquet**	42.6
Italian style: 11 oz / **Banquet**	44.6

GRAMS

Italian style: 13 oz / **Swanson** "TV"	55
Lasagna and meat: 17¾ oz / **Swanson** Hungry-Man	86
Macaroni and beef: 12 oz / **Banquet**	55.1
Macaroni and beef: 10 oz / **Morton**	46
Macaroni and beef: 12 oz / **Swanson** "TV"	56
Macaroni and cheese: 12 oz / **Banquet**	45.6
Macaroni and cheese: 11 oz / **Morton**	52
Macaroni and cheese: 12½ oz / **Swanson** "TV"	55
Meat loaf: 11 oz / **Banquet**	29
Meat loaf: 11 oz / **Morton**	28
Meat loaf: 15 oz / **Morton** Country Table	59
Meat loaf: 10¾ oz / **Swanson** "TV"	48
Meatballs: 11¾ oz / **Swanson** "TV"	35
Mexican style: 16 oz / **Banquet**	73.5
Mexican style combination: 12 oz / **Banquet**	72.1
Mexican / **El Chico**	80
Mexican style combination: 16 oz / **Swanson** "TV"	72
Noodles and chicken: 10¼ oz / **Swanson** "TV"	53
Pepper oriental / **La Choy**	56
Perch, ocean: 8¾ oz / **Banquet**	49.8
Perch, ocean: 16 oz / **Weight Watchers**	15
Polynesian style: 13 oz / **Swanson** "TV"	65
Pork, loin of: 11¼ oz / **Swanson** "TV"	48
Queso / **El Chico**	140
Rib eye: 9 oz / **Morton** Steak House Dinner	38
Salisbury steak	
Banquet / 11 oz	24
Morton / 11 oz	24
Morton Country Table / 15 oz	51
Swanson Hungry-Man / 17 oz	65
Swanson 3 Course / 16 oz	48
Swanson "TV" / 11½ oz	40
Saltillo / **El Chico**	113
Shrimp / **La Choy**	56

Sirloin, chopped: 9½ oz / **Morton** Steak House Dinner	43
Sirloin strip: 9½ oz / **Morton** Steak House Dinner	47
Sole: 16 oz / **Weight Watchers**	17
Spaghetti and meatballs: 11½ oz / **Banquet**	62.9
Spaghetti and meatballs: 11 oz / **Morton**	61
Spaghetti and meatballs: 18½ oz / **Swanson** Hungry-Man	83
Spaghetti and meatballs: 12½ oz / **Swanson** "TV"	57
Swiss steak: 10 oz / **Swanson** "TV"	40
Turbot: 16 oz / **Weight Watchers**	40
Turkey	
Banquet / 11 oz	27.8
Banquet Man Pleaser / 19 oz	73.8
Morton / 11 oz	33
Morton Country Table / 15 oz	88
Swanson Hungry-Man / 19 oz	80
Swanson 3 Course / 16 oz	60
Swanson "TV" / 11½ oz	45
Breast: 10 oz / **Weight Watchers**	32
Veal Parmagian: 11 oz / **Banquet**	42.1
Veal Parmigiana: 10¼ oz / **Morton**	19
Veal Parmigiana: 20½ oz / **Swanson** Hungry-Man	70
Veal Parmigiana: 12¼ oz / **Swanson** "TV"	47
Western: 11 oz / **Banquet**	32.4
Western Round-Up: 11¾ oz / **Morton**	32
Western style: 17¾ oz / **Swanson** Hungry-Man	77
Western style: 11¾ oz / **Swanson** "TV"	41

DINNER MIXES

Ann Page Beef Noodle Dinner / ⅕ prepared dinner	25

Ann Page Cheeseburger Macaroni Dinner /
⅕ prepared dinner   28

Ann Page Chili Tomato Dinner / 1.6 oz
before preparation   32

Ann Page Hash Dinner / ⅕ prepared dinner   25

Ann Page Italian Style Dinner / 2 oz before
preparation   37

Ann Page Potato Stroganoff Dinner / ⅕
prepared dinner   28

Dinner Mexicana, Taco Casserole: 1 pkg before
preparation / **McCormick**   147

Dinner Mexicana, Taco Casserole: 1 pkg before
preparation / **Schilling**   147

Dinner Mexicana, Tamale Pie: 1 pkg before
preparation / **McCormick**   196

Dinner Mexicana, Tamale Pie: 1 pkg before
preparation / **Schilling**   196

Hamburger Helper: ⅕ prepared dinner

   Beef Noodle / **Betty Crocker**   26

   Beef Romanoff / **Betty Crocker**   20

   Cheeseburger Macaroni / **Betty Crocker**   28

   Chili Tomato / **Betty Crocker**   29

   Hamburger Hash / **Betty Crocker**   24

   Hamburger Pizza Dish / **Betty Crocker**   33

   Hamburger Stew / **Betty Crocker**   23

   Lasagne / **Betty Crocker**   32

   Potato Stroganoff / **Betty Crocker**   29

   Rice Oriental / **Betty Crocker** (6½ oz pkg)   27

   Rice Oriental / **Betty Crocker** (8 oz pkg)   35

   Spaghetti / **Betty Crocker**   31

Tuna Helper: ⅕ prepared dinner

   Dumplings and noodles / **Betty Crocker**   31

   Noodles / **Betty Crocker**   31

   Noodles w cheese sauce / **Betty Crocker**   28

Dips

GRAMS

(Ready to serve unless noted)

Bacon and horseradish: 1 oz
Borden	2.9
Kraft Ready	.8
Kraft Teez	1.6
Lucerne	1.8

Bacon and smoke flavor: 1 oz / **Sealtest**
Dip 'n Dressing   1.7
Barbecue: 1 oz / **Borden's** Western Bar BQ   1.8
Bean, chili / **Lucerne**   4.2
Bean, Jalapeno: 1 oz
Fritos	3.4
Gebhardt	4
Granny Goose	4.8
Lucerne	1.9

Blue cheese: 1 oz
Granny Goose Chip-Dip	14
Kraft Ready	1.6
Kraft Teez	1.3
Lucerne Bleu Tang	1.6
Sealtest Dip 'n Dressing	1.5

Casino Dip 'n Dressing: 1 oz / **Sealtest**   2.1
Chipped beef: 1 oz / **Sealtest** Dip 'n Dressing   1.8
Clam: 1 oz
Kraft Ready	1.9
Kraft Teez	1.5
Lucerne	1.4
and lobster / **Borden**	1.6

Dill pickle: 1 oz / **Kraft** Ready   2.5
Garden Spice: 1 oz / **Borden**   2.1
Garlic: 1 oz / **Granny Goose** Chip-Dip   15.7
Garlic: 1 oz / **Kraft** Teez   1.5

	GRAMS
Garlic: 1 oz / **Lucerne**	1.3
Green chili: 1 oz / **Borden**	4.3
Green Goddess: 1 oz / **Kraft** Teez	1.5
Green onion: 1 oz / **Granny Goose** Chip-Dip	16.3
Green onion, mix: ½ oz pkg / **Lawry's**	10
Guacamole: 1 oz / **Lucerne**	1.3
Guacamole, mix: ½ oz pkg / **Lawry's**	5.5
Hickory-smoke flavor: 1 oz / **Lucerne**	1.8
Onion: 1 oz unless noted	
Borden	1.8
Kraft Ready	2
French / **Kraft** Teez	1.5
French / **Lucerne**	1.4
French / **Sealtest** Dip 'n Dressing	2.2
and garlic / **Sealtest** Dip 'n Dressing	2.2
mix: ½ oz pkg / **Lawry's**	9.7
Tasty Tartar: 1 oz / **Borden**	1.8

Eggs

	GRAMS
Chicken egg	
Raw, hard-cooked or poached	
Extra large	.5
Large	.5
Medium	.4
Raw, white only	
Extra large	.3
Large	.3
Medium	.2
1 cup	1.9
Raw, yolk only	
Extra large	.1
Large	.1
Medium	.1
Fried	
Extra large	.2
Large	.1
Medium	.1
Scrambled	
Extra large	1.8
Large	1.5
Medium	1.3
Duck, raw: 1 egg	.5
Goose, raw: 1 egg	1.9
Turkey, raw: 1 egg	1.3
Egg, imitation, frozen: ¼ cup / **Morningstar Farms** Scramblers	2.5
Egg, imitation, mix: ½ pkg / **Eggstra**	4

GRAMS

Egg, imitation, refrigerated: ¼ cup / No-Fat
  Egg Beaters   3

EGG MIXES AND SEASONINGS

	GRAMS
Omelet, prepared: 1 pkg / **Durkee** Puffy	21
Omelet, dry mix: 1 pkg / **Durkee** Puffy	19
Omelet, bacon, prepared: 1 pkg / **Durkee**	20
Omelet, bacon, dry mix: 1 pkg / **Durkee**	18
Omelet, cheese, prepared: 1 pkg / **Durkee**	48
Omelet, cheese, dry mix: 1 pkg / **Durkee**	12
Omelet, cheese: 1¼ oz pkg / **McCormick**	12
Omelet, cheese: 1¼ oz pkg / **Schilling**	12
Omelet, Western: 1 pkg prepared w water only / **Durkee**	9
Omelet, Western: 1 pkg prepared w eggs / **Durkee**	22
Omelet, Western, dry mix: 1 pkg / **Durkee**	20
Omelet, Western: 1¼ oz pkg / **McCormick**	15
Omelet, Western: 1¼ oz pkg / **Schilling**	15
Scrambled: 1 pkg / **Durkee**	4
Scrambled w bacon: 1 pkg / **Durkee**	6

Fish and Seafood

	GRAMS
All fish, all varieties, fresh: any quantity	0
Abalone, raw: 3½ oz	3.4
Abalone, canned: 3½ oz	2.3
Bass, black sea, baked, stuffed: 1 lb	51.7
Bass, striped, oven fried: 1 fillet (8¾ x 4½ x ⅝ in thick)	13.4
Bass, striped, oven fried: 1 oz	1.9
Bass, striped, oven fried: 1 lb	30.4
Bluefish	
Fried: 1 fillet	9.2
Fried: 1 oz	1.3
Caviar, sturgeon, granular: 1 tbsp	.5
Caviar, sturgeon, pressed: 1 tbsp	.8
Clams, hard or round, raw, meat only: 1 pint (1 lb)	26.8
Clams, 4 cherrystone or 5 little neck clams	4.1
Clams, soft, raw, meat only: 1 pint (1 lb)	9.1
Crab, cooked, pieces: 1 cup	.8
Crab, cooked, flaked: 1 cup	.6
Crayfish, freshwater, raw, meat only: 3½ oz	1.2
Eel, raw: 4 oz	0
Frog legs, raw, meat only: 3½ oz	0
Haddock, fried: 1 fillet	6.4
Haddock, fried: 1 oz	1.6
Lobster, northern, cooked pieces: 1 cup	.4
Lobster, whole, steamed, meat only: 3½ oz	.3

	GRAMS
Oysters, raw	
Eastern: 1 cup (13-19 Selects) or	
(27-44 Standards)	8.2
Pacific and Western: 1 cup (about 4-6	
medium) or (6-9 small)	15.4
Cooked, fried: 4 Select (medium)	8.4
Roe, carp, cod, haddock, shad: 3½ oz	1.5
Scallops, bay and sea, raw: 4 oz	3.7
Shrimp, raw, peeled: 4 oz	1.7
Shrimp, french fried: 1 oz	2.8
Snails, raw: 1 oz	.6
Squid, raw, edible portion only: 3½ oz	1.5
Turtle, green, raw, meat only: 3½ oz	0
Whitefish, cooked, stuffed: 1 oz	1.6
Whitefish, smoked: 1 lb	0

CANNED AND FROZEN

Clams	
Chopped or minced, canned: 6 oz can,	
drained / **Doxsee**	1.6
Chopped or minced, canned: 8 oz can,	
drained / **Doxsee**	2.2
Chopped or minced, canned: 10½ oz can,	
drained / **Doxsee**	2.8
Chopped or minced, canned: ½ cup /	
Snow's	2
Fried, frozen: 5 oz / **Howard Johnson's**	45.6
Fried, frozen: 2½ oz / **Mrs. Paul's**	25
Cakes, frozen: 1 cake / **Mrs. Paul's Thins**	16
Deviled, frozen: 1 cake / **Mrs. Paul's**	14
Sticks, frozen: 1 stick / **Mrs. Paul's**	6.4
In cocktail sauce: 4 oz jar / **Sau-Sea**	19.1
Crab	
Canned: 6½ oz can / **Gold Seal** Fancy	2
Canned: 7½ oz can / **Icy Point**	2.3
Canned: 7½ oz can / **Pillar Rock**	2.3

GRAMS

King, in cocktail sauce: 4 oz jar / **Sau-Sea**	18.4
King, frozen: 8 oz / **Ship Ahoy**	1.1
King, frozen: 6 oz / **Wakefield's**	.8
Cakes, frozen: 1 cake / **Mrs. Paul's** Thins	17.5
Deviled, frozen: 1 cake / **Mrs. Paul's**	18
Deviled, frozen: 3⅓ oz / **Mrs. Paul's** Miniatures	26
Fish, frozen	
Cakes: 1 cake / **Mrs. Paul's**	11.5
Cakes: 1 cake / **Mrs. Paul's** Beach Haven	10
Cakes: 1 cake / **Mrs. Paul's** Thins	15.5
Fillets, buttered: 1 fillet (2½ oz) / **Mrs. Paul's**	1
Fillets, fried: 1 fillet (2 oz) / **Mrs. Paul's**	12
Fillets, in light batter: 1 fillet / **Mrs. Paul's**	14
Fillets, in light batter, fried: 1 fillet / **Mrs. Paul's** Supreme	19
In light batter: 3 oz / **Mrs. Paul's** Miniatures	15
Sticks: 1 stick / **Mrs. Paul's**	4
Sticks, in light batter, fried: 1 stick / **Mrs. Paul's**	6
Flounder, fried, frozen: 1 fillet (2 oz) / **Mrs. Paul's**	11
Flounder w lemon butter, frozen: 4½ oz / **Mrs. Paul's**	9
Gelfilte fish, canned or in jars: 1 piece unless noted	
Manischewitz (2-piece, 15½ oz can)	3.7
Manischewitz (4-piece, 1 lb jar)	2.3
Manischewitz (4-piece, 27 oz can)	3.9
Manischewitz (6-piece, 2 lb jar)	2.7
Manischewitz (8-piece, 2 lb jar)	2.4
Mother's (4-piece, 12 oz jar)	2.6
Mother's (4-piece, 1 lb jar)	3.5
Mother's (5-piece, 27 oz jar)	4.8
Mother's (6-piece, 15 oz jar), unsalted	2.2
Mother's (6-piece, 1 lb jar)	2.3

	GRAMS
Mother's (6-piece, 24 oz jar)	3.5
Mother's (8-piece, 24 oz jar)	2.6
Mother's (8-piece, 2 lb jar)	3.5
Mother's (12-piece, 2 lb jar)	2.3
Rokeach (in liquid broth): 1 oz	.2
Rokeach Old Vienna (in jellied broth): 1 oz	1.4
Fishballs, 12-piece, 2 lb jar / **Manischewitz**	1.5
Fishballs, 6-piece, 1 lb jar / **Manischewitz**	1.5
Fishlets, 1 lb and 2 lb jar / **Manischewitz**	trace
Whitefish and pike, 2-piece, 15½ oz can / **Manischewitz**	3.1
Whitefish and pike, 1 lb jar / **Manischewitz**	1.3
Whitefish and pike, 4-piece, 27 oz can / **Manischewitz**	3.3
Whitefish and pike, 2 lb jar / **Manischewitz**	1.5
Whitefish and pike fishlets, 1 lb and 2 lb jar / **Manischewitz** Deluxe	trace
Haddock, fried, frozen: 1 fillet (2 oz) / **Mrs. Paul's**	12
Herring, in jars	
Pickled: 6 oz jar, drained / **Vita** Bismark	5.9
Pickled: 8½ oz jar / **Vita** Cocktail	25.8
Pickled: 8¾ oz jar / **Vita** Lunch	9.8
Pickled: 8¾ oz jar, drained / **Vita** Matjes	18.8
Pickled: 8¾ oz jar, drained / **Vita** Party Snacks	14.1
Pickled: 8¾ oz jar, drained / **Vita** Tastee Bits	19.1
Pickled, in cream sauce: 8⅓ oz jar / **Vita**	18.3
Oysters wo shell, canned: ½ cup / **Bumblebee**	5.5
Perch, fried, frozen: 1 fillet (2 oz) / **Mrs. Paul's**	9
Salmon, canned, all brands	0
Sardines, in mustard sauce: 1 oz / **Underwood**	.6
Sardines, in soya bean oil: 1 oz / **Underwood**	.1
Sardines, in tomato sauce, canned: 7½ oz / **Del Monte**	4
Sardines, in tomato sauce: 1 oz / **Underwood**	1.2

GRAMS

Scallops, fried, frozen: 3½ oz / **Mrs. Paul's**	24
Scallops, in light batter, fried, frozen: 3½ oz / **Mrs. Paul's**	21
Seafood, combination, fried, frozen: 9 oz / **Mrs. Paul's** Platter	57
Seafood croquettes, frozen: 1 cake / **Mrs. Paul's**	24

Shrimp

Baby, solids and liquids: one 4½ oz can / **Bumblebee**	.9
Fancy, tiny: 4½ oz can, drained / **Icy Point**	1
Fancy, tiny: 4½ oz can, drained / **Pillar Rock**	1
Fried, frozen: 3 oz / **Mrs. Paul's**	17
Fried, frozen: 4 oz / **Sau-Sea** Shrimp Fries	22
Frozen, in bag, cooked: 2 oz / **Sau-Sea**	0
Cakes, frozen: 1 cake / **Mrs. Paul's**	17
Cakes, frozen: 1 cake / **Mrs. Paul's** Thins	16.5
Sticks, frozen: 1 stick / **Mrs. Paul's**	5.5
In cocktail sauce: 4 oz jar / **Sau-Sea** Shrimp Cocktail	20.6
Sole w lemon butter, frozen: 4½ oz / **Mrs. Paul's**	10
Tuna, canned, all brands	0

FISH AND SEAFOOD ENTREES, FROZEN

Crepes, clam: 5½ oz / **Mrs. Paul's**	22
Crepes, crab: 5½ oz / **Mrs. Paul's**	24
Crepes, scallop: 5½ oz / **Mrs. Paul's**	25
Crepes, shrimp: 5½ oz / **Mrs. Paul's**	24
Croquette, shrimp w Newburg sauce: 12 oz / **Howard Johnson's**	28.3
Fish Au Gratin: 5 oz / **Mrs. Paul's**	23
Fish Au Gratin: 4 oz / **Mrs. Paul's** Party Pak	15
Fish 'n' Chips: 1 entree / **Swanson** "TV"	25
Fish 'n' Chips, in light batter, fried: 7 oz / **Mrs. Paul's**	45
Fish Parmesan: 5 oz / **Mrs. Paul's**	20

	GRAMS
Fish Parmesan: 4 oz / **Mrs. Paul's** Party Pak	15
Flounder w chopped broccoli, cauliflower, red peppers: 8½ oz / **Weight Watchers**	13
Haddock au Groton: 10 oz / **Howard Johnson's**	11.8
Haddock w stuffing and spinach: 8¾ oz / **Weight Watchers**	14
Perch, ocean w chopped broccoli: 8½ oz / **Weight Watchers**	9
Scallops w butter and cheese: 7 oz / **Mrs. Paul's**	11
Shrimp and Scallops Mariner: 1 pkg / **Stouffer's** 10¼ oz	40
Sole w peas, mushrooms, lobster sauce: 9½ oz / **Weight Watchers**	17
Tuna, creamed w peas: 5 oz / **Green Giant** Boil-in-Bag Toast Toppers	11
Turbot w peas, carrots: 8 oz / **Weight Watchers**	17

Flavorings, Sweet

1 tsp unless noted	GRAMS
Almond extract, pure / **Durkee**	3.3
Anise extract, imitation / **Durkee**	4
Banana extract, imitation / **Durkee**	3.8
Black walnut flavor, imitation / **Durkee**	1
Brandy extract, imitation / **Durkee**	3.8
Chocolate extract / **Durkee**	1.8
Coconut flavor, imitation / **Durkee**	2
Lemon extract, imitation / **Durkee**	4.3
Maple extract, imitation / **Durkee**	1.5
Mocha extract, imitation / **Durkee**	3.5

	GRAMS
Orange extract, imitation / **Durkee**	.4
Peppermint extract, imitation / **Durkee**	3.8
Rum extract, imitation / **Durkee**	3.5
Strawberry extract, imitation / **Durkee**	3
Vanilla extract, imitation / **Durkee**	.8
Vanilla extract, pure / **Durkee**	2

Flour and Meal

FLOUR

	GRAMS
1 cup unless noted	
Biscuit mix / **Bisquick**	76
Buckwheat, dark, sifted	70.6
Buckwheat, light, sifted	77.9
Carob	113
Corn	89.9
Corn: 1 lb	348.4
Lima bean, sifted	79.4
Peanut, defatted	18.9
Rye	
Light	68.6
Medium	65.8
Medium / **Pillsbury**	89
Dark	87.2
Wheat / **Pillsbury** Bohemian	86
Soybean	
Full fat	21.3
Low fat	32.2
Defatted	38.1

	GRAMS
Tortilla, corn: ⅓ cup / **Quaker's Masa Harina**	27.4
Tortilla, wheat: ⅓ cup / **Quaker's Masa Trigo**	24.7
Wheat	
All purpose	104.3
Bread	102.3
Cake or pastry	93.7
Gluten	66.1
Self-rising	92.8
Whole wheat	85.2
Whole wheat / **Pillsbury**	80
White	
Ballard	87
Peavey Family High Altitude Hungarian	87
Peavey Family Occident	87
Peavey Family King Midas	87
Pillsbury All Purpose	87
Cake, self-rising / **Presto**	86.6
Cake / **Softasilk**	88.4
Self-rising: ¼ cup / **Aunt Jemima**	23.6
Self-rising / **Ballard**	84
Self-rising / **Pillsbury**	84
Unbleached / **Pillsbury**	86

MEAL

Almond, partially defatted: 1 oz	8.2
Corn	
White or yellow, whole ground unbolted, dry: 1 cup	89.9
White: 1 oz (2 tbsp and 2 tsp) / **Albers**	22
White: about 3 tbsp / **Aunt Jemima** Enriched	22.2
White: about 3 tbsp / **Quaker** Enriched	22.2
White, bolted, mix: 1/6 cup / **Aunt Jemima**	20.8
White, bolted, self-rising: 1/6 cup / **Aunt Jemima**	20.4
White, self-rising: 1/6 cup / **Aunt Jemima**	21.1

GRAMS

Yellow: 1 oz (2 tbsp and 2 tsp) / **Albers**   22
Yellow: about 3 tbsp / **Aunt Jemima**
  Enriched   22.2
Yellow: about 3 tbsp / **Quaker** Enriched   22.2
Crackermeal: 1 cup / **Sunshine**   83.8

Frostings

GRAMS

Ready to spread: 1 can unless noted

	GRAMS
Cake and cookie decorator, all colors: 1 tbsp / **Pillsbury**	12
Butter pecan / **Betty Crocker**	324
Cherry / **Betty Crocker**	336
Chocolate / **Betty Crocker**	300
Chocolate fudge / **Pillsbury**	288
Chocolate nut / **Betty Crocker**	288
Dark Dutch fudge / **Betty Crocker**	288
Double Dutch / **Pillsbury**	288
Lemon / **Betty Crocker** Sunkist	336
Lemon / **Pillsbury**	324
Milk chocolate / **Betty Crocker**	288
Milk chocolate / **Pillsbury**	288
Orange / **Betty Crocker**	336
Sour cream, chocolate / **Betty Crocker**	300
Sour cream, vanilla / **Pillsbury**	324
Sour cream, white / **Betty Crocker**	324
Strawberry / **Pillsbury**	324
Vanilla / **Betty Crocker**	336
Vanilla / **Pillsbury**	336

GRAMS

1 pkg: prepared

Banana / **Betty Crocker** Chiquita	360
Butter Brickle / **Betty Crocker**	360
Butter pecan / **Betty Crocker**	360
Caramel / **Pillsbury Rich 'n Easy**	348
Cherry / **Betty Crocker**	360
Chocolate / **Betty Crocker** Lite	216
Chocolate fudge / **Betty Crocker**	384
Chocolate fudge / **Pillsbury Rich 'n Easy**	360
Coconut almond / **Pillsbury**	204
Coconut pecan / **Betty Crocker**	216
Coconut pecan / **Pillsbury**	240
Dark chocolate fudge / **Betty Crocker**	360
Double Dutch / **Pillsbury Rich 'n Easy**	360
Lemon / **Betty Crocker** Sunkist	372
Lemon / **Pillsbury Rich 'n Easy**	360
Milk chocolate / **Betty Crocker**	360
Milk chocolate / **Pillsbury Rich 'n Easy**	348
Sour cream, chocolate / **Betty Crocker**	360
Sour cream, white / **Betty Crocker**	372
Strawberry / **Pillsbury Rich 'n Easy**	348
Vanilla / **Betty Crocker** Lite	228
Vanilla / **Pillsbury Rich 'n Easy**	348
White, creamy / **Betty Crocker**	396
White, fluffy / **Betty Crocker** Lite	192
White, fluffy / **Pillsbury**	204

Fruit

FRESH

	GRAMS
Acerola cherries: 10 fruits	5.6
Apples	
w skin: 1 small (about 4 per lb)	15.3
w skin: 1 medium (about 3 per lb)	20
w skin: 1 large (about 2 per lb)	30.7
Peeled: 1 small (about 4 per lb)	13.9
Peeled: 1 medium (about 3 per lb)	18.2
Peeled: 1 large (about 2 per lb)	27.9
Apricots	
Raw, halves: 1 cup	19.8
Raw, halves: 1 lb	58.1
Raw, whole: 3 apricots	13.7
Raw, whole (12 per lb): 1 lb	54.6
Avocados	
California: ½ average	6.5
California, cubed: 1 cup	9
California, puree: 1 cup	13.8
Florida: ½ average	13.5
Florida, cubed: 1 cup	13.2
Florida, puree: 1 cup	20.2
Bananas	
1 small, 7¾ in	21.1
1 medium, 8¾ in	26.2
1 large, 9¾ in	30.2
Mashed: 1 cup	50
Red: 1 banana, 7¼ in	30.7
Red, sliced: 1 cup	35.1
Sliced: 1 cup	33.3
Dehydrated or flakes: 1 tbsp	5.5
Dehydrated or flakes: 1 cup	88.6

Blackberries (including dewberries, boysenberries,
    youngberries), raw: 1 cup   18.6
Blueberries, raw: 1 cup   22.2
Blueberries, raw: 1 lb   69.4
Cherries
    Raw, sour, red: 1 cup   14.7
    Raw, sour, red: 1 lb   58.4
    Raw, sweet: 1 cup   20.4
    Raw, sweet: 1 lb   71
Cranberries, raw, chopped: 1 cup   11.9
Cranberries, raw, whole: 1 cup   10.3
Figs, raw, whole: 1 small   8.1
Figs, raw, whole: 1 medium   10.2
Figs, raw, whole: 1 large   13.2
Grapefruit: half, 3½-in diam   10.3
Grapefruit, sections: 1 cup   24.4
Grapes
    Concord, Delaware, Niagara, Catawba,
      Scuppernong: 10 grapes   4.1
    Flame Tokay, Emperor: 10 grapes   9.9
    Ribier: 10 grapes   11.5
    Thompson Seedless, Malaga, Muscat:
      10 grapes   8.7
Groundcherries (poha or cape-gooseberries):
    1 cup   15.7
Lemons, wedge: 1 from large lemon   2.2
Lemons, whole fruit: 1 large   8.7
Limes, raw: 1 lime   6.4
Loganberries, raw: 1 cup   21.5
Loquats, raw: 10 fruits   15.3
Lychees, raw: 10 fruits   14.8
Mangoes, raw, whole: 1 fruit   38.8
Muskmelons
    Canteloupes, cubed, diced or balls: 1 cup   12
    Canteloupes: half, 5-in diam   20.4
    Casaba, cubed, diced or balls: 1 cup   11.1
    Casaba, whole about 6 lbs: 1 melon   88.5

	GRAMS
Honeydew, cubed, diced or balls: 1 cup	13.1
Honeydew, whole about 5¼ lbs: 1 melon	115.5
Nectarines, raw, 2½-in diam: 1 nectarine	23.6
Oranges	
California navels (winter): 1 small	11.3
California navels (winter): 1 medium	17.8
California navels (winter): 1 large	21.8
California navels, sections: 1 cup	19.1
Valencias (summer): 1 small	12.2
Valencias (summer): 1 medium	15
Valencias (summer): 1 large	23.4
Valencias, sections: 1 cup	22.3
Florida: 1 small	14.5
Florida: 1 medium	18.1
Florida: 1 large	22.6
Florida, sections: 1 cup	22.2
Papaws, raw, whole: 1 papaw	16.4
Papayas, raw, cubed, ½-in pieces: 1 cup	14
Papayas, raw, whole, about 1 lb: 1 papaya	30.4
Peaches	
Raw, pared, sliced: 1 cup	16.5
Raw, whole, peeled: 1 small (about 4 per lb)	9.7
Raw, whole, peeled: 1 large (about 2½ per lb)	14.8
Raw, whole, peeled: 1 lb	38.3
Pears	
Raw, sliced or cubed: 1 cup	25.2
Raw, whole, Bartlett: 1 pear (about 2½ per lb)	25.1
Raw, whole, Boscs: 1 pear (about 3 per lb)	21.6
Raw, whole, D'Anjous: 1 pear (about 2 per lb)	30.6
Persimmons, raw, Japanese or kaki: 1 persimmon	33.1
Persimmons, raw, native: 1 persimmon	8.2
Pineapple, raw, diced pieces: 1 cup	21.2

GRAMS

Pineapple, raw, sliced: 1 slice, ¾-in thick	11.5
Plums	
Raw, whole, Damson: 10 plums, 1-in diam	17.8
Raw, whole, Damson: 1 lb	73.5
Raw, Japanese and hybrid:	
1 plum, 2⅛-in diam	8.1
Raw, Japanese and hybrid: 1 lb	80.7
Prune type, raw: 1 plum, 1½-in diam	5.6
Prune type, raw: 1 lb	84
Pomegranate: 1 pomegranate, 3⅜-in diam	25.3
Raspberries, raw, black: 1 cup	21
Raspberries, raw, red: 1 cup	16.7
Rhubarb, raw, diced: 1 cup	4.5
Rhubarb, cooked w sugar: 1 cup	97.2
Strawberries, raw, whole berries: 1 cup	12.5
Tangerines, raw, whole fruit:	
1 large, 2½-in diam	11.7
Watermelon	
Raw: 1 lb	29
Raw, diced pieces: 1 cup	10.2
Raw, slice, 10-in diam by 1-in thick	27.3
Raw, wedge, 4 in x 8 in radius	27.3

CANNED AND FROZEN

Applesauce in cans or jars	
Del Monte / ½ cup	23.5
Mott's Natural Style / 8 oz	22
S and W Nutradiet / ½ cup	11.5
Stokely-Van Camp / 1 cup	45
Tillie Lewis / ½ cup	15
Town House / 8 oz	47
Unswt: ½ cup / **S and W Nutradiet**	11.5
Apricots: 1 cup unless noted	
Halves / **Del Monte**	52
Halves / **Stokely-Van Camp**	54

GRAMS

Halves / **Tillie Lewis**	30
Halves, in heavy syrup / **Libby's**	54
Halves, in heavy syrup / **Town House**	56
Halves, in light syrup / **Scotch Buy**	40
Halves, in light syrup / **Town House**	40
Whole / **Del Monte**	53
Whole, in heavy syrup / **Town House**	52
Swt: 4 halves / **S and W Nutradiet**	9.1
Unswt: 4 halves / **S and W Nutradiet**	8.7
Swt, whole: 2 whole / **S and W Nutradiet**	6.9
Blackberries, canned, swt:	
½ cup / **S and W Nutradiet**	7.9
Blueberries, unswt, frozen:	
½ cup / **Seabrook Farms**	11
Boysenberries, canned, swt:	
½ cup / **S and W Nutradiet**	7.7
Cherries, canned: 1 cup unless noted	
Tillie Lewis	30
Dark, sweet / **Del Monte**	48
Dark, sweet / **S and W Nutradiet**	25
Dark, sweet, in heavy syrup / **Libby's**	53
Dark, sweet, pitted / **Del Monte**	50
Light, sweet / **Del Monte** Royal Anne	51
Light, sweet, in heavy syrup / **Libby's**	53
Light, sweet, unswt: 14 whole /	
S and W Nutradiet Royal Anne	10.6
Sour, pitted / **Stokely-Van Camp**	22
Cranberry orange, crushed: 2 oz / **Ocean Spray**	26
Cranberry orange relish: 2 oz / **Ocean Spray**	26
Cranberry sauce, jellied: 2 oz / **Ocean Spray**	22
Cranberry sauce, whole: 2 oz / **Ocean Spray**	21
Currants, canned: ½ cup / **Del Monte** Zante	48
Figs, whole, canned: 1 cup / **Del Monte**	55
Figs, whole, swt, canned:	
6 whole / **S and W Nutradiet**	11.5
Figs, whole, unswt, canned:	
6 whole / **S and W Nutradiet**	12.2

	GRAMS
Fruit cocktail, canned: 1 cup	
Del Monte	45
Libby's Juice Pack	39
S and W Nutradiet	45
Stokely-Van Camp	46
Tillie Lewis	26
In heavy syrup / **Libby's**	45
In heavy syrup / **Town House**	46
Unswt / **S and W Nutradiet**	21
Fruit mixed, canned: 5 oz / **Del Monte**	27
Fruit mixed, frozen:	
5 oz / **Birds Eye** Quick Thaw	34
Fruit salad, canned: 1 cup / **Del Monte** Tropical	52
Fruits for salad, canned: 1 cup	
Del Monte	46
Stokely-Van Camp	44
In heavy syrup / **Libby's**	48
Swt / **S and W Nutradiet**	15.8
Unswt / **S and W Nutradiet**	17.4
Grapefruit sections, canned: 1 cup / **Tillie Lewis**	22
Grapefruit sections, in juice, canned:	
1 cup / **Del Monte**	21
Grapefruit sections, in syrup, canned:	
1 cup / **Del Monte**	35
Grapefruit sections, unswt, canned:	
½ cup / **S and W Nutradiet**	7.9
Oranges, Mandarin, canned: 5½ oz / **Del Monte**	25
Oranges, Mandarin, canned:	
½ cup / **Tillie Lewis**	11
Oranges, Mandarin, swt, canned:	
½ cup / **S and W Nutradiet**	7
Oranges, Mandarin, unswt, canned:	
½ cup / **S and W Nutradiet**	6.1
Peaches, canned: 1 cup unless noted	
Stokely-Van Camp	49
Cling / **Del Monte**	45
Cling / **Tillie Lewis**	26

Cling, diced: 5 oz can / **Del Monte**	28
Cling, in heavy syrup / **Libby's**	45
Cling, in heavy syrup / **Town House**	50
Cling, in light syrup / **Highway**	36
Cling, in light syrup / **Scotch Buy**	36
Cling, slices / **Del Monte**	45
Cling, slices, in heavy syrup / **Town House**	50
Cling, slices, in light syrup / **Highway**	36
Cling, slices, in swt juice / **Libby's** Juice Pack	38
Cling, slices, swt / **S and W Nutradiet**	11.2
Cling, unswt: 2 halves / **S and W Nutradiet**	.3
Cling, slices, unswt / **S and W Nutradiet**	10.2
Freestone, halves / **Del Monte**	45
Freestone, halves, in extra heavy syrup / **Town House**	68
Freestone, mixed pieces, in heavy syrup / **Highway**	52
Freestone, mixed pieces, in heavy syrup / **Scotch Buy**	52
Freestone, slices / **Del Monte**	45
Freestone, slices, in extra heavy syrup / **Town House**	68
Freestone, swt: ½ cup / **S and W Nutradiet**	5.9
Slices / **Stokely-Van Camp**	48
Spiced w pits: 7¼ oz / **Del Monte**	40
Peaches, frozen: 5 oz / **Birds Eye** Quick Thaw	34
Peaches, frozen, slices: ½ cup / **Seabrook Farms**	28
Pears, canned: 1 cup unless noted	
Bartlett / **Tillie Lewis**	26
Bartlett, halves / **Del Monte**	43
Bartlett, halves, in light syrup / **Highway**	40
Bartlett, halves, in light syrup / **Scotch Buy**	38
Bartlett, halves, in heavy syrup / **Libby's**	44
Bartlett, halves, in heavy syrup / **Town House**	49
Bartlett, slices / **Del Monte**	43

Bartlett, slices, in heavy syrup /
   Town House   49
Halves / **Stokely-Van Camp**   50
Halves, in swt juice / **Libby's Juice Pack**   39
Halves, swt: 2 halves / **S and W Nutradiet**   6.5
Quartered, swt / **S and W Nutradiet**   12.2
Quartered, unswt / **S and W Nutradiet**   12.8
Slices / **Stokely-Van Camp**   47
Pineapple, canned: 1 cup
   Tillie Lewis   36
Chunks, in juice / **Del Monte**   35
Chunks, in juice / **Dole**   33
Chunks, in juice, unswt / **Town House**   35
Chunks, in syrup / **Del Monte**   49
Chunks, in syrup / **Dole**   44
Chunks, in syrup / **Town House**   49
Chunks, swt / **S and W Nutradiet**   22
Crushed, in juice / **Del Monte**   35
Crushed, in juice, unswt / **Town House**   35
Crushed, in syrup / **Del Monte**   49
Crushed, in syrup / **Town House**   49
Slices, in juice / **Del Monte**   35
Slices, in juice, unswt / **Town House**   35
Slices, in syrup / **Del Monte**   49
Slices, in syrup / **Town House**   49
Slices, swt / **S and W Nutradiet**   26
Slices, unswt / **S and W Nutradiet**   23.4
Tidbits, in syrup / **Town House**   49
Tidbits, swt / **S and W Nutradiet**   22
Tidbits, unswt / **S and W Nutradiet**   33
Plums, canned: 1 cup
   Del Monte   52
   Libby's   56
   S and W Nutradiet   23.8
   Stokely-Van Camp   60
   Tillie Lewis   36
Prunes, stewed, canned: 1 cup / **Del Monte**   60

GRAMS

Raspberries, red, frozen:
   5 oz / **Birds Eye** Quick Thaw   35
Strawberries
       Canned: 1 cup / **S and W Nutradiet**   8.6
       Frozen: 5 oz / **Birds Eye** Quick Thaw   30
       Halves, frozen: 5.3 oz / **Birds Eye**   48
       Slices, frozen: 5 oz / **Birds Eye**   48
       Slices, frozen: ½ cup / **Seabrook Farms** 36
       Whole, frozen: 4 oz / **Birds Eye**   20
       Whole, frozen, unswt: ½ cup /
          Seabrook Farms   10

DRIED

Uncooked

Apples: 2 oz / **Del Monte**   37
Apples: 1 pkg / **Weight Watchers** Apple Snacks 13
Apricots: 2 oz / **Del Monte**   35
Currants: 1 cup / **Del Monte** Zanta   108.4
Dates, chopped: 1 cup / **Dromedary**   114
Dates, diced: 1 cup / **Bordo**   159.6
Dates, whole, pitted: 4 average / **Bordo** 18.2
Dates, whole, pitted: 1 cup / **Dromedary** 111.8
Figs: 1 large (2 in x 1 in)   15
Fruits and peels, glazed: 4 oz / **Liberty** 93
Fruits: 1 pkg / **Weight Watchers** Fruit Snacks 13
Peaches: 2 oz / **Del Monte**   35
Pears: 2 oz / **Del Monte**   40
Prunes, w pits: 2 oz / **Del Monte**   31
Prunes, w pits: 2 oz / **Del Monte** Moist-pak 30
Prunes, pitted: 2 oz / **Del Monte**   36
Raisins, muscat: 3 oz / **Del Monte**   66
Raisins, seedless, golden: 3 oz / **Del Monte** 68
Raisins, seedless, Thompson: 3 oz / **Del Monte** 66

Fruit Drinks and Fruit-Flavored Beverages

	GRAMS
All flavors, mix, w sugar:	
1 env / **Ann Page Cheeri-Aid**	84
All flavors, mix, wo sugar:	
1 env / **Ann Page Cheeri-Aid**	8
All flavors, mix, prepared: 8 fl oz / **Funny Face**	20
All flavors, mix, prepared, swt: 8 fl oz / **Kool-Aid**	23
All flavors, mix, unswt:	
8 fl oz prepared w sugar / **Kool-Aid**	25
Apple, canned: 8 fl oz / **Ann Page**	30
Apple, canned: 6 fl oz / **Hi-C**	23
Apple-grape, canned: 6 fl oz / **Mott's "P.M."**	22
Berry, canned: 8 fl oz / **Cragmont** Wild Berry	31
Cherry	
Canned: 8 fl oz / **Ann Page**	31
Canned: 8 fl oz / **Cragmont**	29
Canned: 6 fl oz / **Hi-C**	23
Mix, prepared: 6 fl oz / **Hi-C**	19
Citrus cooler, canned: 8 fl oz / **Ann Page**	30
Citrus cooler, canned: 8 fl oz / **Cragmont**	29
Citrus cooler, canned: 6 fl oz / **Hi-C**	23
Cranberry juice cocktail	
Bottled: 8 fl oz / **Ann Page**	40
Bottled: 6 fl oz / **Ocean Spray**	26
Bottled: 6 fl oz / **Ocean Spray** Low Calorie	9
Canned: 4 fl oz / **Seneca**	20.4
Canned: 6 fl oz / **Town House**	26
Canned and bottled: 6 fl oz / **Welch's**	28.5
Cranberry-apple drink	
Bottled: 8 fl oz / **Ann Page**	45

GRAMS

Bottled: 6 fl oz / **Ocean Spray Cranapple**	32
Bottled: 6 fl oz /	
Ocean Spray Low Calorie **Cranapple**	7
Canned: 6 fl oz / **Town House**	33
Cranberry-apricot drink, bottled:	
6 fl oz / **Ocean Spray Cranicot**	27
Cranberry-grape drink, bottled:	
6 fl oz / **Ocean Spray Crangrape**	27
Cranberry-prune drink, bottled:	
6 fl oz / **Ocean Spray Cranprune**	29
Fruit, canned: 6 fl oz /	
Mott's "A.M." Fruit Drink	22
Fruit, mix, prepared: 8 fl oz /	
Hawaiian Punch Red	2.5
Grape	
Bottled: 6 fl oz / **Sunshake**	23
Canned: 8 fl oz / **Ann Page**	31
Canned: 6 fl oz / **Hi-C**	22
Canned: 8 fl oz / **Cragmont**	32
Canned: 6 fl oz / **Welchade**	23
Canned: 6 fl oz / **Welchade** Red	23
Mix: 1 heaping tsp /	
Ann Page Instant Breakfast Drink	8
Mix, prepared: 6 fl oz / **Hi-C**	19
Mix, prepared: 4 fl oz / **Tang**	15
Refrigerated: 6 fl oz / **Welch's** Juice Drink	27
Grapefruit, bottled: 6 fl oz / **Ann Page**	
Ready-Made	20
Grapefruit, mix, prepared: 4 fl oz / **Tang**	13
Lemonade	
Frozen, reconstituted: 6 fl oz / **Minute Maid**	19.6
Mix, prepared: 8 fl oz / **Country Time**	22
Mix, prepared: 6 fl oz / **Hi-C**	19
Mix, prepared: 6 fl oz / **Minute Maid**	
Crystals	20
Mix, prepared: 6 fl oz / **Wyler's**	16.8

GRAMS

Pink, mix, prepared: 8 fl oz / **Country Time**	22
Pink, mix, prepared: 6 fl oz / **Minute Maid** Crystals	20
Lemon-limeade, frozen, reconstituted: 6 fl oz / **Minute Maid**	19.6
Limeade, frozen, reconstituted: 6 fl oz / **Minute Maid**	20.1
Orange	
Bottled: 6 fl oz / **A & P** Ready-Made	20
Bottled: 6 fl oz / **Sunshake**	22
Canned: 8 fl oz / **Ann Page**	30
Canned: 8 fl oz / **Cragmont**	32
Canned: 6 fl oz / **Hi-C**	23
Canned: 6 fl oz / **Welchade**	24
Frozen, reconstituted: 6 fl oz / **Birds Eye Orange Plus**	24
Mix: 1 heaping tsp / **Ann Page** Instant Breakfast Drink	8
Mix: 3 rounded tsp / **Town House** Instant Breakfast Drink	24
Mix, prepared: 6 fl oz / **Hi-C**	19
Mix, prepared: 4 fl oz / **Start**	14
Mix, prepared: 4 fl oz / **Tang**	14
Orangeade, frozen, reconstituted: 6 fl oz / **Minute Maid**	22.7
Orange-pineapple, canned: 8 fl oz / **Ann Page**	31
Orange-pineapple, canned: 6 fl oz / **Hi-C**	23
Peach, canned: 6 fl oz / **Hi-C**	23
Peach, mix, prepared: 6 fl oz / **Hi-C**	19
Pineapple-grapefruit, canned: 6 fl oz / **Town House** Juice Drink	24
Pineapple-pink grapefruit, canned: 6 fl oz / **Dole** Drink	23
Pineapple-orange, canned: 8 fl oz / **Cragmont**	32
Punch	
All flavors, canned: 8 fl oz / **Hawaiian Punch**	29

GRAMS

All flavors, frozen, reconstituted:
    8 fl oz / **Hawaiian Punch**   29
All flavors, mix, prepared: 8 fl oz /
    Hawaiian Punch Shelf Concentrate   29
Florida punch, canned: 6 fl oz / **Hi-C**   24
Fruit, canned: 6 fl oz / **Welchade**   24
Tropical fruit, canned: 8 fl oz / **Ann Page**   30
Tropical, canned: 8 fl oz / **Cragmont**   32
    Mix, prepared: 6 fl oz / **Hi-C**   19
Strawberry, canned: 6 fl oz / **Hi-C**   22
Tangerine, canned: 6 fl oz / **Hi-C**   23
Wild berry, canned: 8 fl oz / **Ann Page**   31
Wild berry, canned: 6 fl oz / **Hi-C**   22

Fruit Juices

FRESH

GRAMS

1 cup unless noted

	GRAMS
Acerola cherry	11.6
Grapefruit	22.6
Lemon	19.5
Lemon: 1 tbsp	1.2
Lime: 1 tbsp	1.4
Orange	
California navels	28.1
Florida	24.7
Valcencias	26
Tangerine	24

BOTTLED, CANNED AND FROZEN

GRAMS

6 fl oz unless noted

Apple
Bottled: 8 fl oz / **Ann Page**	30
Canned / **Mott's**	19
Canned / **Mott's** Natural Style	19
Canned / **Pillsbury**	22
Canned and bottled: 4 fl oz / **Seneca**	15.9
Canned from concentrate / **Welch's**	22.5

Apricot nectar
Canned / **Del Monte**	26
Canned / **Libby's**	27
Canned: 4 fl oz / **Seneca**	20.4
Canned / **Town House**	28

Grape
Bottled, canned and frozen concentrate:	
4 fl oz / **Seneca**	18.1
Bottled / **Welch's**	30
Bottled, red / **Welch's**	30
Bottled, red / **Welch's** Sparkling	30
Bottled, white / **Welch's**	30
Bottled, white / **Welch's** Sparkling	30
Frozen, reconstituted **Minute Maid**	25

Grapefruit
Bottled / **Ocean Spray**	16
Canned: 4 fl oz / **Seneca**	13.6
Canned from concentrate / **Welch's**	16.5
Canned, swt / **Del Monte**	21
Canned, swt / **Libby's**	24
Canned, unswt / **Del Monte**	17
Canned, unswt / **Libby's**	18
Canned, unswt: 1 cup / **Treesweet**	24
Frozen, reconstituted / **Minute Maid**	18.3
Frozen, reconstituted: 1 cup / **Treesweet**	24

Grapefruit-orange, canned: 4 fl oz / **Seneca**   14.7

	GRAMS
Lemon, bottled, reconstituted: 2 tbsp / **ReaLemon**	2
Lemon, canned, reconstituted: 1 tbsp / **Town House**	1
Lemon, frozen, reconstituted / **Minute Maid**	13.2
Orange	
Canned: 4 fl oz / **Seneca**	14.7
Canned from concentrate / **Welch's**	22.5
Canned, swt / **Del Monte**	18
Canned, swt / **Libby's**	23
Canned, unswt / **Del Monte**	19
Canned, unswt / **Libby's**	20
Canned, unswt: 1 cup / **Treesweet**	28
Frozen, reconstituted / **Bright and Early**	21.6
Frozen, reconstituted / **Minute Maid**	21.4
Frozen, reconstituted / **Snow Crop**	21.4
Frozen, reconstituted: 1 cup / **Treesweet**	29
Imitation, frozen, reconstituted / **Birds Eye** Awake	21
Orange-grapefruit	
Canned, swt / **Del Monte**	20
Canned, unswt / **Libby's**	19
Canned, unswt / **Del Monte**	12
Frozen, reconstituted / **Minute Maid**	19.1
Peach nectar, canned / **Del Monte**	27
Peach nectar, canned / **Libby's**	23
Pear nectar, canned / **Del Monte**	30
Pear nectar, canned / **Libby's**	25
Pineapple	
Canned / **Del Monte**	25
Canned / **Dole**	22.8
Canned: 4 fl oz / **Seneca**	17
Canned, unswt / **Town House**	25
Frozen, reconstituted / **Minute Maid**	22.7
Pineapple-grapefruit, canned / **Del Monte**	24
Pineapple-orange, frozen, reconstituted / **Minute Maid**	23

GRAMS

Pineapple-pink grapefruit, canned / **Del Monte**	24
Prune	
Bottled / **Ann Page**	34
Bottled / **RealPrune**	32.1
Canned / **Del Monte**	33
Canned / **Mott's**	34
Canned / **Mott's Prune Nectar**	25
Canned: 4 fl oz / **Seneca**	26
Canned or bottled / **Sunsweet**	30
Canned / **Welch's**	36
Canned w pulp / **Mott's**	30
Tangerine, frozen, reconstituted / **Minute Maid**	20.1

Gelatin

	GRAMS
All flavors, mix, prepared: ½ cup / **D-Zerta**	0
All flavors, mix, prepared: ½ cup / **Estee** Low Calorie	9
All flavors, mix, prepared: ½ cup / **Jell-O**	18.2
All flavors, mix, prepared: ½ cup / **Royal**	19
All flavors, unswt, mix, prepared: ½ cup / **Royal Sweet As You Please**	0
Orange-flavored, drinking: 1 env / **Knox** Gelatine	10
Unflavored: 1 pkg (¼ oz) / **Ann Page**	0
Unflavored: 1 env / **Knox** Gelatine	0

Gravies

	GRAMS
¼ cup unless noted	
Au Jus	
Mix, prepared: 1 env / **Ann Page**	16
Mix, prepared / **Durkee**	1.6
Mix w roasting bag: 1 pkg / **Durkee** Roastin' Bag	14
Mix, prepared / **French's**	2

Mix, prepared / **French's** Pan Rich	1
Mix, prepared: ½ cup / **McCormick**	.8
Mix, prepared: ½ cup / **Schilling**	.8
Beef, canned: ⅕ can / **Ann Page**	4
Beef, canned: 2 oz / **Franco-American**	3
Brown	
Mix, prepared: 1 env / **Ann Page**	12
Mix, prepared / **Durkee**	2.5
Mix, prepared / **French's**	3
Mix, prepared / **French's** Pan Rich	4
Mix, prepared / **McCormick**	3.2
Mix, prepared / **McCormick** Lite	1
Mix, prepared / **Pillsbury**	3
Mix, prepared / **Schilling**	3.2
Mix, prepared / **Schilling** Lite	2
Mix, prepared: 1 fl oz / **Spatini** Family Style	3
Mix, prepared / **Weight Watchers**	1
Herb-flavored, mix, prepared / **McCormick**	2.5
Herb-flavored, mix, prepared / **Schilling**	2.5
w mushroom broth, canned: 1 oz / **Dawn Fresh**	2
w mushrooms, mix, prepared / **Durkee**	2.7
w mushrooms, mix, prepared / **Weight Watchers**	2
w onions, canned: 2 oz / **Franco-American**	4
w onions, mix, prepared / **Durkee**	3.2
w onions, mix, prepared / **Weight Watchers**	2
Chicken	
Canned: 2 oz / **Franco-American**	3
Mix, prepared: 1 env / **Ann Page**	16
Mix, prepared / **Durkee**	3.5
Mix, prepared / **Durkee** Creamy	3.5
Mix w roasting bag: 1 pkg / **Durkee** Roastin' Bag	24
Mix w roasting bag: 1 pkg / **Durkee** Roastin' Bag Italian Style	31

	GRAMS
Mix, prepared / **French's**	4
Mix, prepared / **French's** Pan Rich	4
Mix, prepared / **McCormick**	3.5
Mix, prepared / **McCormick** Lite	1
Mix, prepared / **Pillsbury**	4
Mix, prepared / **Schilling**	3.5
Mix, prepared / **Schilling** Lite	1
Mix, prepared / **Weight Watchers**	2
Mix, creamy w roasting bag: 1 pgk / **Durkee** Roastin' Bag	22
Chicken giblet, canned: 2 oz / **Franco-American**	3
Homestyle, mix, prepared / **Durkee**	2.7
Homestyle, mix, prepared / **French's**	4
Homestyle, mix, prepared / **Pillsbury**	3
Meatloaf, mix w roasting bag: 1 pkg / **Durkee** Roastin' Bag	18
Mushroom	
Canned: 2 oz / **Franco-American**	4
Mix, prepared: 1 env / **Ann Page**	12
Mix, prepared / **French's**	3
Mix, prepared / **McCormick**	3.2
Mix, prepared / **Schilling**	3.2
Onion, mix, prepared: 1 env / **Ann Page**	20
Onion, mix, prepared / **Durkee**	3.7
Onion, mix, prepared / **French's**	4
Onion, mix, prepared / **French's** Pan Rich	4
Onion pot roast, mix w roasting bag: 1 pkg / **Durkee** Roastin' Bag	24
Pork, mix, prepared / **Durkee**	3.5
Pork, mix w roasting bag: 1 pkg / **Durkee** Roastin' Bag	26
Pork, mix, prepared / **French's**	3
Pot roast stew, mix w roasting bag: 1 pkg / **Durkee** Roastin' Bag	25
Sparerib sauce, mix w roasting bag: 1 pkg / **Durkee** Roastin' Bag	37
Swiss steak, mix, prepared / **Durkee**	2.7

	GRAMS
Swiss steak, mix w roasting: 1 pkg / **Durkee** Roastin' Bag	28
Turkey, mix, prepared / **Durkee**	3.5
Turkey, mix, prepared / **French's**	4
Turkey, mix, prepared / **McCormick**	3.8
Turkey, mix, prepared / **Schilling**	3.8

Health Foods

Flour, Meal, Rice and Yeast

Flour, soy: ¼ cup / **Loma Linda**	7
Meal, almond: 2 tbsp / **Roberts**	3.7
Meal, coconut: 2 tbsp / **Roberts**	4.4
Meal, millet seed: 2 tbsp / **Roberts**	14.6
Meal, sesame, 2 tbsp / **Roberts**	3.3
Meal, sunflower: 2 tbsp / **Roberts**	3.8
Rice, brown: ¼ cup raw / **Datetree**	38.9
Rice, brown: ¼ cup raw / **Roberts**	38.9
Yeast, brewer's: 1 rounded tbsp / **Datetree**	4.4
Yeast, brewer's: 1 rounded tbsp /**Roberts**	4.4

Granola Bars

w cinnamon: 1 bar / **Nature Valley**	16
w coconut: 1 bar / **Nature Valley**	15
w oats and honey: 1 bar / **Nature Valley**	16
Peanut: 1 bar / **Nature Valley**	15

Seasonings and Gravy

Gravy, mix, brown: 1/6 pkg / **Loma Linda** Gravy Quick	2.3
Seasoning, chicken: 1 tbsp / **Loma Linda**	1

Soy Milk

Soyagen, all purpose: 1 cup prepared / **Loma Linda**	13

Soyagen, carob: 1 cup prepared / **Loma Linda**	13
Soyalac, concentrated: 6 fl oz prepared / **Loma Linda**	11.4
Soyalac, powder: 6 fl oz prepared / **Loma Linda**	11.4
I-Soyalac, concentrated: 6 fl oz prepared / **Loma Linda**	11.4

Soybeans and Legumes

Beans, brown, canned: ½ cup / **Loma Linda**	21.8
Beans, in tomato sauce, canned: ½ cup / **Loma Linda**	7.8
Garbanzo beans, canned: ½ cup / **Loma Linda**	25.5
Lentils, canned: ¾ cup / **Loma Linda**	15
Soy beans	
Boston style, canned: ½ cup / **Loma Linda**	14.9
Cooking: ½ cup raw / **Datetree**	34.8
Cooking: ½ cup raw / **Roberts**	34.8
Dry roasted: 1 oz / **Soy Ahoy**	6.5
Dry roasted: 1 oz / **Soy Town**	6.5
Green, canned: ½ cup / **Loma Linda**	7.9
Oil roasted: 1 oz / **Soy Ahoy**	5.1
Oil roasted: 1 oz / **Soy Town**	5.1
Roasted: ¼ cup / **Datetree**	8.3
Roasted: ¼ cup / **Roberts**	8.3

Spreads and Sandwich Fillings

Almond butter: 1 tbsp / **Roberts**	3.1
Cashew butter: 1 tbsp / **Roberts**	4.7
Marmalade, orange: 1 tbsp / **Datetree**	13

Mayonnaise: 1 tbsp / **Datetree**	.4
Peanut butter: 1 tbsp / **Datetree**	3.3
Peanut butter: 1 tbsp / **Roberts**	3.3
Preserves: 1 tbsp	
Blackberry / **Datetree**	13
Grape / **Datetree**	13
Red raspberry / **Datetree**	14.2
Rose hip / **Datetree**	13
Strawberry / **Datetree**	14.2
Sandwich filling: ½-in slice /	
Loma Linda Vegelona	5.2
Sandwich spread: 3 tbsp / **Loma Linda**	6
Sesame butter: 1 tbsp / **Roberts**	2.8
Soy bean cheese: ½-in slice /	
Loma Linda Vegechee	1.8

Sweets, Nuts and Snacks: Natural

Almonds, raw: ¼ cup / **Datetree**	6.2
Almonds, raw: ¼ cup / **Roberts**	6.2
Apricot chew: ¼ bar / **Datetree**	13.5
Apricot chew: ¼ bar / **Roberts**	13.5
Cashews, raw: ¼ cup / **Datetree**	9.4
Cashews, raw: ¼ cup / **Roberts**	9.4
Coconut shreds: 2 tbsps / **Datetree**	4.1
Coconut shreds: 2 tbsps / **Roberts**	4.1
Date 'n' seed chew: ¼ bar / **Roberts**	13.5
Fruit 'n' nut chew: ¼ bar / **Datetree**	13.5
Fruit 'n' nut chew: ¼ bar / **Roberts**	13.5
Pistachio nuts, natural: ¼ cup / **Datetree**	4.8
Protein, bar: ¼ bar / **Roberts** Hi	
Protein Bar	12.4
Raisin nut mix: ½ cup / **Datetree**	36
Raisin nut mix: ½ cup / **Roberts**	36
Raisin 'n' peanut chew: ¼ bar / **Roberts**	12.7
Rose hip chew: ¼ bar / **Datetree**	12.7

	GRAMS
Rose hip chew: ¼ bar / **Roberts**	12.7
Seeds	
Millet: ¼ cup / **Datetree**	32.1
Millet: ¼ cup / **Roberts**	32.1
Pepitas: ¼ cup / **Datetree**	4.8
Pumpkin: ¼ cup / **Datetree**	4.8
Pumpkin: ¼ cup / **Roberts**	4.8
Sesame: ¼ cup / **Datetree**	8.4
Sesame: ¼ cup / **Roberts**	8.4
Squash, dry, hulled: 1 oz	4.5
Sunflower: 1 oz / **Frito Lay**	5
Sunflower: 1 oz / **Granny Goose**	4.2
Sunflower, dry roasted: 1 oz / **Planters**	5
Sunflower, unsalted: 1 oz / **Planters**	5
Sunflower, raw or roasted: ¼ cup / **Datetree**	6.4
Sunflower, raw or roasted: ¼ cup / **Roberts**	6.4
Sunflower, whole: 1 oz / **Granny Goose**	4.2
Sesame carob chew: ¼ bar / **Datetree**	12.7
Sesame carob chew: ¼ bar / **Roberts**	12.7
Sesame 'n' almond bar: ¼ bar / **Roberts**	12.7
Sesame 'n' cashew bar: ¼ bar / **Roberts**	12.7
Sesame 'n' coconut bar: ¼ bar / **Roberts**	12.7
Sesame 'n' fruit bar: ¼ bar / **Roberts**	12.7
Sesame 'n' honey bar: ¼ bar / **Roberts**	12.7

Sweeteners

Honey, tupelo: 1 tbsp / **Datetree**	16.4
Honey, wildflower: 1 tbsp / **Datetree**	16.4
Molasses, blackstrap: 1 tbsp / **Datetree**	11
Sugar, turbinado: 1 tsp / **Datetree**	3.8
Sugar, turbinado: 1 tsp / **Roberts**	3.8

Wheat and Wheat Germ

	GRAMS
Bulgur, club wheat: 1 cup	139.1
Bulgur, hard red winter wheat: 1 cup	128.7
Bulgur, white wheat: 1 cup	121.1
Wheat, oven cooked: ½ cup / **Loma Linda**	53.1
Wheat germ: ¼ cup / **Kretschmer** Regular	12.6
Wheat germ: ¼ cup / **Kretschmer** Sugar 'N Honey	16.9
Wheat germ, natural and toasted: 2 tbsp / **Loma Linda**	9.3
Wheat germ, raw: 2 rounded tbsp / **Datetree**	7.9
Wheat germ, raw: ¼ cup / **Pillsbury**	12
Wheat germ, raw: 2 rounded tbsp /**Roberts**	7.9
Wheat germ, toasted: ¼ cup / **Pillsbury**	13

Vegetarian meat substitutes (gluten base unless noted)

	GRAMS
Bologna: ½-in slice / **Loma Linda**	6
Burgers: 1 burger /**Loma Linda** Sizzle Burgers	10
Chicken (4-in diameter): ½-in slice / **Loma Linda**	7
Frankfurters: 1 frank / **Loma Linda** Big Franks	5
Linketts: 1 link / **Loma Linda**	3.5
Little Links: 1 link / **Loma Linda**	1.5
Meatballs: 1 ball / **Loma Linda**	2.2
Nuteena (peanut-butter base): (½-in slice / **Loma Linda**	10
Proteena (gluten-peanut-butter base): ½-in slice / **Loma Linda**	6
Redi-Burger: ½-in slice / **Loma Linda**	9
Roast beef: ½-in slice /**Loma Linda**	4
Salami: ½-in slice / **Loma Linda**	4
Sausage: 1 link / **Loma Linda** Breakfast Links	1.3

GRAMS

Sausage: 1 piece / **Loma Linda**	
Breakfast Sausage	3.6
Stew Pac: 2 oz / **Loma Linda**	6
Swiss Steak: 1 steak / **Loma Linda**	6
Tender Bits: 1 bit /**Loma Linda**	2.2
Tender Rounds: 1 round / **Loma Linda**	2
Turkey: ½-in slice / **Loma Linda**	7
Vegeburger: ½ cup / **Loma Linda**	8
Vegeburger, unsalted: ½ cup / **Loma Linda**	8
Vegelona: ½-in slice /**Loma Linda**	13

Ice Cream and Similar Frozen Products

GRAMS

Frozen dessert: 5 fl oz / Weight Watchers Dietary	19
Frozen dessert: 6 fl oz / Weight Watchers Frosted Treat	22
Ice cream: ½ cup unless noted	
Black raspberry / Breyers	18
Black walnut / Meadow Gold	16
Butter almond / Sealtest	16
Butter almond, chocolate / Breyers	17
Butter brickle / Sealtest	19
Butter pecan / Meadow Gold	16
Butter pecan / Sealtest	16
Caramel pecan crunch / Breyers	18
Cherry nugget / Sealtest	16
Cherry-vanilla / Breyers	17
Cherry-vanilla / Meadow Gold	18
Cherry-vanilla / Sealtest	17
Chocolate / Breyers	18.8
Chocolate: 4 oz / Howard Johnson's	29
Chocolate / Meadow Gold	18
Chocolate / Sealtest	18
Chocolate / Swift's	16
Chocolate almond / Breyers	18
Chocolate almond / Sealtest	18
Chocolate chip / Meadow Gold	17

GRAMS

Chocolate chip / **Sealtest**	17
Chocolate Revel / **Meadow Gold**	19
Coconut / **Sealtest**	18
Coffee / **Breyers**	15
Coffee / **Sealtest**	16
Dutch chocolate almond / **Breyers**	18
Lemon / **Sealtest**	16
Maple walnut / **Sealtest**	16
Mint chocolate chip / **Breyers**	17
Peach / **Meadow Gold**	16
Peach / **Sealtest**	18
Pineapple / **Sealtest**	17
Southern pecan butterscotch / **Breyers**	18
Strawberry / **Breyers**	17
Strawberry: 4 oz / **Howard Johnson's**	26.5
Strawberry / **Meadow Gold**	19
Strawberry / **Sealtest**	18.6
Strawberry / **Swift's**	15
Vanilla / **Breyers**	15
Vanilla: 4 oz / **Howard Johnson's**	24.3
Vanilla / **Meadow Gold**	16
Vanilla / **Meadow Gold** Golden	16
Vanilla / **Sealtest**	16
Vanilla / **Swift's**	16
Vanilla, French / **Sealtest**	16
Vanilla-flavored cherry / **Sealtest** Royale	19
Vanilla-flavored red raspberry / **Sealtest** Royale	20
Vanilla fudge / **Breyers**	18.4
Ice milk: ½ cup	
Banana-strawberry Twirl / **Sealtest Light N' Lively**	21
Chocolate / **Sealtest Light N' Lively**	19
Chocolate / **Swift** Light'n Easy	18
Coffee / **Sealtest Light N' Lively**	17
Fudge Twirl / **Sealtest Light N' Lively**	20
Neapolitan / **Sealtest Light N' Lively**	18

GRAMS

Peach / **Sealtest Light N' Lively**	18
Strawberry / **Sealtest Light N' Lively**	18
Strawberry / **Swift** Light'n Easy	18
Vanilla / **Sealtest Light N' Lively**	17
Vanilla / **Swift** Light'n Easy	17
Sherbet: ½ cup unless noted	
Lemon / **Sealtest**	30
Lemon-lime / **Sealtest**	30
Lime / **Meadow Gold**	27
Lime / **Sealtest**	30
Orange: 4 oz / **Howard Johnson's**	33
Orange / **Meadow Gold**	27
Orange / **Sealtest**	30
Pineapple / **Meadow Gold**	29
Pineapple / **Sealtest**	30
Rainbow / **Sealtest**	30
Red raspberry / **Sealtest**	30
Strawberry / **Sealtest**	30

ICE CREAM BARS

1 bar or piece

Almond, toasted / **Eskimo**	15.4
Almond, toasted / **Eskimo** Almond Crunch	16.3
Almond, toasted / **Good Humor**	21
Banana: 2½ fl oz bar / **Fudgsicle**	23.5
Banana fudge: 2½ oz / **Eskimo**	15.5
Banana fudge: 3 oz / **Eskimo**	18.6
Bell / **Eskimo**	13.2
Cherry / **Eskimo** Super Rocket	17.3
Chocolate: 2½ fl oz bar / **Bi-Sicle**	21.4
Chocolate / **Eskimo** Party Slice	16.7
Chocolate w stick / **Eskimo** Pie	14.5
Chocolate, stickless / **Eskimo** Pie	14.5
Chocolate: 2½ fl oz bar /**Fudgsicle**	23.7
Chocolate eclair /**Eskimo**	17.1
Chocolate eclair / **Good Humor**	25

	GRAMS
Chocolate fudge: 2½ oz / **Eskimo**	15.5
Chocolate fudge: 3 oz /**Eskimo**	18.6
Chocolate fudge / **Eskimo** Super Rocket	24.8
Chocolate malted flavor / **Eskimo** Do-Nut	9.8
Choco Nana Bar / **Eskimo**	12.8
Christmas Tree / **Eskimo**	13.2
Creamsicle / 2½ fl oz bar	12.8
Dietetic / **Eskimo**	9
Double Crunch Bar / **Eskimo**	12.5
Double fudge: 3¼ oz / **Eskimo**	20.2
Double fudge: 4 oz / **Eskimo**	24.8
Dreamsicle / 2½ fl oz bar	13.1
Drumstick, ice cream	22.7
Drumstick, ice milk	24.3
English toffee / **Eskimo** Bar	13.6
Eskimo Pie Juniors	8.5
Eskimo Pie Miniatures	4.7
Fiddlesticks Fudges, all flavors / **Eskimo**	13
Fiddlesticks Pops / **Eskimo**	11.5
Fudge / **Eskimo** Kooler	15.8
Fudge-banana / **Eskimo** Triple	18.5
Fudge-caramel / **Eskimo** Triple	18.6
Fudge-chocolate / **Eskimo** Triple	18.6
Icy Whammy, assorted flavors / **Good Humor**	13
Kreme Kooler Bar / **Eskimo**	14.3
La Mode / **Eskimo**	14.4
Mint / **Eskimo**	8
Mod-Pop / **Eskimo**	17.2
Orange: 2½ oz / **Eskimo** Kooler	12
Orange : 3 oz / **Eskimo** Kooler	14.2
Orange cream: 2 fl oz bar / **Sealtest**	11
Orange Treat: 3 fl oz bar / **Sealtest**	18
Penguin Bar / **Eskimo**	11.7
Peppermint / **Eskimo** Patty	14.3
Popsicle, all fruit flavors / 3 fl oz	16.5
Rocket Bar / **Eskimo**	10.8
Sandwich / **Good Humor**	34

	GRAMS
Santa / **Eskimo**	10.1
Slush Stik, all flavors / **Eskimo**	18.6
Strawberry / **Eskimo** Party Slice	16.5
Strawberry eclair / **Eskimo**	16.4
Strawbery Shortcake / **Good Humor**	21
Summer Treats / **Eskimo**	18.7
Super Rocket Crunch / **Eskimo**	20.1
Super Rocket Pops, all flavors: 4 oz / **Eskimo**	22.9
Twin Pops, all flavors: 3 oz / **Eskimo**	17.2
Twin Pops, all flavors: 4 oz / **Eskimo**	22.9
Whammy Assorted Ice Cream / **Good Humor**	9
Whammy Chip Crunch / **Good Humor**	10
Vanilla, chocolate coated / **Good Humor**	12
Vanilla w stick / **Eskimo** Pie	13.6
Vanilla, stickless / **Eskimo** Pie	13.6
Vanilla / **Eskimo** Party Slice	15.6
Vanilla ice milk / **Eskimo** Do-Nut	9.7

Italian Foods

See also Pizza and Spaghetti

	GRAMS
Cannelloni Florentine w veal, spinach, cheese and sauce, frozen: 13 oz / **Weight Watchers**	54
Eggplant Parmigiana, frozen: 4 oz / **Buitoni**	19.4
Eggplant Parmigiana, frozen: 13 oz / **Weight Watchers**	25
Lasagna	
Canned: 10 oz / **Hormel**	30
Canned: 7½ oz can / **Hormel Short Orders**	22.9
Frozen: 4 oz / **Buitoni** 26 oz	12
Frozen: 4 oz / **Buitoni** Family Size	20.8

GRAMS

Frozen: 7 oz / **Green Giant** Oven Bake Entrees	28
Frozen: 9 oz / **Green Giant** Boil-in-Bag Entrees	33
Frozen: 10½ oz / **Stouffer's**	36
Frozen: 1 entree / **Swanson** Hungry-Man	51
Frozen w cheese, veal and sauce: 13 oz / **Weight Watchers**	39
Frozen w meat sauce: 4 oz / **Buitoni** 14 oz	20.8
Mix, prepared: ⅛ pkg / **Golden Grain** Stir-n-Serve	26
Manicotti, frozen w sauce: 4 oz / **Buitoni**	20.1
Manicotti, frozen wo sauce: 4 oz / **Buitoni**	21.6
Ravioli	
Beef, in sauce, canned: 7½ oz / **Franco-American**	36
Beef, in sauce, canned: 7½ oz / **Franco-American** Raviolos	32
Cheese, canned: ½ can /**Buitoni**	33
Cheese, frozen: 4 oz / **Buitoni** 12 Count Round	30.4
Cheese, frozen: 4 oz / **Buitoni** 40 Count	48.8
Meat, canned: ½ can / **Buitoni**	30
Meat, frozen: 4 oz / **Buitoni** 40 Count	48.8
Meat, frozen: 4 oz / **Buitoni** Raviolettes	60.6
Ravioli Parmigiana, cheese, frozen: 4 oz / **Buitoni**	23.5
Ravioli Parmigiana, meat, frozen: 4 oz / **Buitoni**	20.6
Rotini, in tomato sauce, canned: 7½ oz / **Franco-American**	36
Rotini and meatballs, in tomato sauce, canned: 7¼ oz / **Franco-American**	27
Sausage and peppers w rigati, frozen: 4 oz / **Buitoni**	11.9
Shells w sauce, frozen: 4 oz / **Buitoni**	24.9
Shrimp Marinara w shells, frozen: 4 oz / **Buitoni**	19

GRAMS

	GRAMS
Spaghetti, in sauce w veal: 1 entree / **Swanson** "TV" 8¼ oz	24
Veal Parmigiana	
Frozen: 5 oz / **Banquet** Cookin' Bag	19.5
Frozen: 7 oz / **Green Giant** Oven Bake Entrees	19
Frozen w spaghetti twists: 4 oz / **Buitoni**	16.5
Frozen w tomato sauce:	
32 oz / **Banquet** Buffet Supper	119.1
Frozen w zucchini:	
9½ oz / **Weight Watchers**	14
Ziti, baked w sauce, frozen:	
4 oz / **Buitoni**	25.8
Ziti w veal and sauce, frozen:	
13 oz / **Weight Watchers**	44

Jams, Jellies, Preserves, Butters, Marmalade

	GRAMS
Butters	
Apple: 1 tbsp / **Bama**	7.7
Apple, cider: 1 tsp / **Smucker's**	3
Apple, spiced: 1 tsp / **Smucker's**	3
Peach: 1 tsp / **Smucker's**	4
Jams	
All flavors: 1 tsp / **Ann Page**	4.5
All flavors: 1 tsp / **Kraft**	4
All flavors: 1 tsp / **Smucker's**	5
All flavors, imitation:	
1 tsp / **Smucker's Slenderella Low Calorie**	2
Apricot: 1 tbsp / **Bama**	12.7
Apricot-pineapple, swt:	
1 tbsp / **Diet Delight**	5.1
Blackberry, swt: 1 tbsp / **Diet Delight**	5.1
Blackberry, swt:	
1 tbsp / **S and W Nutradiet**	2.4
Peach: 1 tbsp / **Bama**	12.7
Pear: 1 tbsp / **Bama**	12.7
Plum: 1 tbsp / **Bama**	12.7
Raspberry, swt: 1 tbsp / **Diet Delight**	5.4
Raspberry, art swt:	
1 tbsp / **S and W Nutradiet**	2.4
Strawberry, swt: 1 tbsp / **Diet Delight**	4.8

Strawberry, art swt:
    1 tbsp / **S and W Nutradiet**   3
Strawberry, imitation, art swt:
    1 tsp / **Smucker's**   1

Jellies

All flavors: 1 tsp / **Ann Page**   4.5
All flavors: 1 tbsp / **Bama**   12.7
All flavors: 1 tsp / **Empress**   4.5
All flavors: 1 tsp / **Kraft**   4
All flavors except low calorie:
    1 tbsp / **Kraft**   11.7
All flavors: 1 tsp / **Smucker's**   5
All flavors, imitation:
    1 tsp / **Smucker's Slenderella** Low Calorie   2
Apple: 1 tbsp / **Kraft** Low Calorie   5.4
Apple, swt: 1 tbsp / **Diet Delight**   5.4
Apple, art swt: 1 tbsp/**S and W Nutradiet**   3.3
Blackberry-apple:
    1 tbsp / **Kraft** Low Calorie   5.4
Blackberry, imitation:
    ⅜ oz / **Smucker's** Single Service   1
Cherry, imitation:
    ⅜ oz / **Smucker's** Single Service   1
Grape: 1 tsp / **Home Brands**   4.5
Grape: 1 tbsp / **Kraft** Low Calorie   5.3
Grape, swt: 1 tbsp / **Diet Delight**   5.4
Grape, art swt: 1 tbsp / **S and W Nutradiet**   2.4
Grape, imitation: 1 tsp / **Kraft** Low Calorie   2
Grape, imitation, art swt: 1 tsp / **Smucker's**   1
Grape, imitation, art swt:
    ⅜ oz / **Smucker's** Single Service   1

Marmalade

All flavors: 1 tsp / **Ann Page**   4.5
Orange: 1 tbsp / **Bama**   13.5
Orange: 1 tbsp / **Kraft**   13.6
Orange: 1 tbsp / **Kraft** Low Calorie   6.1
Orange: 1 tsp / **Smucker's**   5

Orange, art swt: 1 tbsp / **S and W Nutradiet**	2.4
Orange, imitation:	
1 tsp / **Smucker's Slenderella** Low Calorie	2

Preserves

All flavors: 1 tsp / **Ann Page**	4.5
All flavors: 1 tsp / **Empress**	4.5
All flavors: 1 tsp / **Kraft**	4
All flavors: 1 tbsp / **Kraft** Regular	13.6
All flavors: 1 tsp / **Smucker's**	5
Apricot: 1 tbsp / **Bama**	12.7
Apricot-pineapple, art swt:	
1 tbsp / **S and W Nutradiet**	2.4
Boysenberry, art swt:	
1 tbsp / **S and W Nutradiet**	2.4
Cherry, art swt: 1 tbsp / **S and W Nutradiet**	2.4
Peach: 1 tbsp / **Bama**	12.7
Peach: 1 tbsp / **Kraft** Low Calorie	6.1
Pear: 1 tbsp / **Bama**	12.7
Plum: 1 tbsp / **Bama**	12.7
Raspberry, black:	
1 tbsp / **Kraft** Low Calorie	6.2
Strawberry: 1 tsp / **Home Brands**	4.5
Strawberry, imitation:	
1 tsp / **Kraft** Low Calorie	2

Spreads

All fruit flavors:	
1 tsp / **Smucker's** Low Sugar	2
All fruit flavors: 1 tsp / **Tillie Lewis**	1

Liqueurs and Brandies

Brandies: 1 fl oz	
Leroux Deluxe	.1
Apricot / **Leroux**	8.6
Blackberry / **Leroux**	8.3
Blackberry / **Leroux Polish** type	8.6
Cherry / **Leroux**	8.3
Cherry / **Leroux Kirschwasser**	0
Coffee / **Leroux**	8.3
Ginger / **Leroux**	4.4
Peach / **Leroux**	8.9
Liqueurs: 1 fl oz	
Anesone / **Leroux**	2.8
Anisette / **Leroux**	9.9
Apricot / **Leroux**	8.9
Aquavit / **Leroux**	0
Banana / **Leroux**	11.4
Blackberry / **Leroux**	7.1
Cherry / **Kijafa**	5.1
Cherry / **Leroux**	7.5
Cherry / **Leroux Cherry Karise**	7.5
Chocolate, cherry / **Cheri-Suisse**	10.2
Chocolate, minted / **Vandermint**	10.2
Chocolate, orange / **Sabra**	10.4
Claristine / **Leroux**	10.8
Coffee / **Pasha Turkish Coffee**	13.4
Creme de Cacao, brown / **Leroux**	14.3
Creme de Cacao, white / **Leroux**	13.3

GRAMS

Creme de Cafe / **Leroux**	13.6
Creme de Cassis / **Leroux**	14.9
Creme de Menthe, green / **Leroux**	15.2
Creme de Menthe, white / **Leroux**	12.8
Creme de Noya / **Leroux**	14.6
Curacao / **Leroux**	9.5
Gold-O-Mint / **Leroux**	15.2
Grenadine / **Leroux**	15.2
Kummel / **Leroux**	4.1
Lochan Ora Scotch	7.8
Maraschino / **Leroux**	9.7
Peach / **Leroux**	8.9
Peppermint Schnapps / **Leroux**	9.2
Raspberry / **Leroux**	8.3
Rock and Rye / **Leroux**	10.5
Rock and Rye-Irish Moss / **Leroux**	13
Sloe gin / **Leroux**	6
Strawberry / **Leroux**	8.3
Triple Sec / **Leroux**	8.9

Macaroni

GRAMS

plain, cooked to firm stage "al dente":
1 cup	39.1
plain, cooked to tender stage: 1 cup	32.2

and beef, in tomato sauce, canned:
7½ oz / **Franco-American** Beefy Mac	28

and beef, frozen:
32 oz / **Banquet** Buffet Supper	106.4

and beef w tomato sauce, frozen:
9 oz / **Green Giant** Boil-in-Bag Entrees	31

and beef w tomatoes, frozen:
½ pkg / **Stouffer's** 11½ oz	20

and cheese
Canned: 7¼ oz / **Franco-American**	23
Canned: 7½ oz can / **Hormel** Short Orders	28.6
Frozen: 8 oz / **Banquet**	35.9
Frozen: 32 oz / **Banquet** Buffet Supper	110.9
Frozen: 8 oz / **Banquet** Cookin' Bag	28.6
Frozen: 9 oz / **Green Giant** Boil-in-Bag Entrees	36
Frozen: 8 oz / **Green Giant** Oven Bake Entrees	32
Frozen: 10 oz / **Howard Johnson's**	50.1
Frozen: 19 oz / **Howard Johnson's**	95.3
Frozen: 1 pkg / **Morton** Casserole	33
Frozen: ½ pkg / **Stouffer's** 12 oz	24
Frozen / **Swanson** 7 oz	26
Mix, dry: 1.8 oz / **Ann Page**	37

Mix, prepared: ¼ pkg / **Betty Crocker**   38
Mix, prepared: 1 pouch / **Betty Crocker**
  Mug-O-Lunch   40
Mix, prepared: ¼ pkg / **Golden Grain**
  Macaroni and Cheddar   38
Mix, prepared: ¾ cup / **Kraft**   30
Mix, prepared:
  ½ cup / **Pennsylvania Dutch Brand**   25
and meatballs, in tomato sauce, canned:
  7½ oz / **Franco-American** Meatball Mac   27

Mayonnaise

GRAMS

1 tbsp

Ann Page   0
Best   .2
Hellmann's   .2
Kraft Real   0
Mrs. Filbert's Real   0
Nu Made   0
Piedmont   0
Sultana   0
Flavored / **Durkee** Famous Sauce   2.2
Imitation
  Mrs. Filbert's   1
  Piedmont   0
  Weight Watchers   1
Miracle Whip / **Kraft**   2
w relish / **Mrs. Filbert's** Relish Spread   2

Meat

FRESH

	GRAMS
Beaver, roasted: 3 oz	0
Beef, ground, lean (10% fat), raw: 4 oz	0
Beef, ground, regular (21% fat), raw: 4 oz	0
Beef, roast, oven-cooked, no liquid added:	
relatively fat, such as rib:	
3 oz lean and fat	0
1.8 oz lean only	0
relatively lean, such as heel of round:	
3 oz lean and fat	0
2.7 oz lean only	0
Brains, all varieties, raw: 4 oz	.9
Hamburger (ground beef), broiled:	
3 lean oz	0
3 regular oz	0
Heart	
Beef, lean, cooked: 4 oz	.8
Beef, lean, raw: 4 oz	.8
Calf, cooked: 4 oz	2
Calf, raw: 4 oz	2
Lamb, cooked: 4 oz	1.1
Lamb, raw: 4 oz	1.1
Kidney, beef, cooked: 4 oz	.9
Kidney, beef, raw: 4 oz	1
Kidney, lamb, raw: 4 oz	1
Lamb, cooked:	
Chop, 4.8 oz thick w bone, broiled	0
4.0 oz lean and fat, broiled	0
2.6 oz lean only, broiled	0
Leg, roasted:	
3 oz lean and fat	0
2.5 oz lean only	0

Shoulder, roasted:

3 oz lean and fat	0
2.3 oz lean only	0

Liver

Beef, fried: 4 oz	6
Beef, raw: 4 oz	6
Calf, fried: 4 oz	4.6
Calf, raw: 4 oz	4.6
Lamb, broiled: 4 oz	3.3
Lamb, raw: 4 oz	3.3

Pork, fresh, cooked:

Chop, 3.5 oz thick w bone	0
2.3 oz lean and fat	0
1.7 lean only	0

Roast, oven-cooked, no liquid added:

3 oz lean and fat	0
2.4 oz lean only	0

Cuts, simmered:

3 oz lean and fat	0
2.2 oz lean only	0
Quail: 8 oz dressed, ready to cook	0
Rabbit, domesticated: 1 lb dressed, ready to cook	0
Rabbit, wild: 1 lb dressed, ready to cook	0

Steak, broiled

relatively fat such as sirloin:

3 oz lean and fat	0
2 oz lean only	0

relatively lean such as round:

3 oz lean and fat	0
2.4 oz lean only	0

Sweetbreads, 4 oz cooked

Beef	0
Calf	0
Lamb	0
Tongue, beef, cooked: 4 oz	.5
Tongue, calf, cooked: 4 oz	1.1
Tongue, lamb, cooked: 4 oz	.6

Veal, med fat, cooked, bone removed:
Cutlet, 3 oz	0
Roast, 3 oz	0

CANNED, CURED, PROCESSED

Bacon, cooked	
Hormel Black Label / 1 slice	.2
Hormel Range Brand / 1 slice	0
Hormel Red Label / 1 slice	0
Oscar Mayer / 1 slice	.5
Swift Lazy Maple / 1 slice	0
Swift Premium / 1 slice	0
Wilson's Certified / 1 oz	.3
Canadian: 1 slice / **Oscar Mayer**	.5
Canadian: 1 oz / **Wilson's** Certified	trace
Bacon bits, canned, cooked: 1 oz / **Wilson's**	1
Banquet loaf: 1 slice / **Eckrich** 8 oz pkg	1.5
Banquet loaf: 1 slice / **Eckrich** Beef Smorgas Pac	1
Bar-B-Q Loaf: 1 slice / **Oscar Mayer**	2
Beef, chopped: 1 slice / **Eckrich** Slender-Sliced	.6
Beef, chopped, canned:	
1 oz / **Wilson's** Certified Bif	.5
Beef, corned, canned: 3 oz / **Dinty Moore**	0
Beef, corned, canned: 2.3 oz / **Libby's**	1.3
Beef, corned, canned: 1 oz / **Safeway**	1
Beef, corned brisket, cooked:	
3½ oz / **Swift** Premium for Oven Roasting	0
Beef, corned brisket, canned:	
1 oz / **Wilson's** Certified	.3
Beef, corned, chopped:	
1 slice / **Eckrich** Slender-Sliced	1.4
Beef, dried, chunked and formed:	
¾ oz / **Swift** Premium	0
Beef, smoked, sliced: 1 oz / **Safeway**	1
Beef, smoked, sliced: 1 oz / **Safeway** Spicy	1
Beef roast, canned: 1 oz / **Wilson's** Certified	0
Beef steaks, breaded, frozen: 4 oz / **Hormel**	13

GRAMS

Bologna

Eckrich 12 oz pkg / 1 slice	1.5
Eckrich 16 oz pkg / 1 slice	1.5
Eckrich Smorgas Pac / 1 slice	1.5
Eckrich thick-sliced / 1 slice (12 oz pkg)	3
Eckrich thick-sliced / 1 slice (16 oz pkg)	3
Hormel / 1 oz	.5
Swift Premium / 1 oz	1.5
Wilson's Certified / 1 oz	.5
Beef: 1 slice / **Eckrich** 8 oz pkg	1.5
Beef: 1 slice / **Eckrich** 12 oz pkg	1.5
Beef: 1 slice / **Eckrich** Beef Smorgas Pac	1
Beef: 1 slice / **Oscar Mayer**	.5
Coarse ground: 1 oz / **Hormel**	1
Fine ground: 1 oz / **Hormel**	.5
Garlic: 1 slice / **Eckrich**	1.5
Ring: 2 oz / **Eckrich**	3
Ring, garlic: 1 slice / **Eckrich**	1.5
Ring, pickled: 2 oz / **Eckrich**	3
Braunschweiger: 1 oz / **Oscar Mayer**	1
Braunschweiger: 1 oz / **Wilson's** Certified	.7
Breakfast strips: 1 strip / **Swift Sizzlean**	0

Frankfurters: 1 frank

Eckrich 12 oz pkg	2
Eckrich Jumbo	3
Eckrich Skinless 16 oz pkg	3
Hormel Range Brand Wranglers Smoked Franks	1
Hormel Wieners 12 oz pkg	.5
Hormel Wieners 16 oz pkg	1
Oscar Mayer Wieners	2
Wilson's Certified Skinless	.8
Beef / **Eckrich**	3
Beef / **Eckrich** Jumbo	3
Beef / **Hormel** Wieners 12 oz pkg	.5
Beef / **Hormel** Wieners 16 oz pkg	1
Beef / **Hormel Wranglers** Smoked Franks	2

	GRAMS
Beef / **Oscar Mayer**	2
Beef / **Wilson's** Certified	.8
Frozen, batter-wrapped / **Hormel Corn Dogs**	22
Frozen, batter-wrapped / **Hormel Tater Dogs**	15
Gourmet Loaf: 1 slice / **Eckrich**	2
Gourmet Loaf: 1 slice / **Eckrich** Beef Smorgas Pac	1.5
Ham, luncheon type	
Cooked: 1 slice / **Eckrich**	1
Cooked: 1 oz / **Hormel**	0
Cooked, sliced: 1 oz / **Safeway**	1
Cooked, smoked: 1 slice / **Oscar Mayer**	0
Chopped: 1 oz / **Hormel**	1
Chopped: 2 oz / **Hormel** 8 lb can	1
Chopped: 1 slice / **Oscar Mayer**	1
Chopped, smoked: 1 slice / **Eckrich** Slender-Sliced	.6
Ham, whole, canned	
Oscar Mayer Jubilee / 4 oz	1
Swift Premium / 3½ oz	1
Swift Premium Hostess / 3½ oz	1
Wilson's Certified Boned and Rolled / 1 oz	0
Wilson's Certified Fully Cooked / 1 oz	.3
Wilson's Certified Tender-Made / 1 oz	.3
Ham, whole, plastic or other wrap	
Hormel Bone-In / 6 oz	1
Hormel Cure 81 / 6 oz	0
Hormel Curemaster / 6 oz	2
Swift Premium Hostess / 3½ oz	1
Smoked, aged: 1 oz / **Wilson's** Certified Festival Ham	.3
Ham slice, smoked: 4 oz / **Oscar Mayer** Jubilee	1
Ham steaks: 1 slice / **Oscar Mayer** Jubilee	0
Ham patties: 1 patty / **Hormel**	.5

GRAMS

Ham patties:
1 patty / **Swift** Premium Brown 'n Serve	1
Ham and cheese loaf: 1 slice / **Oscar Mayer**	.5
Honey loaf: 1 slice / **Eckrich**	2
Honey loaf: 1 slice / **Eckrich** Smorgas Pac	2.5
Honey loaf: 1 slice / **Oscar Mayer**	1.5

Liver, beef, thin sliced:
2.6 oz / **Swift's** Tru Tender	3
Liver cheese: 1 slice / **Oscar Mayer**	1
Luncheon meat: 1 slice / **Oscar Mayer**	1
Luncheon meat, spiced: 1 oz / **Hormel**	1
Old fashioned loaf: 1 slice / **Eckrich**	2

Old fashioned loaf:
1 slice / **Eckrich** Smorgas Pac	2
Old fashioned loaf: 1 slice / **Oscar Mayer**	2.5
Olive loaf: 1 slice / **Oscar Mayer**	2.5

Pastrami, chopped:
1 slice / **Eckrich** Slender-Sliced	1.4
Pastrami, sliced: 1 oz / **Safeway**	1
Pepperoni: 1 oz / **Swift**	1
Pepperoni, sliced: 1 oz / **Hormel**	0
Pickle loaf: 1 slice / **Eckrich** 8 oz pkg	1.5
Pickle loaf: 1 slice / **Eckrich** Smorgas Pac	1.5

Pickle loaf, beef:
1 slice / **Eckrich** Smorgas Pac	1

Pickle and pimento loaf:
1 slice / **Oscar Mayer**	3
Picnic, smoked: 1 oz / **Wilson's** Certified	0

Polish sausage:
1 link / **Eckrich** Polska Kielbasa Skinless	2

Polish sausage, ring:
2 oz / **Eckrich** Polska Kielbasa	1
Polish sausage ring: 3 oz / **Hormel** Kolbase	1

Polish sausage, smoked beef:
1 oz / **Frito-Lay**	1
Pork, chopped, canned: 1 oz / **Wilson's** Mor	.5

GRAMS

Pork butt, cured smoked:
  1 oz / **Wilson's** Certified Smoked Tasty Meat   0
Pork loin, chipped, smoked:
  1 slice / **Eckrich** Slender-Sliced   .6
Pork roast, canned: 1 oz / **Wilson's** Certified   0
Pork steaks, breaded, frozen: 3 oz / **Hormel**   11
Salami
    Hormel Dairy Hard / 1 oz   0
    Hormel Di Lusso Genoa / 1 oz   1
    Oscar Mayer Beef Cotto / 1 slice   .5
    Oscar Mayer for Beer / 1 slice   .5
    Oscar Mayer Cotto / 1 slice   .5
    Oscar Mayer Hard / 1 slice   .3
    Swift Premium Genoa / 1 oz   0
    Swift Premium Hard / 1 oz   1
Sausage, beef, smoked: 2 oz / **Eckrich**   1
Sausage, pork bulk:
  1 oz / **Wilson's** Certified   .3
Sausage, pork, smoked:
  3 oz / **Hormel** No-Link   1
Sausage links
    Hormel Brown 'n Serve / 1 sausage   0
    Hormel Little Sizzlers / 1 sausage   0
    Hormel Midget Links / 1 sausage   1
    Oscar Mayer Little Friers / 1 link   .5
    Swift's The Original / 1 link   .5
    Swift Premium Bacon 'n Sausage / 1 link   .5
    Swift Premium Brown 'n Serve
      Kountry Kured / 1 link   .5
    Beef: 1 link / **Swift**
      Premium Brown 'n Serve   .5
Sausage links, smoked
    Eckrich 16 oz pkg / 1 link   2
    Eckrich Skinless / 1 link   1
    Eckrich Smok-Y-Links / 1 link   1
    Eckrich Skinless Smok-Y-Links / 1 link   1

GRAMS

Hormel Smokies / 1 sausage	.5
Oscar Mayer / 1 link	1
Wilson's Certified Smokies / 1 oz	.5
Beef: 1 link / **Eckrich** Smok-Y-Links	1
Sausage sticks	
Beef: 1¼ oz / **Slim Jim** Polish Sausage	.4
Beef: ⅝ oz / **Cow-Boy Jo's**	.9
Beef, smoked:	
¼ oz / **Cow-Boy Jo's** Smok-O-Roni	.3
Beef, smoked: ½ oz / **Slim Jim**	.4
Pickled: 1¼ oz / **Lowrey's** Hot Sausage	1.4
Pickled: ⅝ oz / **Lowrey's** Polish Sausage	.4
Scrapple, in tube: 1 oz / **Oscar Mayer**	1.8
Scrapple, Philadelphia style, canned:	
1 oz / **Oscar Mayer**	2.4
Spam: 3 oz / **Hormel**	3
Spam w cheese chunks: 3 oz / **Hormel**	2
Spam, smoke-flavored: 3 oz / **Hormel**	1
Substitute, meat, BV in glass jars:	
1 oz / **Wilson's** Certified	2.5
Summer sausage: 1 slice / **Oscar Mayer**	
Thuringer Cervelat	.5
Summer sausage, beef: 1 slice / **Oscar Mayer**	.5
Summer sausage, beef: 1 oz / **Swift** Premium	1
Thuringer: 1 oz / **Hormel Old Smokehouse**	0
Tripe, canned: 5 oz / **Libby's**	.9
Veal steaks, frozen: 4 oz / **Hormel**	2
Veal steaks, breaded, frozen: 4 oz / **Hormel**	13
Vienna sausage, canned: 1 piece / **Hormel**	.5
Vienna sausage, canned: 1 sausage / **Libby's**	.5
Vienna sausage, canned, in barbecue sauce:	
1 sausage / **Libby's**	.3

MEAT ENTREES, CANNED

Beef w barbecue sauce:	
5 oz / **Morton House**	19

Beef, corned w cabbage: 8 oz / **Hormel**	7
Beef goulash:	
7½ oz can / **Hormel Short Orders**	17.1
Beef, sliced w gravy:	
6¼ oz can / **Morton House**	8
Beef stew	
Dinty Moore / 7½ oz	13
Dinty Moore Short Orders / 7½ oz	14.3
Libby's / 1 cup	32
Morton House / 8 oz	17
Swanson / 7½ oz	18
Hash, beef w potatoes:	
7½ oz can / **Dinty Moore Short Orders**	28.6
Hash	
Corned beef: 7½ oz / **Ann Page**	20
Corned beef: 7½ oz / **Mary Kitchen**	21
Corned beef: 3 oz / **Libby's**	8
Corned beef:	
7½ oz can / **Mary Kitchen Short Orders**	20
Roast beef: 7½ oz / **Mary Kitchen**	18
Roast beef:	
7½ oz can / **Mary Kitchen Short Orders**	17.1
Pork, sliced w gravy: 6¼ oz / **Morton House**	9
Salisbury steak w mushroom gravy:	
4 1/6 oz / **Morton House**	7
Sloppy Joe: 7½ oz can / **Hormel Short Orders**	17.1
Sloppy Joe, beef: 1/3 cup / **Libby's**	6
Sloppy Joe, pork: 1/3 cup / **Libby's**	6
Stew, meatball: 6¼ oz / **Morton House**	18
Stew, meatball: 1 cup / **Libby's**	25
Stew, Mulligan:	
7½ oz can / **Dinty Moore Short Orders**	14.3

MEAT ENTREES, FROZEN

Beef, chipped, creamed:	
5 oz / **Banquet** Cookin' Bag	10.5

GRAMS

Beef, chipped, creamed:
  1 pkg / **Stouffer's** 5½ oz 10
Beef, sirloin, chopped w green beans,
  cauliflower and sauce: 9½ oz /
  Weight Watchers 18
Beef, sliced: 1 entree / **Swanson** Hungry-Man 23
Beef, sliced w barbecue sauce:
  5 oz / **Banquet** Cookin' Bag 12.5
Beef, sliced w gravy:
  32 oz / **Banquet** Buffet Supper 34.5
Beef, sliced w gravy:
  5 oz / **Banquet** Cookin' Bag 4.8
Beef, sliced w gravy:
  5 oz / **Green Giant** Boil-in-Bag Toast Toppers 7
Beef, sliced w gravy and whipped potatoes:
  1 entree / **Swanson** "TV" 23
Beef stroganoff: 1 pkg / **Stouffer's** 9¾ oz 31
Green pepper steak:
  1 pkg / **Stouffer's** 10½ oz 35
Meat loaf
  Banquet Buffet Supper / 32 oz 46.4
  Banquet Cookin' Bag / 5 oz 13.6
  Banquet Man Pleaser / 19 oz 63.6
  Morton Country Table / 1 entree 32
  w tomato sauce and whipped potatoes:
    1 entree / **Swanson** "TV" 27
Meatballs w gravy and whipped potatoes:
  1 entree / **Swanson** "TV" 26
Noodles and beef:
  32 oz / **Banquet** Buffet Supper 83.6
Salisbury steak
  Banquet Man Pleaser / 19 oz 71.7
  Morton Country Table / 1 entree 35
  Stouffer's 12 oz / ½ pkg 5
  Swanson Hungry-Man / 1 entree 39
  w crinkle-cut potatoes:
    1 entree / **Swanson** "TV" 28

w gravy: 32 oz / **Banquet** Buffet Supper	48.2
w gravy: 5 oz / **Banquet** Cookin' Bag	7.8
w gravy: 7 oz / **Green Giant** Oven Bake Entrees	14
w tomato sauce: 9 oz / **Green Giant** Boil-in-Bag Entrees	22
Sausage, cheese and tomato pies:	
7 oz / **Weight Watchers**	39
Sloppy Joe: 5 oz / **Banquet** Cookin' Bag	11.2
Sloppy Joe: 5 oz / **Green Giant** Boil-in-Bag Toast Toppers	15
Steak, beef, chopped w carrots, green peppers and mushroom sauce: 10 oz / **Weight Watchers**	17
Stew, beef: 32 oz / **Banquet** Buffet Supper	90.9
Stew, beef: 9 oz / **Green Giant** Boil-in-Bag Entrees	20
Stew, beef: 1 pkg / **Stouffer's** 10 oz	16
Stew, beef w biscuits:	
7 oz / **Green Giant** Oven Bake Entrees	21
Stuffed cabbage w beef, in tomato sauce:	
7 oz / **Green Giant** Oven Bake Entrees	17
Stuffed green pepper w beef:	
7 oz / **Green Giant** Oven Bake Entrees	18

MEAT SUBSTITUTES

Breakfast Links: 1 link / **Morningstar Farms**	.3
Breakfast patties:	
1 pattie / **Morningstar Farms**	3.2
Breakfast strips: 1 strip / **Morningstar Farms**	.2
Grillers: 1 griller / **Morningstar Farms**	5
Luncheon slices: 1 slice / **Morningstar Farms**	1.4

Mexican Foods

	GRAMS
Beans	
Refried, canned:	
½ cup / **Ortega** Lightly Spicy	25
Refried, canned:	
½ cup / **Ortega** True Bean	25
Burritos, beef, canned: 4 oz / **Hormel**	28
Chiles, diced, canned: 1 oz / **Ortega**	1.1
Chiles, in strips, canned: 1 oz / **Ortega**	1.1
Chiles, whole, canned: 1 oz / **Ortega**	1.1
Chili con carne, canned	
w beans: 8 oz / **A & P**	29
w beans: 7½ oz / **Hormel**	24
w beans: 7½ oz can / **Hormel Short Orders**	22.9
w beans: 1 cup / **Libby's**	33
w beans: 7½ oz / **Morton House**	27
w beans: 7¾ oz / **Swanson**	28
w beans, hot:	
7½ oz can / **Hormel Short Orders**	22.9
w beans, low sodium: 7¾ oz / **Campbell**	30
wo beans: 7½ oz / **Hormel**	8
wo beans:	
7½ oz can / **Hormel Short Orders**	8.6
wo beans: 1 cup / **Libby's**	11
wo beans: 7½ oz / **Morton House**	14
Chili Mac, canned:	
7½ oz can / **Hormel Short Orders**	17.1
Enchiladas	
Frozen: 1 dinner / **El Chico**	118
Frozen, beef w cheese and chili gravy:	
32 oz / **Banquet** Buffet Supper	118.2
Frozen, beef and cheese w gravy:	
3 enchiladas / **El Chico**	98

GRAMS

Frozen, beef w gravy:
   3 enchiladas / **El Chico**   89
Frozen, beef w sauce:
   6 oz / **Banquet** Cookin' Bag   28.9
Mexican dinner, frozen: 1 dinner / **El Chico**   46
Queso dinner, frozen: 1 dinner / **El Chico**   140
Peppers, hot, diced, canned:
   1 oz / **Ortega**   1.6
Peppers, hot, whole, canned:
   1 oz / **Ortega**   1.6
Salsa, green chile, canned: 1 oz / **Ortega**   1.2
Saltillo dinner, frozen: 1 dinner / **El Chico**   150
Tacos, beef, frozen: 3 tacos / **El Chico**   51
Tacos, prepared: 1 taco / **Ortega**   13
Taco shell: 1 shell / **Lawry's**   5.1
Taco shell: 1 shell / **Ortega**   7.3
Tamales
   Beef, canned: 1 tamale / **Hormel**   4.5
   Beef, canned:
      7½ oz can / **Hormel Short Orders**   17.1
   Beef, in jar: 2 tamales / **Swift** Derby   13
Tomatoes and hot green chiles, canned:
   1 oz / **Ortega**   1.4
Tostada shells: 1 shell / **Lawry's**   5.1

Milk

GRAMS

Buttermilk: 8 fl oz (1 cup)
   .1% fat / **Borden**   12.5
   .2% fat / **Sealtest** Skimmilk   9.3

GRAMS

.5% fat / **Borden**	9.5
.5% fat / **Meadow Gold**	12
.8% fat / **Golden Nugget**	10
.8% fat / **Light n' Lively**	10.5
1% fat / **Borden**	12.4
1.5% fat / **Borden**	9.5
1.5% fat / **Lucerne**	11.6
2% fat / **Borden**	9.5
2% fat / **Sealtest** Lowfat	9.3
2.2% fat / **Borden**	12.5
3.5% fat / **Borden**	11.9
Condensed, swt: ¼ cup / **Borden** Dime Brand	42
Condensed, swt: 1 oz / **Borden** Eagle Brand	20.6
Condensed, swt:	
¼ cup / **Borden** Magnolia Brand	42
Dry, nonfat	
¼ cup / **Carnation**	9.4
Reconstituted: 8 oz glass / **Borden**	11.6
Reconstituted: 8 oz glass / **Carnation**	12.5
Reconstituted: 8 oz glass / **Lucerne**	12
Reconstituted: 8 oz glass / **Sannalec**	11
Evaporated, canned: 8 fl oz (1 cup)	
Borden's	24.2
Carnation	24.9
Carnation Skimmed	27.9
Lucerne	25
Pet / ½ cup	12
Evaporated skim: ½ cup / **Pet**	14
Imitation milk: 8 fl oz / **Lucerne**	11
Skim or nonfat: 8 fl oz	
0% fat / **Lucerne**	11.8
.1% fat / **Sealtest**	11.3
.4% fat / **Sealtest** Diet Skim	13.8
.5% fat / **Meadow Gold**	13
1% fat / **Lucerne** 1-10	13
2% fat / **Lucerne** 2-10	13
2% fat / **Meadow Gold** Viva	14

GRAMS

Fortified, .1% fat / **Borden** 11.2
Fortified, .1% fat / **Borden** Vitamin A & D 11.2
Fortified, 1% fat / **Light n' Lively** Lowfat 13.6
Fortified, 1.5% fat / **Borden** 15.2
Fortified, 1.75% fat / **Borden** Lite Line 14
Fortified, 2% fat / **Borden** Hi-Protein 13.9
Fortified, 2% fat / **Sealtest** Vita-lure 13.6
Whole: 8 fl oz
    3.25% fat / **Sealtest** 10.8
    3.3% fat / **Meadow Gold** 12
    3.5% fat / **Borden** 12
    3.5% fat / **Lucerne** 11.5
    3.5% fat / **Sealtest** 11
    3.7% fat / **Borden** Cream Line 11.2
    3.7% fat / **Sealtest** 11.1
    3.8% fat / **Lucerne** 11.5
    4% fat / **Borden** 11.9
    Fortified / **Sealtest** Multivitamin Milk 11

FLAVORED MILK BEVERAGES

All flavors, canned:
    10 fl oz / **Carnation** Slender 34
All flavors, mix:
    1 env / **Lucerne** Instant Breakfast 35
Cherry-vanilla, canned:
    8 fl oz / **Borden** Milk Shake 37.4
Chocolate, canned:
    9½ fl oz / **Borden's** Dutch 32.1
Chocolate, dairy pack, 3.5% fat:
    8 fl oz / **Borden's** Dutch Chocolate Milk 26.1
Chocolate fudge, canned:
    8 fl oz / **Borden's** Frosted Shake 40
Chocolate mixes
    Carnation Instant Breakfast / 1 env 23
    Carnation Slender / 1 env 20
    Ovaltine / ¾ oz 16
    PDQ / 3½ tsp 14.6

GRAMS

Pillsbury Instant Breakfast / 1 pouch	38
Safeway / 2 tsp dry	21
Safeway (w 8 fl oz whole milk) / 2 tsp	27
Dutch, mix: 1 env / **Carnation** Slender	20
Malt, mix: 2 heaping tsp / **Borden**	16
Malt, mix: 1 env /	
Carnation Instant Breakfast	22
Malt, mix: 1 env / **Carnation** Slender	20
Malt, mix, prepared:	
1 pouch / **Pillsbury** Instant Breakfast	38
Coffee	
Canned: 8 fl oz / **Borden's** Frosted Shake	22.8
Canned: 8 fl oz / **Borden's** Milk Shake	37.4
Mix: 1 env / **Carnation** Instant Breakfast	24
Mix: 1 env / **Carnation** Slender	21
Eggnog	
Dairy case, 4.7% fat:	
½ cup / **Borden**	16.3
Dairy case, 6% fat: ½ cup / **Borden**	16.3
Dairy case, 8% fat: ½ cup / **Borden**	16.3
Mix: 1 env / **Carnation** Instant Breakfast	23
Mix: 2 heaping tbsp / **PDQ**	27.5
Malt-flavored	
Instant: 3 heaping tsp / **Carnation**	15.6
Mix: 2 heaping tsp / **Borden**	13.4
Mix: ¾ oz / **Ovaltine**	17
Chocolate, instant:	
3 heaping tsp / **Carnation**	18
Mocha, canned: 8 fl oz / **Borden's** Milk Shake	37.4
Strawberry	
Canned: 8 fl oz / **Borden's** Frosted Shake	39
Canned: 8 fl oz / **Borden's** Milk Shake	37.4
Mix: 1 env / **Carnation** Instant Breakfast	24
Mix: 3½ tsp / **PDQ**	15
Mix, prepared:	
1 pouch / **Pillsbury** Instant Breakfast	39
Wild, mix: 1 env / **Carnation** Slender	21

GRAMS

Vanilla

    Canned: 8 fl oz / **Borden's** Frosted Shake   39

    Mix: 1 env / **Carnation** Instant Breakfast   24

    Mix, prepared:

      1 pouch / **Pillsbury** Instant Breakfast   39

    French, mix: 1 env / **Carnation** Slender   21

Muffins: English and Sweet

GRAMS

1 muffin unless noted

Apple cinnamon, mix, prepared / **Betty Crocker**	26
Apple cinnamon, refrigerator, to bake / **Pillsbury**	18
Banana nut, mix, prepared / **Betty Crocker** Chiquita	25
Blueberry	
Thomas' Toast-R-Cakes	17
Frozen / **Howard Johnson's** Toasties	16.7
Frozen / **Morton**	23
Frozen / **Morton** Rounds	21
Frozen / **Pepperidge Farm**	22
Mix, prepared / **Betty Crocker**	19
Bran / **Oroweat** Bran'nola	30
Bran / **Thomas'** Toast-R-Cakes	20
Corn	
Thomas'	26
Thomas' Toast-R-Cakes	18
Frozen / **Howard Johnson's** Toasties	20.4
Frozen / **Morton**	20

GRAMS

Frozen / **Morton** Rounds   21
Frozen / **Pepperidge Farm**   21
Frozen / **Thomas'** Toast-R-Cakes   18
Mix, prepared / **Betty Crocker**   25
Mix, prepared / **Flako**   23
Refrigerator, to bake / **Pillsbury**   20
English
    Arnold   25
    Earth Grains / 2 1/3 oz   33
    Home Pride   25
    Pepperidge Farm   24
    Thomas'   26
    Wonder   26
    Frozen / **Thomas'**   26
    Cinnamon-raisin / **Pepperidge Farm** 27
    Onion / **Thomas'**   26
    Sour dough / **Oroweat**   30
    Wheat / **Home Pride**   25
    Honeyberry wheat / **Oroweat**   30
    Honey butter / **Oroweat**   30
Orange, frozen / **Howard Johnson's** Toasties   16.4
Orange, mix, prepared / **Betty Crocker** Sunkist   26
Pineapple, mix, prepared / **Betty Crocker**   20
Raisin / **Oroweat**   30
Raisin / **Wonder** Rounds   28
Raisin bran, frozen / **Pepperidge Farm**   21
Sour dough / **Wonder**   27
Wild blueberry, mix, prepared / **Duncan Hines**   17

Noodles and Noodle Dishes

	GRAMS
Plain, cooked: 1 cup	37.3
Almondine, mix, prepared:	
¼ pkg / **Betty Crocker**	27
w beef, canned: 7½ oz can /	
Hormel Short Orders Noodles 'n Beef	17.1
w beef sauce, mix, prepared: ½ cup /	
Pennsylvania Dutch Brand	24
w beef-flavored sauce, mix, prepared: 1 pouch /	
Betty Crocker Mug-O-Lunch	30
w butter sauce, mix, prepared: ½ cup /	
Pennsylvania Dutch Brand	23
w cheese, mix, prepared: ⅛ pkg /	
Noodle-Roni Parmesano	23
w cheese sauce, mix, prepared: ½ cup /	
Pennsylvania Dutch Brand	24
w chicken, canned: 7½ oz can / **Dinty Moore**	
Short Orders	14.3
w chicken sauce, mix, prepared: ½ cup /	
Pennsylvania Dutch Brand	25
Romanoff, frozen: ⅓ pkg / **Stouffer's**	16
Romanoff, mix, prepared: ¼ pkg / **Betty Crocker**	23
Stroganoff, mix: 2 oz / **Pennsylvania**	
Dutch Brand	40

GRAMS

Stroganoff, mix, prepared: ¼ pkg / **Betty Crocker**	26
w tuna, frozen: ½ pkg / **Stouffer's** 11½ oz	18

Nuts

SALTED AND FLAVORED

GRAMS

1 oz unless noted (1 oz = about ⅕ cup)

Almonds / **Granny Goose**	7.5
Almonds, dry roasted / **Planters**	6
Cashews	
Frito-Lay	9
Granny Goose	7
Planters	8
Planters Unsalted	9
Dry roasted, in jar / **A & P**	8
Dry roasted / **Planters**	9
Dry roasted / **Skippy**	8
Mixed	
Excel	5
Granny Goose	5.7
w peanuts / **Planters**	6
wo peanuts / **A & P** Fancy	6
wo peanuts / **Planters**	6
Unsalted / **Planters**	7
Dry roasted, in jar / **A & P**	7
Dry roasted / **Planters**	7
Dry roasted / **Skippy**	5.4
Peanuts	
A & P	5

	GRAMS
Frito-Lay	6
Planters Old Fashioned	5
Unsalted / **Planters**	5
Cocktail halves / **Excel**	5
Cocktail / **Planters**	5
Dry roasted, in jar / **A & P**	6
Dry roasted / **Planters**	6
Dry roasted / **Skippy**	4.1
In shell: 1 oz edible portion / **A & P**	6
In shell: 1 oz edible portion / **A & P** Raw Fancies	5
In shell: 1 oz edible portion / **Frito-Lay**	6
Spanish / **A & P**	5
Spanish / **Frito-Lay**	7
Spanish / **Granny Goose**	4
Spanish / **Planters**	5
Spanish, dry roasted / **Planters**	6
Virginia / **Granny Goose**	4.6
Virginia redskin / **Planters**	5
Pecans, pieces and chopped / **A & P**	4
Pecans / **Granny Goose**	3.1
Pecans, dry roasted / **Planters**	5
Pistachios: 1 oz of edible portion / **Frito-Lay**	6
Pistachios / **Granny Goose**	5
Pistachios, dry roasted / **Planters** Natural	6
Sesame Nut Mix / **Planters**	8
Soybeans, dry roasted / **Malt-O-Meal**	6
Soybeans, oil roasted / **Malt-O-Meal**	5
Soy nuts / **Planters**	10
Tavern / **Planters**	6

UNSALTED AND UNFLAVORED

Almonds	
Dried, in shell: 10 nuts	2
Dried, in shell: 1 cup	6.1
Dried, shelled, chopped: 1 tbsp	1.6

	GRAMS
Dried, shelled, chopped: 1 cup	25.4
Dried, shelled, slivered: 1 cup	22.4
Dried, shelled, whole: 1 cup	27.7
Roasted, in oil: 1 cup	30.6
Beechnuts, in shell: 1 lb	56.2
Beechnuts, shelled: 1 lb	92.1
Brazil nuts, in shell: 1 cup	6.4
Brazil nuts, shelled: 1 oz or 6-8 kernels	3.1
Brazil nuts, shelled: 1 cup	15.3
Butternuts, in shell: 1 lb	5.3
Butternuts, shelled: 1 lb	38.1
Cashew nuts, roasted in oil: 1 cup	41
Cashew nuts, roasted in oil: 1 lb	132.9
Chestnuts	
Fresh, in shell: 1 cup	40.9
Fresh, in shell: 1 lb	154.7
Fresh, shelled: 1 cup	64.7
Fresh, shelled: 1 lb	191
Filberts, in shell: 1 lb	34.9
Filberts, shelled, chopped: 1 cup	19.2
Filberts, shelled, whole: 1 cup	22.5
Peanuts	
Roasted, in shell: 10 jumbo nuts	3.7
Roasted, in shell: 1 lb	62.6
Roasted (Spanish and Virginia): 1 lb	225.9
Roasted (Spanish and Virginia), chopped: 1 cup	27.1
Hickory nuts, shelled: 1 oz	3.8
Macadamia nuts, shelled: 1 oz	4.7
Pecans	
In shell: 10 large (64-77 per lb)	5
In shell: 10 extra large (56-63 per lb)	5.9
In shell: 10 oversize (55 or fewer per lb)	6.4
Chopped or pieces: 1 tbsp	1.1
Chopped or pieces: 1 cup	17.2
Halves: 10 large (451-550 per lb)	1.3

GRAMS

Halves: 10 jumbo (301-350 per lb)	2
Halves: 10 mammoth (250 or fewer per lb)	2.6
Pinenuts, Pignolias, shelled: 1 oz	3.3
Pinenuts, Piñon, shelled: 1 oz	5.8
Pistachio nuts, in shell: 1 lb	43.1
Pistachio nuts, shelled: 1 lb	86.2
Walnuts	
Black, in shell: 1 lb	14.8
Black, shelled, chopped or broken kernels: 1 tbsp	1.2
Black, shelled, chopped or broken kernels: 1 cup	18.5
Persian or English, in shell: 1 lb	32.2
Persian or English, shelled, halves: 1 cup	15.8
Persian or English: 10 large nuts	7.8
Persian or English, chopped: 1 tbsp	1.3

Oils

Corn, olive, peanut, safflower, vegetable: any quantity, all brands	0
Corn / **Mrs. Tucker's** Salad Oil	0
Corn / **Nu Made**	0
Peanut / **Planters**	0
Popcorn / **Planters**	0
Safflower / **Nu Made**	0
Soybean / **Mrs. Tucker's** Salad Oil	0
Sunflower / **Sunlight**	0
Vegetable	
Crisco	0
Puritan	0
Swift Hi Lite	0
Swift Pour 'n Fry	0
Wesson	0
Vegetable-cottonseed / **Swift** Jewel	0
Vegetable-soybean / **Swift** Jewel	0

Olives

GRAMS

Green	
10 small	.5
10 large	.5
10 giant	.9

GRAMS

Ripe, black

	GRAMS
Ascolano: 10 extra large	1.2
Ascolano: 10 giant	1.8
Ascolano: 10 jumbo	2.1
Manzanillo: 10 small	.8
Manzanillo: 10 medium	.9
Manzanillo: 10 large	1
Manzanillo: 10 extra large	1.2
Mission: 10 small	.9
Mission: 10 medium	1.1
Mission: 10 large	1.3
Mission: 10 extra large	1.5
Sevillano: 10 giant	1.9
Sevillano: 10 jumbo	2.2
Sevillano: 10 colossal	2.8
Sevillano: 10 supercolossal	3.3
Greek style: 10 medium	1.7
Greek style: 10 extra large	2.3

Pancakes, Waffles and Similar Breakfast Foods

	GRAMS
Breakfast, frozen, French toast w sausages: 1 entree / **Swanson "TV"**	22
Breakfast, frozen, pancakes w sausages: 1 entree / **Swanson "TV"**	50
Breakfast, frozen, scrambled eggs w sausage and coffee cake: 1 entree / **Swanson "TV"**	22
Breakfast bars, chocolate chip: 1 bar / **Carnation**	24
Breakfast bars, chocolate crunch: 1 bar / **Carnation**	23
Breakfast bars, peanut butter crunch: 1 bar / **Carnation**	22
Breakfast squares: 1 bar / **General Mills**	22.5
Crepes, mix, prepared: 2 crepes 6-in diam / **Aunt Jemima**	15
French toast, frozen: 1 slice / **Aunt Jemima**	13
French toast, frozen: 1 slice / **Downyflake**	15
French toast w cinnamon, frozen: 1 slice / **Aunt Jemima** Cinnamon Swirl	15.5
Fritters, apple, frozen: 1 fritter / **Mrs. Paul's**	16
Fritters, corn, frozen: 1 fritter / **Mrs. Paul's**	15.5
Pancakes, frozen: 1 pancake / **Downyflake**	10
Pancake batter, frozen: 3 cakes 4-in diam / **Aunt Jemima**	43

157

GRAMS

Pancake batter, frozen: 3 cakes 4-in diam /
  Aunt Jemima Blueberry — 44
Pancake batter, frozen: 3 cakes 4-in diam /
  Aunt Jemima Buttermilk — 43
Pancake, mix, prepared
  Hungry Jack Complete / 3 cakes 4-in diam — 42
  Hungry Jack Extra Lights /
    3 cakes 4-in diam — 26
  Tillie Lewis / 3 cakes 4-in diam — 26
  Blueberry: 3 cakes 4-in diam /
    Hungry Jack — 43
  Buttermilk: 3 cakes 4-in diam /
    Betty Crocker — 39
  Buttermilk: 3 cakes 4-in diam /
    Betty Crocker Complete — 41
  Buttermilk: 3 cakes 4-in diam /
    Hungry Jack — 29
  Buttermilk: 3 cakes 4-in diam /
    Hungry Jack Complete — 34
Pancake-waffle, mix, prepared
  Aunt Jemima Complete / 3 cakes 4-in diam — 38
  Aunt Jemima Original / 3 cakes 4-in diam — 26
  Log Cabin Complete / 3 cakes 4-in diam — 33
  Log Cabin Regular / 3 cakes 4-in diam — 26
  Buckwheat: 3 cakes 4-in diam /
    Aunt Jemima — 25
  Buttermilk: 3 cakes 4-in diam /
    Aunt Jemima — 40
  Buttermilk: 3 cakes 4-in diam /
    Aunt Jemima Complete — 46
  Buttermilk: 3 cakes 4-in diam /
    Log Cabin — 32
  Whole wheat: 3 cakes 4-in diam /
    Aunt Jemima — 32
Waffles, frozen: 1 waffle
  Aunt Jemima Jumbo Original — 14
  Downyflake — 10

GRAMS

Downyflake Hot 'n Buttery | 11
Downyflake Jumbo | 15
Eggo | 17
Blueberry / **Aunt Jemima** Jumbo | 14
Blueberry / **Downyflake** | 16
Blueberry / **Eggo** | 18
Bran / **Downyflake** | 8
Bran / **Eggo** | 20
Buttermilk / **Aunt Jemima** Jumbo | 14
Buttermilk / **Downyflake** | 15
Buttermilk / **Downyflake** Round | 17
Strawberry / **Eggo** | 18

Pastry

FROZEN

GRAMS

Donuts: 1 donut
　Morton Mini | 16
　Bavarian creme / **Morton** | 22
　Boston creme / **Morton** | 28
　Chocolate iced / **Morton** | 20
　Glazed / **Morton** | 19
　Jelly / **Morton** | 23
Dumplings, apple: 1 dumpling /
　Pepperidge Farm | 31
Pie tarts, frozen: 1 tart
　Apple / **Pepperidge Farm** | 33
　Blueberry / **Pepperidge Farm** | 35
　Cherry / **Pepperidge Farm** | 35

	GRAMS
Lemon / **Pepperidge Farm**	37
Raspberry / **Pepperidge Farm**	34
Strudel, apple: 3 oz / **Pepperidge Farm**	31
Turnovers: 1 turnover	
Apple, frozen / **Pepperidge Farm**	30
Apple, refrigerator / **Pillsbury**	22
Blueberry, frozen / **Pepperidge Farm**	32
Blueberry, refrigerator / **Pillsbury**	22
Cherry, frozen / **Pepperidge Farm**	30
Cherry, refrigerator / **Pillsbury**	24
Peach, frozen / **Pepperidge Farm**	33
Raspberry, frozen / **Pepperidge Farm**	37

TOASTER PASTRIES

1 portion

Cinnamon brown sugar, frosted / **Town House**	40
Pop-Tarts	
Blueberry / **Kellogg's**	36
Brown sugar-cinnamon / **Kellogg's**	34
Cherry / **Kellogg's**	35
Concord grape / **Kellogg's**	36
Raspberry / **Kellogg's**	36
Strawberry / **Kellogg's**	36
Pop-Tarts, frosted	
Blueberry / **Kellogg's**	36
Brown sugar-cinnamon / **Kellogg's**	33
Cherry / **Kellogg's**	36
Chocolate fudge / **Kellogg's**	35
Chocolate-peppermint / **Kellogg's**	35
Chocolate-vanilla creme / **Kellogg's**	34
Concord grape / **Kellogg's**	37
Dutch apple / **Kellogg's**	36
Raspberry / **Kellogg's**	37
Strawberry / **Kellogg's**	36

Pickles and Relishes

	GRAMS
Capers: 1 tbsp / **Crosse & Blackwell**	1
Cauliflower, sweet: 2 buds / **Smucker's**	11
Chow-Chow: 1 tbsp / **Crosse & Blackwell**	1
Onions, cocktail: 1 tbsp / **Crosse & Blackwell**	.3
Peppers	
Chile: ¼ cup / **Del Monte**	2.1
Chile: 1 oz / **Ortega** Jalapenos	1.2
Chile, green: 1 oz / **Ortega**	1.1
Hot: 1 4-in / **Smucker's**	2.1
Mild sweet, wax: ¼ cup / **Del Monte**	2.3
Red, bell: 1 oz / **Ortega**	1.9
Pickles, dill	
Slices: 3 / **Heinz** Hamburger Dill Slices	.1
Slices: 3 / **Smucker's** Hamburger Dill Slices	.3
Spears: 1 piece / **Bond's** Fresh-Pack	.2
Spears: 1 piece / **Bond's** Fresh-Pack Kosher	.2
Sticks, candied: 1 4-in / **Smucker's**	11.2
Whole: 1 / **Bond's** Flavor Pack	.2
Whole: 1 / **Bond's** Fresh-Pack Kosher	.2
Whole: 1 large / **Del Monte**	1.4
Whole: 1 4-inch / **Heinz** Genuine Dill	1.1
Whole: 1 3-in / **Heinz** Processed Dill	.1
Whole: 1 large / **L & S**	2
Whole: 1 large / **L & S** Fresh-Pack Kosher	2
Whole: 1 3½-in / **Smucker's**	1.4
Whole: 2 2¾-in / **Smucker's** Fresh Pack Baby	1
Whole: 1 3½-in / **Smucker's** Kosher	1.4
Whole: 1 3½-in / **Smucker's** Kosher Fresh Pack	1.4
Pickles, mixed, hot: 4 pieces / **Smucker's**	1
Pickles, sour, whole: 1 large / **Del Monte**	2

GRAMS

Pickles, sweet
Chips: 3 / **Smucker's** Fresh Pack	7.7
Chips: 3 / **Smucker's** Sweet Pickle Chips	7.7
Mixed: 3 pieces / **Heinz**	5.6
Pieces, mixed: 4 / **Smucker's**	11.6
Slices: 3 / **Bond's** Fresh-Pack Cucumber Slices	5
Slices: 3 / **Heinz** Cucumber Slices	4.7
Slices: 6 / **Lutz & Schramm** Fresh Cucumber Slices	4
Sticks: 1 4-in / **Smucker's** Fresh Pack	6.8
Whole: 1 pickle / **Bond's** Sweet Gherkins	3
Whole: 1 2-in / **Heinz** Sweet Gherkin	3.9
Whole: 1 med / **L & S** Sweet Pickles	7
Whole: 2 2½-in / **Smucker's**	8.4
Whole, candied: 2 2-in / **Smucker's** Midgets	7
Pimientos: 4 oz / **Dromedary**	4.8
Pimientos, canned: 4 oz / **Ortega**	6
Pimientos: ½ cup / **Stokely-Van Camp**	6.3

Relishes: 1 tbsp
Barbecue / **Crosse & Blackwell**	5.4
Barbecue / **Heinz**	8.5
Corn / **Crosse & Blackwell**	3.6
Hamburger / **Crosse & Blackwell**	4.7
Hamburger / **Del Monte**	8.9
Hamburger / **Heinz**	3.6
Hot Dog / **Crosse & Blackwell**	5.4
Hot Dog / **Del Monte**	6.9
Hot Dog / **Heinz**	3.9
Hot Pepper / **Crosse & Blackwell**	5.4
India / **Crosse & Blackwell**	6.3
India / **Heinz**	3.9
Piccalilli / **Crosse & Blackwell**	6.3
Piccalilli / **Heinz** Green Tomato	5.3
Sweet / **Cross & Blackwell**	6.3
Sweet / **Del Monte**	9.2
Sweet / **Heinz**	6.6

	GRAMS
Sweet / **Lutz & Schramm**	4
Sweet / **Smucker's**	5.6
Watermelon rind / **Crosse & Blackwell**	9.3

Pies

FROZEN

	GRAMS
1 whole pie	
Apple	
Banquet 20 oz	213.2
Morton 24 oz	246
Morton Mini 8 oz	88
Mrs. Smith's 8 in	240
Mrs. Smith's (natural juice) 8 in	390
Dutch / **Mrs. Smith's** 8 in	270
Tart / **Mrs. Smith's** 8 in	252
Banana cream	
Banquet 14 oz	119.6
Morton 16 oz	120
Morton Mini 3½ oz	26
Mrs. Smith's 8 in	168
Mrs. Smith's Light 13.8 oz	162
Blueberry	
Banquet 20 oz	225.1
Morton 24 oz	234
Morton Mini 8 oz	86
Mrs. Smith's 8 in	240
Mrs. Smith's (natural juice) 8 in	282
Mrs. Smith's (natural juice) 9 in	390
Boston cream / **Mrs. Smith's** 8 in	312

GRAMS

Cherry
Banquet 20 oz	203
Morton 24 oz	252
Morton Mini 8 oz	87
Mrs. Smith's 8 in	258
Mrs. Smith's (natural juice) 8 in	282
Mrs. Smith's (natural juice) 9 in	390
Chocolate / **Mrs. Smith's** Light 13.8 oz	186

Chocolate cream
Banquet 14 oz	131
Morton 16 oz	138
Morton Mini 3½ oz	29
Mrs. Smith's 8 in	198
Coconut / **Mrs. Smith's** Light 13.8 oz	168

Coconut cream
Banquet 14 oz	114.7
Morton 16 oz	132
Morton Mini 3½ oz	29
Mrs. Smith's 8 in	192
Coconut custard / **Banquet** 20 oz	169.5
Coconut custard / **Morton** Mini 6½ oz	53
Coconut custard / **Mrs. Smith's** 8 in	192
Custard / **Banquet** 20 oz	190.5
Egg custard / **Mrs. Smith's** 8 in	258
Lemon / **Mrs. Smith's** 8 in	270

Lemon cream
Banquet 14 oz	131
Morton 16 oz	132
Morton Mini 3½ oz	28
Mrs. Smith's 8 in	192
Lemon Krunch / **Mrs. Smith's** 8 in	342
Lemon meringue / **Mrs. Smith's** 8 in	240
Lemon yogurt / **Mrs. Smith's** 15.6 oz	162
Mince / **Morton** 24 oz	276
Mince / **Morton** Mini 8 oz	92
Mince / **Mrs. Smith's** 8 in	312
Mincemeat / **Banquet** 20 oz	230.8

GRAMS

Neapolitan cream / **Morton** 16 oz	138
Neapolitan cream / **Mrs. Smith's** 8 in	198
Peach	
Banquet 20 oz	179.2
Morton 24 oz	234
Morton Mini 8 oz	82
Mrs. Smith's 8 in	252
Mrs. Smith's (natural juice) 8 in	258
Mrs. Smith's (natural juice) 9 in	372
Pecan / **Morton** Mini 6½ oz	81
Pecan / **Mrs. Smith's** 8 in	348
Pineapple / **Mrs. Smith's** 8 in	252
Pineapple-cheese / **Mrs. Smith's** 8 in	210
Pumpkin	
Banquet 20 oz	193.9
Morton 24 oz	216
Morton Mini 8 oz	72
Mrs. Smith's 8 in	210
Raisin / **Mrs. Smith's** 8 in	282
Strawberry cream / **Banquet** 14 oz	135.2
Strawberry cream / **Morton** 16 oz	132
Strawberry cream / **Mrs. Smith's** 8 in	180
Strawberry-rhubarb / **Mrs. Smith's** 8 in	282
Strawberry-rhubarb / **Mrs. Smith's** (natural juice) 8 in	240
Strawberry-rhubarb / **Mrs. Smith's** (natural juice) 9 in	342
Strawberry yogurt / **Mrs. Smith's** 15.6 oz	150

PIE MIXES

Prepared: 1 whole pie

Boston cream / **Betty Crocker**	384
Chocolate creme / **Pillsbury** No Bake	318
Lemon chiffon / **Pillsbury** No Bake	324
Vanilla marble / **Pillsbury** No Bake	324

PIE CRUSTS AND PASTRY SHELLS

	GRAMS
Pastry sheets, frozen: 1 sheet / **Pepperidge Farm**	36
Pastry shells: 1 piece / **Stella D'Oro**	16
Patty shells, frozen: 1 shell / **Pepperidge Farm**	15
Pie crust, prepared	
Mix: double crust / **Betty Crocker**	160
Mix: 1 whole crust / **Flako**	174
Mix: double crust / **Pillsbury**	162
Stick: 1 stick / **Betty Crocker**	80
Pie shells, deep, frozen: 1 shell / **Pepperidge Farm**	40
Pie shells, shallow bottom, frozen: 1 bottom / **Pepperidge Farm**	36
Pie shells, top, frozen: 1 top / **Pepperidge Farm**	60
Pot shells: 1 piece / **Stella D'Oro**	28.2
Tart shells, frozen: 1 shell / **Pepperidge Farm**	10

PIE FILLING

Apple: 21 oz can / **Wilderness**	180
Apple, French: 21 oz can / **Wilderness**	168
Apricot: 21 oz can / **Wilderness**	180
Banana cream, mix, prepared: whole 8-in pie / **Jell-O**	108
Blueberry: 21 oz can / **Wilderness**	168
Cherry: 21 oz can / **Wilderness**	174
Key Lime, mix, prepared: ½ cup / **Royal** Cooked	30
Lemon: 22 oz can / **Wilderness**	234
Lemon, mix, prepared: whole 8-in pie / **Jell-O**	228
Lemon, mix, prepared: ½ cup / **Royal** Cooked	30
Mince: 22 oz can / **Wilderness**	270
Mincemeat: ⅓ cup / **None Such**	50
Peach: 21 oz can / **Wilderness**	150
Pumpkin, canned: 1 cup / **Stokely-Van Camp**	89
Pumpkin mix, canned: 1 cup / **Libby's**	56

GRAMS

Raisin: 22 oz can / **Wilderness**   186
Strawberry: 21 oz can / **Wilderness**   186

PIE AND PASTRY SNACKS

1 piece

Apple pastry / **Stella D'Oro** Dietetic	13
Apple pie / **Hostess**	54
Berry pie / **Hostess**	51
Blueberry pie / **Hostess**	49
Cherry pie / **Hostess**	59
Fig pastry / **Stella D'Oro** Dietetic	14
Guava pastry / **Stella D'Oro**	23
Lemon pie / **Hostess**	53
Peach pie / **Hostess**	53
Peach-apricot pastry / **Stella D'Oro**	14.5
Peach-apricot pastry / **Stella D'Oro** Dietetic	13
Pecan pie: 3 oz / **Frito-Lay**	53
Prune pastry / **Stella D'Oro** Dietetic	13.5

Pizza

GRAMS

1 whole pizza unless noted

Beef and cheese w enchilada seasoning, frozen / **El Chico** Mexican	84
Beef and cheese w taco seasoning, frozen / **El Chico** Mexican	88
Canadian bacon, frozen / **Totino's** Party Cheese	94
Frozen: 4 oz / **Buitoni**	37.4

	GRAMS
Frozen / **Celeste** 7 oz	64
Frozen / **Celeste** 19 oz	144
Frozen / **Celeste** Sicilian Style 20 oz	192
Frozen / **Jeno's** 13 oz	108
Frozen / **Jeno's** Deluxe 20 oz	171
Frozen / **La Pizzeria** 20 oz	132
Frozen, thick crust / **La Pizzeria** 18.5 oz	138
Frozen: ½ pkg / **Stouffer's**	43
Frozen / **Totino's** Crisp Party	104
Frozen / **Totino's** Party	106
Mix, prepared / **Jeno's**	124
w mushroom, frozen / **Celeste** 8 oz	64
w mushroom, frozen / **Celeste** 21 oz	120
Chili and cheese, frozen / **El Chico** Mexican	90
Combination	
Frozen / **Celeste** Deluxe 9 oz	56
Frozen / **Celeste** Deluxe 23½ oz	136
Frozen / **Jeno's** Deluxe 23 oz	165
Frozen / **La Pizzeria** 13.5 oz	86
Frozen / **La Pizzeria** 24½ oz	156
Frozen: ½ pkg / **Stouffer's** Deluxe	46
Frozen / **Totino's** Classic	153
Frozen, deep crust / **Totino's** Classic	198
Hamburger, frozen / **Jeno's**	114
Hamburger, frozen / **Totino's** Crisp Party	102
Hamburger, frozen / **Totino's** Party	102
Open face, frozen: 4 oz / **Buitoni**	39
Pepperoni	
Frozen / **Celeste** 7½ oz	52
Frozen / **Celeste** 20 oz	128
Frozen / **Jeno's** 13 oz	114
Frozen / **La Pizzeria** 21 oz	168
Frozen: ½ pkg / **Stouffer's**	42
Frozen, deep crust / **Totino's** Classic	204
Frozen / **Totino's** Crisp Party	100
Frozen / **Totino's** Party	104

GRAMS

Mix, prepared / **Jeno's**	134
w mushroom, frozen / **Totino's** Classic	153
Pizza rolls, frozen	
Cheeseburger: 3 oz / **Jeno's**	27
Pepperoni and cheese: 3 oz / **Jeno's**	25
Sausage and cheese: 3 oz / **Jeno's**	25
Shrimp and cheese: 3 oz / **Jeno's**	23
Refried bean and cheese, frozen / **El Chico** Mexican	88
Regular, mix, prepared / **Jeno's**	134
Sausage	
Frozen / **Celeste** 8 oz	52
Frozen / **Celeste** 22 oz	136
Frozen / **Jeno's** 13 oz	114
Frozen / **Jeno's** Deluxe 21 oz	159
Frozen / **La Pizzeria** 13 oz	82
Frozen / **La Pizzeria** 23 oz	164
Frozen, deep crust / **Totino's** Classic	198
Frozen / **Totino's** Crisp Party	106
Frozen / **Totino's** Party	108
Mix, prepared / **Jeno's**	132
w mushrooms, frozen / **Celeste** 9 oz	58
w mushrooms, frozen / **Celeste** 21 oz	140
w mushrooms, frozen / **Totino's** Classic	141

Popcorn

GRAMS

**Note: 1 oz candy-coated popcorn =
a little over ¾ cup**

Plain, popped: 1 cup / **Pops-Rite**	5
Plain, popped: 1 cup / **Jolly Time**	10.7

GRAMS

Plain, popped: 1 cup / **TNT**	6.5
Butter flavor, ready to eat: 1 cup / **Wise**	5.8
Caramel-coated: 1 oz / **Old London**	22.2
Caramel-coated: ½ cup / **Wise**	14.8
Caramel-coated w peanuts: 1 oz / **Wise Pixies**	23
Caramel Corn: 1 oz / **Granny Goose**	25.8
Cheese flavor, ready to eat: ½ cup / **Wise**	2.8
Cheese flavor, ready to eat: 1 oz / **Old London**	21.9
Cracker Jack: 1⅜ oz pkg	32.4
Cracker Jack: 6 oz pkg	131
Fiddle Faddle, almond: 1 oz	23.4
Fiddle Faddle, coconut: 1 oz	21.8
Fiddle Faddle, peanut: 1 oz	23.1
Krazy Korn: 1 oz	20.2
Screaming Yellow Zonkers: 1 oz	23.1

Pot Pies

GRAMS

Frozen: 1 whole pie

Beef

Banquet 8 oz	40.9
Morton 8 oz	31
Stouffer's 10 oz	38
Swanson 8 oz	43
Swanson Hungry-Man 16 oz	65

Chicken

Banquet 8 oz	39
Morton 8 oz	32
Stouffer's 10 oz	40
Swanson 8 oz	44
Swanson Hungry-Man 16 oz	66

GRAMS

Sirloin Burger / **Swanson** Hungry-Man 16 oz	55
Tuna	
Banquet 8 oz	42.7
Morton 8 oz	36
Turkey	
Banquet 8 oz	40.6
Morton 8 oz	32
Stouffer's 10 oz	35
Swanson 8 oz	40
Swanson Hungry-Man 16 oz	60

Poultry and Poultry Entrees

FRESH

GRAMS

Chicken, all cuts (fresh), raw or cooked, except organs	0
Duck, all cuts (fresh), raw or cooked, except organs	0
Goose, all cuts (fresh), raw or cooked, except organs	0
Turkey, all cuts (fresh), raw or cooked, except organs	0
Gizzard, chicken, cooked: 4 oz	.8
Gizzard, goose, cooked: 4 oz	0
Heart, chicken, cooked: 4 oz	.1
Heart, turkey, cooked: 4 oz	.2
Liver, chicken, cooked: 4 oz	3.5
Liver, goose, raw: 4 oz	6.1
Liver, turkey, cooked: 4 oz	3.5

CANNED, FROZEN AND PROCESSED

	GRAMS
Chicken a la King, canned: 5¼ oz / **Swanson**	9
Chicken a la King, frozen	
Banquet Cookin' Bag / 5 oz	10.4
Green Giant Boil-in-Bag Toast Toppers / 5 oz	8
Stouffer's 9½ oz / 1 pkg	38
Chicken, boned, canned: 3 oz / **Hormel Tender Chunk**	1
Chicken, boned, canned, white chunk: 2½ oz / **Swanson**	0
Chicken, boned, canned w broth: 2½ oz / **Swanson**	0
Chicken, chopped, pressed: 1 slice / **Eckrich** Slender Sliced	1.4
Chicken and biscuits, frozen: 7 oz / **Green Giant** Oven Bake Entrees	19
Chicken breast Parmigiana and spinach, frozen: 9 oz / **Weight Watchers**	8
Chicken, creamed, frozen: 1 pkg / **Stouffer's** 6½ oz	6
Chicken creole, frozen: 13 oz / **Weight Watchers**	17
Chicken croquette w sauce, frozen: 12 oz / **Howard Johnson's**	38.6
Chicken divan, frozen: 1 pkg / **Stouffer's** 8½ oz	14
Chicken w dumplings, canned: 7½ oz / **Swanson**	18
Chicken w dumplings, frozen: 32 oz / **Banquet** Buffet Supper	128.2
Chicken, escalloped, frozen: ½ pkg / **Stouffer's** 11½ oz	16
Chicken, fried	
Frozen: 2 lb / **Banquet**	117.3
Frozen: 6.4 oz / **Morton** 32 oz	41
Frozen: 1 entree / **Morton** Country Table 12 oz	26

GRAMS

Frozen, assorted pieces: 3.2 edible oz / **Swanson**	10
Frozen, breast portions: 3.2 edible oz / **Swanson**	8
Frozen, thighs and drumsticks: 3.2 edible oz / **Swanson**	7
Frozen, wing sections: 3.2 edible oz / **Swanson** Nibbles	12
Chicken livers w broccoli, frozen: 10½ oz / **Weight Watchers**	15
Chicken Nibbles w french fries: 1 entree / **Swanson** "TV" 6 oz	31
Chicken and noodles, frozen: 32 oz / **Banquet** Buffet Supper	79.1
Chicken and noodles, frozen: 9 oz / **Green Giant** Boil-in-Bag Entrees	24
Chicken, smoked, sliced: 1 oz / **Safeway**	1
Chicken stew, canned: 7½ oz / **Swanson**	18
Chicken stew w dumplings, canned: 1 cup / **Libby's**	20
Chicken, white meat w peas, onions, frozen: 9 oz / **Weight Watchers**	16
Turkey, boned, canned: 3 oz / **Hormel Tender Chunk**	0
Turkey, boned, canned w broth: 2½ oz / **Swanson**	0
Turkey slices	
Canned w gravy: 6¼ oz / **Morton House**	7
Frozen entree / **Morton** Country Table 12¼ oz	36
Frozen entree / **Swanson** Hungry-Man 13¼ oz	35
Frozen entree / **Swanson** "TV" 8¾ oz	27
Frozen w giblet gravy: 32 oz / **Banquet** Buffet Supper	28.2
Frozen w giblet gravy: 5 oz / **Banquet** Cookin' Bag	5.3

GRAMS

Frozen w gravy: 5 oz / **Green Giant** Boil-in-Bag Toast Toppers	7
Turkey tetrazzini, frozen: ½ pkg / **Stouffer's** 12 oz	17
Turkey tetrazzini w mushrooms, red peppers, frozen: 13 oz / **Weight Watchers**	43
Turkey, roast, frozen, cooked	
Dark meat: 3½ oz / **Swift** Butterball	1
White meat: 3½ oz / **Swift** Butterball	0
White and dark meat w skin: 3½ oz / **Swift** Butterball	0
Roll, boneless white and dark meat: 3½ oz / **Swift** Park Lane	3
Roll, boneless white and dark meat: 3½ oz / **Swift** Premium Perfect Slice	1
Roll, white meat: 3½ oz / **Swift** Park Lane	4
Roll, white meat: 3½ oz / **Swift** Premium Perfect Slice	0
Turkey, smoked, chopped: 1 slice / **Eckrich** Slender Sliced	1.4
Turkey, smoked, sliced: 1 oz / **Safeway**	1

Pretzels

1 oz   GRAMS

Bavarian / **Granny Goose**	23.4
Mini / **Granny Goose**	22.9
Ring / **Granny Goose**	23
Stick	
Granny Goose	22.9
Pepperidge Farm Thin	19
Planters	22

GRAMS

Twists	
Granny Goose	22.7
Pepperidge Farm Tiny	19
Planters	22
Rold Gold	23

Pudding

GRAMS

½ cup unless noted

All flavors, mix, prepared / **Estee** Low Calorie	16
Banana	
Canned, ready to serve: 5 oz can /	
Del Monte	30
Canned: 8 oz can / **Sego**	39
Mix, prepared / **Ann Page**	28
Mix, prepared / **Jell-O** Instant	30
Mix, prepared / **Royal**	27
Mix, prepared / **Royal** Instant	29
Butter pecan, mix, prepared / **Jell-O** Instant	29
Butterscotch	
Canned, ready to serve: 5 oz can /	
Del Monte	31
Canned: 8 oz can / **Sego**	39
Mix, prepared / **Ann Page**	32
Mix, prepared / **Ann Page** Instant	28
Mix, prepared / **Jell-O**	30
Mix, prepared / **Jell-O** Instant	30
Mix, prepared / **My-T-Fine**	28
Mix, prepared / **Royal**	27
Mix, prepared / **Royal** Instant	29

GRAMS

Mix, prepared w nonfat milk / **D-Zerta**	13
Mix, as packaged / **D-Zerta**	6
Chocolate	
Canned, ready to serve / **Betty Crocker**	30
Canned, ready to serve: 5 oz can / **Del Monte**	31
Canned: 8 oz can / **Sego**	41
Mix, prepared / **Ann Page**	29
Mix, prepared / **Ann Page** Instant	32
Mix, prepared / **Jell-O**	29
Mix, prepared / **Jell-O** Instant	34
Mix, prepared / **My-T-Fine**	28
Mix, prepared / **Royal**	33
Mix, prepared / **Royal** Instant	35
Mix, prepared w nonfat milk / **D-Zerta**	12
Mix, as packaged / **D-Zerta**	5
Almond, mix, prepared / **My-T-Fine**	27
Fudge, canned, ready to serve / **Betty Crocker**	30
Fudge, canned, ready to serve: 5 oz can / **Del Monte**	31
Fudge, mix, prepared / **Jell-O**	28
Fudge, mix, prepared / **Jell-O** Instant	33
Fudge, mix, prepared / **My-T-Fine**	27
Milk, mix, prepared / **Jell-O**	29
Chocolate fudge: 8 oz can / **Sego**	41
Chocolate marshmallow: 8 oz can / **Sego**	41
Coconut	
Mix, prepared / **Royal** Instant	30
Cream, mix, prepared / **Ann Page**	25
Cream, mix, prepared / **Jell-O**	17
Cream, mix, prepared / **Jell-O** Instant	28
Toasted, mix, prepared / **Ann Page**	26
Coffee, mix, prepared / **Royal** Instant	29
Custard, mix, prepared / **Royal**	22
Custard, egg, mix, prepared / **Ann Page**	21
Custard, egg, mix, prepared / **Jell-O** Americana	24

GRAMS

Custard, rennet, all flavors, mix, prepared / **Junket**	16.8
Dark 'N Sweet, mix, prepared / **Royal**	33
Dark 'N Sweet mix, prepared / **Royal** Instant	35
Flan, mix, prepared / **Royal**	22
Lemon	
Mix, prepared / **Ann Page**	32
Mix, prepared / **Ann Page** Instant	31
Mix, prepared / **Jell-O** Instant	31
Mix, prepared / **My-T-Fine**	30
Mix, prepared / **Royal** Instant	29
Pineapple cream, mix, prepared / **Jell-O** Instant	31
Pistachio, mix, prepared / **Ann Page** Instant	29
Pistachio, mix, prepared / **Jell-O** Instant	30
Pistachio nut, mix, prepared / **Royal** Instant	30
Plum pudding, canned, ready to serve / **R & R**	68
Rice, canned, ready to serve / **Betty Crocker**	25
Rice, mix, prepared / **Jell-O** Americana	30
Tapioca	
Minute Tapioca: 1 tbsp	10
Minute (Fluffy Pudding recipe)	20.1
Canned, ready to serve / **Betty Crocker**	22
Chocolate, mix, prepared / **Ann Page**	29
Chocolate, mix, prepared / **Jell-O** Americana	28
Chocolate, mix, prepared / **Royal**	33
Vanilla, mix, prepared / **Ann Page**	28
Vanilla, mix, prepared / **Jell-O** Americana	28
Vanilla, mix, prepared / **My-T-Fine**	28
Vanilla, mix, prepared / **Royal**	27
Vanilla	
Canned, ready to serve / **Betty Crocker**	29
Canned, ready to serve: 5 oz can / **Del Monte**	32
Canned: 8 oz can / **Sego**	39
Mix, prepared / **Ann Page**	28
Mix, prepared / **Jell-O**	27

	GRAMS
Mix, prepared / **Jell-O** Instant	31
Mix, prepared / **My-T-Fine**	28
Mix, prepared / **Royal**	27
Mix, prepared / **Royal** Instant	29
Mix, prepared w nonfat milk / **D-Zerta**	13
Mix, as packaged / **D-Zerta**	7
French, mix, prepared / **Jell-O**	30
French, mix, prepared / **Jell-O** Instant	30

Rice and Rice Dishes

	GRAMS
Brown, long grain, parboiled: ⅔ cup cooked / **Uncle Ben's**	26.4
Brown and wild, seasoned, mix, prepared: ½ cup / **Uncle Ben's**	24.7
White: ⅔ cup cooked / **Minute**	27
White, long grain, parboiled: ⅔ cup cooked / **Uncle Ben's**	28.9
White, precooked: ⅔ cup cooked / **Uncle Ben's** Quick	27.4
White and wild, frozen: 1 cup / **Green Giant** Boil-in-Bag	43
White and wild, w bean sprouts, pea pods and water chestnuts, frozen: 1 cup / **Green Giant** Boil-in-Bag Oriental	40
White and wild, w peas, celery, mushrooms and almonds, frozen: 1 cup / **Green Giant** Boil-in-Bag Medley	47
White, long grain and wild, mix, prepared: ½ cup / **Uncle Ben's**	20.6
White, long grain and wild, mix, prepared: ½ cup / **Uncle Ben's** Fast Cooking	20.1
Beef-flavored, mix, prepared	
1/6 pkg / **Ann Page** Rice 'n Easy	27
½ cup / **Minute** Rice Rib Roast	25
1/6 pkg / **Rice-A-Roni**	27
½ cup / **Uncle Ben's**	20.4
w bell peppers and parsley, frozen: 1 cup / **Green Giant** Boil-in-Bag Verdi	47

GRAMS

w broccoli, in cheese sauce, frozen: 1 cup /
    Green Giant Boil-in-Bag 40
Chicken-flavored, mix, prepared
    1/6 pkg / **Ann Page** Rice 'n Easy 27
    ⅛ pkg / **Rice-A-Roni** 33
    ½ cup / **Uncle Ben's** 20.9
Curried, mix, prepared: ½ cup / **Uncle Ben's** 20.9
Fried, mix, prepared: ½ cup / **Minute** 25
w green beans and almonds, frozen: 1 cup /
    Green Giant Boil-in-Bag Continental 35
w peas, mushrooms, frozen: 2.3 oz /
    Bird's Eye Combinations 22
w peas, mushrooms, frozen: 1 cup / **Green Giant**
    Boil-in-Bag Medley 35
Pilaf, mix, prepared: ½ cup / **Uncle Ben's** 21.7
Pilaf, w mushrooms and onions, frozen: 1 cup /
    Green Giant Boil-in-Bag 45
Poultry-flavored, mix, prepared: ½ cup /
    Minute Drumstick 25
Spanish
    Canned: 1 cup / **Libby's** 28
    Mix, prepared: ½ cup / **Minute** 25
    Mix, prepared: 1/6 pkg / **Rice-A-Roni** 26
    Mix, prepared: ½ cup / **Uncle Ben's** 22

Rolls and Buns

GRAMS

1 roll or bun unless noted

Bagel, egg, 3-in diam 28
Bagel, water, 3-in diam 30

Buns for sandwiches
Arnold Dutch Egg Buns	22
Arnold Francisco Sandwich Rolls	31
Arnold Soft Sandwich	18
w poppy seeds / **Arnold** Soft Sandwich	18
w sesame seeds / **Arnold** Soft Sandwich	19
w sesame seeds / **Pepperidge Farm**	19
Hamburger / **Arnold** 8's	21
Hamburger: 2 oz / **Colonial**	30
Hamburger: 2 oz / **Kilpatrick's**	30
Hamburger: 2 oz / **Manor**	30
Hamburger / **Mrs. Wright's** 12 oz pkg	23
Hamburger / **Mrs. Wright's** 16 oz pkg	20
Hamburger / **Pepperidge Farm**	20
Hamburger: 2 oz / **Rainbo**	30
Hamburger / **Wonder**	29
Hamburger w sesame seeds / **Mrs. Wright's**	22
Hot dog / **Arnold**	20
Hot dog: 2 oz / **Colonial**	30
Hot dog: 2 oz / **Kilpatrick's**	30
Hot dog / **Mrs. Wright's** 11 oz pkg	20
Hot dog / **Mrs. Wright's** 13½ oz pkg	19
Hot dog: 2 oz / **Manor**	30
Hot dog / **Pepperidge Farm**	20
Hot dog: 2 oz / **Rainbo**	30
Hot dog / **Wonder**	29

Dinner and soft rolls
Arnold Deli-Twist	17
Arnold Finger 24's	10
Arnold Francisco Variety	20
Arnold Party Finger 12's	10
Arnold Party Parkerhouse 12's	10
Arnold Party Rounds 12's	10
Arnold Party Tea 20's	6
Arnold 12's	9.5
Arnold 24's	9.5
Colonial	11.5

	GRAMS
Home Pride	13.5
Kilpatrick's	11.5
Mrs. Wright's Buttermilk	16
Mrs. Wright's Cloverleaf	15
Mrs. Wright's Flaky Gem	15
Mrs. Wright's Twin	15
Manor	11.5
Pepperidge Farm Butter Crescent	15
Pepperidge Farm Dinner	10
Pepperidge Farm Finger	9
Pepperidge Farm Finger w poppy seeds	9
Pepperidge Farm Finger w sesame seeds	9
Pepperidge Farm Golden Twist	15
Pepperidge Farm Old-Fashioned	5
Pepperidge Farm Parkerhouse	10
Pepperidge Farm Party	6
Pepperidge Farm Party Pan	6
Rainbo Dinner	12.5
Wonder Buttermilk	13
Wonder Gem Style Dinner	13.5
Wonder Half & Half Dinner	13
Wonder Home Bake Dinner	13
Wonder Pan	17
Mix, prepared / **Pillsbury** Hot Roll Mix	15.5
Refrigerator / **Ballard** Crescent	13
Refrigerator / **Pillsbury** Butterflake	17
Refrigerator / **Pillsbury** Crescent	12.5
Hard rolls	
Club / **Pepperidge Farm**	23
Deli / **Pepperidge Farm**	34
French / **Wonder**	13.5
French, four / **Pepperidge Farm**	43
French, large: ½ roll / **Pepperidge Farm**	38
French, nine / **Pepperidge Farm**	19
French, small: ½ roll / **Pepperidge Farm**	25
French sourdough / **Arnold** Francisco	19

GRAMS

French sourdough / **Arnold** Francisco Brown and Serve	18
Hearth / **Pepperidge Farm**	11
Italian: 2 oz / **Pepperidge Farm**	27
Kaiser: 2 oz / **Earth Grains**	27
Kaiser & Hoagie Rolls: 6 oz / **Wonder**	82
Onion: 2 oz / **Earth Grains**	30
Sandwich / **Pepperidge Farm**	26
Sesame Crisp / **Pepperidge Farm**	12
Popovers, mix, prepared: 1 popover / **Flako**	25

SWEET ROLLS

1 roll unless noted

Caramel, refrigerated / **Pillsbury** Danish	20
Cinnamon, refrigerated / **Ballard**	17
Cinnamon w icing, refrigerated / **Hungry Jack Butter Tastin**	19.5
Cinnamon w icing, refrigerated / **Pillsbury**	17.5
Cinnamon-nut: 3 oz / **Rainbo**	52
Cinnamon-raisin, refrigerated / **Merico**	26
Cinnamon-raisin, refrigerated / **Pillsbury** Danish	21
Danish, apple: 2 oz / **Earth Grains**	26
Danish Bear Claws: 2 oz / **Earth Grains**	27
Danish, cinnamon: 2 oz / **Earth Grains** Pastry	29
Danish, cherry: 2 oz / **Earth Grains** Pastry	26
Danish, fruit, refrigerated / **Merico**	27
Danish Horns: 2 oz / **Earth Grains**	26
Honey Buns / **Hostess**	63
Honey Buns: 3 oz / **Rainbo**	41
Honey Buns, frozen / **Morton**	31
Honey Buns, frozen / **Morton** Mini	14
Orange, refrigerated / **Pillsbury** Danish	21

Salad Dressings

GRAMS

Bottled unless noted: 1 tbsp unless noted

Ann Page Salad Dressing	2
Mrs. Filbert's Salad Dressing	2
Nu Made Salad Dressing	2
Piedmont Salad Dressing	2
Sultana Salad Dressing	2
Avocado / **Kraft**	2
Bacon, mix: ¾ oz pkg / **Lawry's**	12
Blue cheese	
Ann Page Low Calorie	1
Kraft Chunky	2
Kraft Low Calorie	1
Kraft Low Calorie Chunky	3
Lawry's	.7
Nu Made	1
Roka	1
Seven Seas Real	1
Tillie Lewis / 1 tsp	0
Wish-Bone Chunky	1
Mix: ¾ oz pkg / **Lawry's**	4.6
Mix, prepared / **Weight Watchers**	1
Caesar	
Kraft Golden	1
Lawry's	.6
Nu Made	1
Pfeiffer / 1 oz	1
Pfeiffer Low-Cal / 1 oz	2

Seven Seas	1
Wish-Bone	1
Mix: ¾ oz pkg / **Lawry's**	8.8
Canadian bacon-flavored / **Lawry's**	.6
Chef Style / **Ann Page** Low Calorie	3
Chef Style / **Kraft** Low Calorie	3
Coleslaw dressing / **Kraft**	4
Coleslaw dressing / **Kraft** Low Calorie	4
Cucumber, creamy / **Kraft**	1
Cucumber, creamy / **Kraft** Low Calorie	1
French	
Casino	3
Kraft	2
Kraft Casino Garlic	3
Kraft Catalina	4
Kraft Herb and Garlic	0
Kraft Low Calorie	2
Kraft Miracle	3
Lawry's	1.5
Lawry's San Francisco French	.7
Lawry's Sherry French	1
Nu Made Low Calorie	3
Nu Made Savory	4
Nu Made Zesty	4
Pfeiffer / 1 oz	7
Pfeiffer Low-Cal / 1 oz	5
Seven Seas Creamy	2
Seven Seas Family Style	3
Seven Seas Low Calorie	2
Wish-Bone Deluxe	2
Wish-Bone Garlic French	3
Wish-Bone Low Calorie	4
Wish-Bone Sweet 'n Spicy	3
Mix: ⅖ oz pkg / **Lawry's** Old Fashioned	15
Mix, prepared / **Weight Watchers**	1
French Style / **Ann Page** Low Calorie	2
French Style / **Kraft** Low Calorie	2

GRAMS

French Style: 1 tsp / **Tillie Lewis**	1
Garlic, creamy / **Kraft**	1
Garlic, creamy / **Wish-Bone**	1
Green Goddess	
Kraft	1
Lawry's	.7
Nu Made	1
Seven Seas	0
Wish-Bone	1
Mix: ¾ oz pkg / **Lawry's**	13
Green onion / **Kraft**	1
Hawaiian / **Lawry's**	5.3
Herbs and spices / **Seven Seas**	1
Italian	
Ann Page Low Calorie	1
Kraft	1
Kraft Golden Blend	1
Kraft Low Calorie	1
Lawry's	.9
Nu Made	1
Nu Made Low Calorie	1
Pfeiffer Chef / 1 oz	1
Pfeiffer Low-Cal / 1 oz	3
Seven Seas	1
Seven Seas Family Style	0
Seven Seas Low Calorie	1
Seven Seas Viva	1
Tillie Lewis / 1 tsp	0
Wish-Bone	1
Wish-Bone Low Calorie	1
Cheese / **Lawry's**	4.7
Creamy / **Kraft**	1
Creamy / **Seven Seas Creamy**	1
Creamy / **Weight Watchers**	2
Mix, prepared / **Good Seasons** Low Calorie	2
Mix: ⅗ oz pkg / **Lawry's**	9.5
Mix, prepared / **Weight Watchers**	0

GRAMS

Mix, cheese: ¾ oz pkg / **Lawry's**	9.5
Mix, creamy, prepared / **Weight Watchers**	1
Lemon garlic, mix: ⅞ oz pkg / **Lawry's**	15
May Lo Naise / **Tillie Lewis**	1
Oil and vinegar	
Kraft	1
Lawry's	4.1
Nu Made	4
Red Wine / **Seven Seas** Viva	1
Onion / **Wish-Bone** California	1
Red wine: 1 oz / **Pfeiffer** Low-Cal	2
Russian	
Kraft Low Calorie	4
Nu Made	7
Pfeiffer / 1 oz	4
Pfeiffer Low-Cal / 1 oz	4
Seven Seas Creamy	1
Tellis Lewis / 1 tsp	1
Weight Watchers	2
Wish-Bone	7
Wish-Bone Low Calorie	5
Creamy / **Kraft**	2
w honey / **Kraft**	5
Mix, prepared / **Weight Watchers**	1
Salad Secret / **Kraft**	2
Sour Treat: 1 oz **Friendship**	1.5
Spin Blend / **Hellmann's**	2.7
Thousand Island	
Ann Page Low Calorie	2
Kraft	2
Kraft Low Calorie	2
Lawry's	2.1
Nu Made	3
Nu Made Low Calorie	2
Pfeiffer / 1 oz	4
Pfeiffer Low-Cal / 1 oz	4
Seven Seas	2

GRAMS

Tillie Lewis / 1 tsp	1
Weight Watchers	2
Wish-Bone	2
Wish-Bone Low Calorie	3
Mix: ⅞ oz pkg / Lawry's	18
Mix, prepared / Weight Watchers	1
Whipped / Tillie Lewis	2
Yogonaise / Henri's	2
Yogowhip / Henri's	3
Yogurt	
Bleu cheese / Henri's	4
Creamy garlic / Henri's	5
Cucumber and onion / Henri's	5
French / Henri's	6
Italian / Henri's	5
Thousand Island / Henri's	4

Sauces

GRAMS

A la King, mix, prepared: ½ cup / Durkee	7
Barbecue, bottled or canned: 1 tbsp	
Chris' and Pitt's	4
French's	3
Open Pit	6.3
Hickory smoke flavor / French's Smoky	3
Hickory smoke flavor / Open Pit	6.5
Hot / French's	3
Hot / Open Pit Hot 'n Spicy	6.3
w onions / Open Pit	6.3
Cheese, mix, prepared: ½ cup / Durkee	9.5
Cheese, mix, prepared: ¼ cup / French's	7

	GRAMS
Cheese, mix, prepared: ¼ cup / **McCormick**	5
Cheese, mix, prepared: ¼ cup / **Schilling**	5
Enchilada	
Mix: 1⅝ oz pkg / **Lawry's**	27
Mix: 1½ oz pkg / **McCormick**	24
Mix: 1½ oz pkg / **Schilling**	24
Hollandaise, mix, prepared: ¾ cup / **Durkee**	11
Hollandaise, mix, prepared: 3 tbsp / **French's**	2
Hollandaise, mix, prepared: ½ cup / **McCormick**	5.5
Hollandaise, mix, prepared: ½ cup / **Schilling**	5.5
Horseradish sauce: 1 tbsp / **Kraft**	2
Italian, canned: 2 fl oz / **Contadina** Cookbook	7.3
Italian, red, in jar: 5 oz / **Ragu**	6
Lasagna, mix: 1⅝ oz pkg / **Lawry's**	30
Lemon-butter-flavored, mix, prepared: 1 tbsp / **Weight Watchers**	1
Mushroom steak, canned: 1 oz / **Dawn Fresh**	2
Pizza, canned: 4 oz / **Buitoni**	6.5
Pizza, in jar: 5 oz / **Ragu**	15
Sour cream, mix, prepared: ⅔ cup / **Durkee**	15
Sour cream, mix, prepared: 2½ tbsp / **French's**	5
Sour cream, mix, prepared: ¼ cup / **McCormick**	6.3
Sour cream, mix, prepared: ¼ cup / **Schilling**	6.3
Spaghetti	
Canned: 4 oz / **Ann Page**	13
Canned: 4 oz / **Buitoni**	6.8
Canned: ½ cup / **Town House**	12
In jar: 5 oz / **Ragu** Extra Thick	13
In jar: 5 oz / **Ragu** Plain	14
Mix, prepared: 1 env / **Ann Page**	28
Mix, prepared: ½ cup / **Durkee**	10.4
Mix, prepared: ⅝ cup / **French's** Italian Style	15
Mix: 1½ oz pkg / **Lawry's**	22.5
Mix, prepared: ½ cup / **McCormick**	8.7
Mix, prepared: ½ cup / **Schilling**	8.7
Mix, prepared: 4 fl oz / **Spatini**	16

	GRAMS
Clam, canned: 5 oz / **Ragu**	14
Clam, red, canned: 4 oz / **Buitoni**	4.8
Clam, white, canned: 4 oz / **Buitoni**	2.8
Marinara, canned: 4 oz / **Ann Page**	13
Marinara, canned: 4 oz / **Buitoni**	6
Marinara, in jar: 5 oz / **Ragu**	15
Meat flavor, canned: 4 oz / **Ann Page**	12
Meat flavor, canned: 4 oz / **Buitoni**	7.6
Meat flavor, canned: ½ cup / **Town House**	12
Meat flavor, in jar: 5 oz / **Ragu**	14
Meat flavor, in jar: 5 oz / **Ragu** Extra Thick	14
w meatball seasonings, mix: 3¼ oz pkg / **Lawry's**	61
w mushrooms, canned: 4 oz / **Ann Page**	13
w mushrooms, canned: 4 oz / **Buitoni**	8.4
w mushrooms, canned: ½ cup / **Town House**	14
w mushrooms, in jar: 5 oz / **Ragu**	13
w mushrooms, in jar: 5 oz / **Ragu** Extra Thick	14
w mushrooms, mix, prepared: 1 env / **Ann Page**	28
w mushrooms, mix, prepared: ⅔ cup / **Durkee**	12
w mushrooms, mix, prepared: ⅝ cup / **French's**	13
Pepperoni flavor, in jar: 5 oz / **Ragu**	14
Stroganoff	
Mix, prepared: 1 cup / **Durkee**	6.5
Mix, prepared: ⅓ cup / **French's**	11
Mix: 1½ oz pkg / **Lawry's**	23
Mix, prepared: ½ cup / **McCormick**	26
Mix, prepared: ½ cup / **Schilling**	26
Sweet and sour, canned: 2 fl oz / **Contadina** Cookbook	16.1
Sweet and sour, canned: 1 cup / **La Choy**	128

	GRAMS
Sweet and sour, mix, prepared: 1 cup / **Durkee**	45
Sweet and sour, mix, prepared: ½ cup / **French's**	14
Swiss steak, canned: 2 fl oz / **Contadina** Cookbook	5
Teriyaki, mix, prepared: 2 tbsp / **French's**	7
Tomato, canned	
Contadina / 1 cup	19
Del Monte / 1 cup	17
Hunt's / 4 oz	8
Hunt's Prima Salsa Regular / 4 oz	20
Hunt's Special / 4 oz	10
Stokely-Van Camp / 1 cup	13
Town House Spanish Style / 8 oz	18
w bits: 4 oz / **Hunt's**	8
w cheese: 4 oz / **Hunt's**	10
w herbs: 4 oz / **Hunt's**	12
Meat-flavored: 4 oz / **Hunt's** Prima Salsa	20
w mushrooms: 1 cup / **Del Monte**	22
w mushrooms: 4 oz / **Hunt's**	9
w mushrooms: 4 oz / **Hunt's** Prima Salsa	20
w onion: 1 cup / **Del Monte**	23
w onions: 4 oz / **Hunt's**	10
w tidbits: 1 cup / **Del Monte**	19
Tuna casserole, mix, prepared: ½ cup / **McCormick**	11.8
Tuna casserole, mix, prepared: ½ cup / **Schilling**	11.8
White, mix, prepared: ½ cup / **Durkee**	20.5
Wine, burgundy, mix: 1 oz / **Lawry's**	16
Wine, sherry, mix: 1 oz / **Lawry's**	21
Wine, white, mix: 1 oz / **Lawry's**	25

Seasonings

GRAMS

1 tsp unless noted

Allspice, ground / **McCormick**	1.1
Allspice, ground / **Schilling**	1.1
Anise seed / **McCormick**	.9
Anise seed / **Schilling**	.9
Bacon, imitation, crumbled: 1 tbsp	
Ann Page	2
Baco's	2
Durkee Bacon Bits	.5
French's Bacon Crumbles	0
Lawry's Baconion	6.2
McCormick Bacon Bits	2
McCormick Bacon Chips	2
Schilling Bacon Bits	2
Schilling Bacon Chips	2
Barbecue / **French's**	1
Basil leaves / **McCormick**	.3
Basil leaves / **Schilling**	.3
Bay leaf (laurel), crumbled: 6 small / **McCormick**	.3
Bay leaf (laurel), crumbled: 6 small / **Schilling**	.3
Caraway seed / **McCormick**	.8
Caraway seed / **Schilling**	.8
Celery seed / **McCormick**	.5
Celery seed / **Schilling**	.5
Chili powder / **Lawry's**	1.2
Cinnamon, ground / **McCormick**	1
Cinnamon, ground / **Schilling**	1
Cloves, ground / **McCormick**	1
Cloves, ground / **Schilling**	1
Cloves, whole: 1 tsp (about 28) / **McCormick**	1.2
Cloves, whole: 1 tsp (about 28) / **Schilling**	1.2
Cumin, ground / **McCormick**	.5

	GRAMS
Cumin, ground / **Schilling**	.5
Dill seed / **McCormick**	.8
Dill seed / **Schilling**	.8
Fennel seed / **McCormick**	.6
Fennel seed / **Schilling**	.6
Garlic concentrate: 1 tbsp / **Lawry's**	1.4
Garlic powder / **McCormick**	1.1
Garlic powder / **Schilling**	1.1
Ginger, ground / **McCormick**	1.1
Ginger, ground / **Schilling**	1.1
Herb blend / **Lawry's**	.9
Lemon pepper marinade / **Lawry's**	1.3
Mace, ground / **McCormick**	.7
Mace, ground / **Schilling**	.7
Marjoram, ground / **McCormick**	.5
Marjoram, ground / **Schilling**	.5
Marjoram, leaves / **McCormick**	.3
Marjoram, leaves / **Schilling**	.3
Meat tenderizer / **French's**	0
Meat tenderizer, seasoned / **French's**	0
Nutmeg, ground / **McCormick**	.8
Nutmeg, ground / **Schilling**	.8
Onion powder / **McCormick**	1.7
Onion powder / **Schilling**	1.7
Oregano / **McCormick**	.2
Oregano / **Schilling**	.2
Paprika / **McCormick**	.7
Paprika / **Schilling**	.7
Pepper, black, ground / **McCormick**	1.2
Pepper, black, ground / **Schilling**	1.2
Pepper, black, whole / **McCormick**	1.8
Pepper, black, whole / **Schilling**	1.8
Pepper, red / **McCormick**	.6
Pepper, red / **Schilling**	.6
Pepper, white, ground / **McCormick**	1.3
Pepper, white, ground / **Schilling**	1.3

GRAMS

Pepper, lemon-flavored / **French's** Lemon and Pepper Seasoning	1
Pepper, seasoned / **French's**	1
Pepper, seasoned / **Lawry's**	1.5
Pizza / **French's**	1
Rosemary / **McCormick**	.6
Rosemary / **Schilling**	.6
Sage, rubbed / **McCormick**	.4
Sage, rubbed / **Schilling**	.4
Salad / **Durkee**	.7
Salad / **French's** Salad Lift	1
Salad w cheese / **Durkee**	.4
Salt	
Butter flavor, imitation / **French's**	0
Celery / **French's**	0
Garlic / **French's**	1
Garlic-flavored / **Lawry's**	1.4
Garlic, parslied / **French's**	1
Hickory smoke / **French's**	0
Onion / **French's**	1
Onion-flavored / **Lawry's**	.9
Seasoned / **French's**	1
Seasoned / **Lawry's**	.1
Savory, ground / **McCormick**	.7
Savory, ground / **Schilling**	.7
Seafood / **French's**	0
Sesame seed / **McCormick**	.1
Sesame seed / **Schilling**	.1
Stock base, chicken-flavored / **French's**	1
Stock base, beef-flavored / **French's**	2
Sugar, cinnamon-flavored / **French's**	4
Thyme, leaves / **McCormick**	.4
Thyme, leaves / **Schilling**	.4
Thyme, ground / **McCormick**	.6
Thyme, ground / **Schilling**	.6
Tumeric, ground / **McCormick**	1.1
Tumeric, ground / **Schilling**	1.1

SEASONING MIXES

	GRAMS
Beef	
Lawry's Beef Olé / 1¼ oz pkg	24
Lawry's Marinade / 1 1/16 oz pkg	9.9
Stew, mix, prepared: 1 cup / **Durkee**	16.7
Stew, dry mix: 1 pkg / **Durkee**	22
Stew: 1 env / **French's**	36
Stew: 1 ⅔ oz pkg / **Lawry's**	24
Stew: 1½ oz pkg / **McCormick**	19
Stew: 1½ oz pkg / **Schilling**	19
Burger: ⅓ oz / **Lipton** Make-A-Better-Burger	3
Burger, onion: ⅓ oz / **Lipton**	
Make-A-Better-Burger	3
Chili: 1 env / **Ann Page**	30
Chili: 1 env / **French's** Chili-O	30
Chili con carne	
Mix, prepared: 1 cup / **Durkee**	31.2
Mix, dry: 1 pkg / **Durkee**	33
Lawry's / 1⅝ oz pkg	23
McCormick / 1¼ oz pkg	42
Schilling / 1¼ oz pkg	42
Chop suey, prepared: 1 cup / **Durkee**	12
Chop suey, dry mix: 1 pkg / **Durkee**	19
Enchilada, prepared: 1 cup / **Durkee**	12.5
Enchilada, dry mix: 1 pkg / **Durkee**	18
Enchilada: 1 env / **French's**	20
Fried rice, prepared: 1 cup / **Durkee**	46.5
Fried rice, dry mix: 1 pkg / **Durkee**	11
Goulash: 1 ⅝ pkg / **Lawry's**	23
Ground beef	
Mix, prepared: 1 cup / **Durkee**	9
Mix, dry: 1 pkg / **Durkee**	18
French's Hamburger Seasoning / 1 env	20
w onions: 1 env / **Ann Page**	24
w onions, prepared: 1 cup / **Durkee**	6.5
w onions, dry mix: 1 pkg / **Durkee**	13
w onions: 1 env / **French's**	24

	GRAMS
Hamburger, prepared: 1 cup / **Durkee**	7.5
Hamburger, dry mix: 1 pkg / **Durkee**	15
Meatball: 1 env / **French's**	28
Meatball, Italian, prepared: 1 cup / **Durkee**	4.5
Meatball, Italian, dry mix: 1 pkg / **Durkee**	9
Meatball, Italian w cheese, prepared: 1 cup / **Durkee**	4.5
Meatball, Italian w cheese, dry mix: 1 pkg / **Durkee**	9
Meatloaf	
Contadina / 1 env	72.8
French's / 1 env	40
Lawry's / 3½ oz pkg	66
McCormick / 1½ oz pkg	29
Schilling / 1½ oz pkg	29
Meat marinade, prepared: ½ cup / **Durkee**	9
Meat marinade: 1 env / **French's**	16
Sloppy Joe	
Ann Page / 1 env	32
Durkee / 1 cup prepared	24
Durkee / dry mix: 1 pkg	29
French's / 1 env	32
Lawry's / 1½ oz pkg	27
McCormick / 1 5/16 oz pkg	25
Schilling / 1 5/16 oz pkg	25
Pizza flavor, prepared: 1 cup / **Durkee**	20.8
Pizza flavor, dry mix: 1 pkg / **Durkee**	12
Spanish rice, prepared: 1 cup / **Durkee**	44.6
Spanish rice, dry mix: 1 pkg / **Durkee**	25
Spanish rice: 1½ oz pkg / **Lawry's**	20
Swiss steak: 1 oz pkg / **McCormick**	10
Swiss steak: 1 oz pkg / **Schilling**	10
Taco	
Mix, prepared: 1 cup / **Durkee**	7.5
Mix, dry: 1 pkg / **Durkee**	15
French's / 1 env	30

GRAMS

McCormick / 1¼ oz pkg	15
Schilling / 1¼ oz pkg	15

Shortening

GRAMS

Solid

Lard: 1 cup	0
1 tbsp	0
Vegetable: 1 tbsp / **Crisco**	0
Vegetable: 1 tbsp / **Fluffo**	0
Vegetable: 1 tbsp / **Mrs. Tucker's**	0
Vegetable: 1 tbsp / **Snowdrift**	0

Soft Drinks

GRAMS

8 fl oz unless noted

All flavors: 6 fl oz / **Weight Watchers** Dietary Carbonated Beverages	.5
Birch beer / **Canada Dry**	28
Bitter lemon / **Canada Dry**	26
Bitter lemon / **Schweppes**	26.4
Black cherry	
Canada Dry Low Calorie	.3
No-Cal	0

	GRAMS
Shasta	28.6
Shasta Diet	0
Tab	0
Black raspberry / **No-Cal**	0
Bubble Up	24.5
Bubble Up Sugar Free	.3
Cactus Cooler / **Canada Dry**	29
Chocolate / **Canada Dry** Low Calorie	1
Chocolate / **No-Cal**	0
Chocolate / **Shasta** Diet	0
Chocolate mint / **No-Cal**	0
Club soda / **Canada Dry**	0
Club soda / **Schweppes**	0
Club soda / **Shasta**	0
Coffee / **No-Cal**	0
Cola	
Canada Dry Low Calorie	.8
Coca-Cola	24
Diet-Rite	.8
Jamaica cola / **Canada Dry**	27
No-Cal	0
Pepsi-Cola	26.4
Pepsi-Cola, Diet	.1
Pepsi Light	12
Royal Crown	25.9
Shasta	26
Shasta Diet	0
Tab	0
Collins mixer / **Shasta**	21.3
Cream / **No-Cal**	0
Cream / **Shasta**	27.3
Cream / **Shasta** Diet	0
Dr. Nehi	25.2
Dr. Pepper	24.8
Dr. Pepper Sugar Free	.2
Fresca	0

	GRAMS
Ginger ale	
Canada Dry	21
Canada Dry Golden	24
Canada Dry Low Calorie	0
Fanta	21
Nehi	22
No-Cal	0
Schweppes	21.6
Shasta	21.3
Shasta Diet	0
Tab	0
Ginger beer / **Schweppes**	22.4
Grape	
Canada Dry	32
Canada Dry Low Calorie	0
Crush	32
Fanta	29
Nehi	29
No-Cal	0
Patio	32
Schweppes	31.2
Shasta	31.3
Shasta Diet	0
Tab	0
Grapefruit / **Shasta**	28.6
Grapefruit / **Shasta** Diet	.5
Half and Half / **Canada Dry**	26
Hi Spot / **Canada Dry**	25
Kick	29.5
Lemon / **Canada Dry** Low Calorie	0
Lemon-lime / **Shasta**	25.3
Lemon-lime / **Shasta** Diet	0
Lemon-lime / **Tab**	0
Lime / **Canada Dry**	33
Mello Yello	30
Mr. PiBB	25
Mr. PiBB wo sugar	.2

GRAMS

Mountain Dew	29.6
Orange	
Canada Dry Low Calorie	.2
Canada Dry Sunripe	33
Crush	31.2
Fanta	30
Nehi	31
No-Cal	0
Patio	32
Schweppes Sparkling	28.8
Shasta	31.3
Shasta Diet	0
Tab	0
Pineapple / **Canada Dry**	26
Purple Passion / **Canada Dry**	30
Raspberry / **Canada Dry** Low Calorie	0
Red creme / **Schweppes**	28
Red Pop / **No-Cal**	0
Root beer	
A & W	27
A & W Sugar Free	4
Berks County	29.1
Canada Dry Barrelhead	26
Canada Dry Barrelhead Low Calorie	1
Canada Dry Low Calorie	1
Canada Dry Rooti	26
Dad's	26.1
Diet **Dad's**	.2
Fanta	27
Hires	27.2
Hires Sugar Free	.2
No-Cal	0
Patio	28
Schweppes	25.6
Shasta	27.3
Shasta Diet	0
Tab	.2

GRAMS

7 Up	24
7 Up Diet	2
Shape-Up / **No-Cal**	0
Sprite	24
Sprite wo sugar	0
Strawberry	
Canada Dry California	30
Canada Dry Low Calorie	0
Crush	31.2
Nehi	29
Shasta	26
Shasta Diet	0
Tab	0
Sun-Drop	32
Sun-Drop Sugar Free	.3
Teem	17.6
TNT / **No-Cal**	0
Tahitian Treat / **Canada Dry**	32
Tiki	27.3
Tiki Diet	0
Tonic water	
Canada Dry	22
Canada Dry Low Calorie	0
No-Cal	0
Schweppes	21.6
Shasta	17.8
Upper 10	25.4
Vanilla cream / **Canada Dry**	32
Vanilla cream / **Canada Dry** Low Calorie	.3
Wild cherry / **Canada Dry**	32
Wink / **Canada Dry**	30
Wink / **Canada Dry** Low Calorie	0

Soups

	GRAMS
Alphabet vegetable, mix, prepared: 6 fl oz / **Lipton** Cup-A-Soup	6
Asparagus, cream of, condensed, prepared: 10 oz / **Campbell**	12
Bean, canned	
Condensed, prepared: 8 oz / **Manischewitz**	17.5
Semi-condensed, prepared: 1 can / **Campbell** Soup for One	28
w bacon, condensed, prepared: 1 cup / **Ann Page**	18
w bacon, condensed, prepared: 10 oz / **Campbell**	26
w bacon, condensed, prepared: 1 cup / **Town House**	20.1
Black, condensed, prepared: 10 oz / **Campbell**	22
Black, ready to serve: ½ can / **Crosse & Blackwell**	18
w ham, ready to serve: ½ can / **Campbell** Chunky 9½ oz	31
w ham, ready to serve, individual service size: 1 can / **Campbell** Chunky 10¾ oz	35
w hot dogs, condensed, prepared: 10 oz / **Campbell**	25
Lima, condensed, prepared: 8 oz / **Manischewitz**	15.2
Beef	
Condensed, prepared: 10 oz / **Campbell**	14
Ready to serve: ½ can / **Campbell** Chunky 9½ oz	20
Ready to serve, individual service size: 1 can / **Campbell** Chunky 10¾ oz	22

GRAMS

Flavor, mix, prepared: 8 oz / **Lipton** Lite-Lunch	30
Barley, mix, prepared: 6 oz serving / **Wyler's**	10
Cabbage, condensed, prepared: 8 oz / **Manischewitz**	9.1
Low sodium, ready to serve, individual service size: 1 can / **Campbell** Chunky 7¼ oz	16
Mushroom, mix, prepared: 8 fl oz / **Lipton**	7
Noodle, condensed, prepared: 10 oz / **Campbell**	10
Noodle, condensed, prepared: 8 oz / **Manischewitz**	7.9
Noodle, condensed, prepared: 1 cup / **Town House**	6.7
Noodle, mix, prepared: 1 env / **Souptime**	4
Noodle, mix, prepared: 6 oz serving / **Wyler's**	7
Vegetable, condensed, prepared: 8 oz / **Manischewitz**	8.9

Bouillon

Beef: 1 cube / **Herb-Ox**	1
Beef: 1 cup / **Maggi**	0
Beef: 1 cube / **Wyler's**	.4
Beef-flavored: 1 cube / **Wyler's**	1
Beef-flavored, powder: 1 tsp / **Wyler's** Instant	1
Beef, powder: 1 tsp / **Wyler's** Instant	.4
Chicken: 1 cube / **Herb-Ox**	1
Chicken: 1 cube / **Maggi**	1
Chicken-flavored: 1 cube / **Wyler's**	1
Chicken-flavored, powder: 1 tsp / **Wyler's** Instant	1
Chicken, powder: 1 tsp / **Wyler's** Instant	.8
Onion: 1 cube / **Herb-Ox**	1
Onion: 1 cube / **Wyler's**	1.2

	GRAMS
Vegetable: 1 cube / **Herb-Ox**	1
Vegetable: 1 cube / **Wyler's**	.3
Vegetable-flavored, powder: 1 tsp / **Wyler's** Instant	1
Broth	
Beef: 1 packet / **Herb-Ox**	1
Beef: 1 tsp / **Herb-Ox** Instant	1
Beef, canned: 6¾ oz / **Swanson**	1
Beef, condensed, prepared: 10 oz / **Campbell**	3
Beef, mix: 1 packet / **Weight Watchers**	2
Chicken: 1 packet / **Herb-Ox**	2
Chicken: 1 tsp / **Herb-Ox** Instant	1
Chicken, canned: 6¾ oz / **Swanson**	2
Chicken, condensed, prepared: 10 oz / **Campbell**	3
Chicken, mix, prepared: 6 fl oz / **Lipton** Cup-A-Broth	3
Chicken, mix: 1 packet / **Weight Watchers**	2
Onion: 1 packet / **Herb-Ox**	2
Onion, mix: 1 packet / **Weight Watchers**	2
Vegetable: 1 packet / **Herb-Ox**	2
Vegetable: 1 tsp / **Herb-Ox** Instant	1
Celery, cream of, condensed, prepared: 1 cup / **Ann Page**	8
Celery, cream of, condensed, prepared: 10 oz / **Campbell**	10
Celery, cream of, condensed, prepared: 1 cup / **Town House**	9
Cheddar cheese, condensed, prepared: 10 oz / **Campbell**	12
Chickarina, canned, ready to serve: 8 fl oz / **Progresso**	8
Chicken	
Canned, ready to serve: ½ can / **Campbell** Chunky 9½ oz	20

Canned, ready to serve, individual service size: 1 can / **Campbell** Chunky 10¾ oz	22
Flavor, mix, prepared: 8 oz / **Lipton** Lite-Lunch	30
Alphabet, condensed, prepared: 10 oz / **Campbell**	15
Barley, condensed, prepared: 8 oz / **Manischewitz**	12.4
Cream of, condensed, prepared: 1 cup / **Ann Page**	8
Cream of, condensed, prepared: 10 oz / **Campbell**	10
Cream of, condensed, prepared: 1 cup / **Town House**	8.3
Cream of, mix, prepared: 6 fl oz / **Lipton** Cup-A-Soup	10
Cream of, mix, prepared: 1 env / **Souptime**	8
w dumplings, condensed, prepared: 10 oz / **Campbell**	7
Gumbo, condensed, prepared: 10 oz / **Campbell**	10
Kasha, condensed, prepared: 8 oz / **Manischewitz**	5.3
Low sodium, ready to serve: 1 can / **Campbell** Chunky 7½ oz	13
Noodle, condensed, prepared: 1 cup / **Ann Page**	9
Noodle, condensed, prepared: 1 cup / **A & P** "O" Style	9.2
Noodle, condensed, prepared: 10 oz / **Campbell**	11
Noodle, condensed, prepared: 10 oz / **Campbell** Noodle-O's	12
Noodle, condensed, prepared: 8 oz / **Manischewitz**	4.1
Noodle, condensed, prepared: 1 cup / **Town House**	9.5

Noodle, condensed, prepared: 1 cup /
Town House Star Noodle   7.9

Noodle, semi-condensed, prepared: 1 can /
Campbell Soup for One 11⅝ oz   14

Noodle, mix, prepared: 6 fl oz /
Lipton Cup-A-Soup   6

Noodle, mix, prepared: 8 fl oz /
Lipton Noodle   9

Noodle, mix, prepared: 8 fl oz /
Lipton Ripple Noodle   12

Noodle, mix, prepared: 1 env / **Souptime**   4

Noodle, mix, prepared: 6 oz serving /
Wyler's   4

Rice, canned, ready to serve: ½ can /
Campbell Chunky 9½ oz   16

Rice, condensed, prepared: 1 cup /
Ann Page   5

Rice, condensed, prepared: 10 oz /
Campbell   9

Rice, condensed, prepared: 8 oz /
Manischewitz   5.4

Rice, condensed, prepared: 1 cup /
Town House   6.7

Rice, mix, prepared: 8 fl oz / **Lipton**   8

Rice, mix, prepared: 6 fl oz / **Lipton**
Cup-A-Soup   9

Rice, mix, prepared: 6 oz serving / **Wyler's**   6

w stars, condensed, prepared: 1 cup /
Ann Page   8

w stars, condensed, prepared: 10 oz /
Campbell   9

Vegetable, canned, ready to serve: ½ can /
Campbell Chunky 9½ oz   21

Vegetable, condensed, prepared: 1 cup /
Ann Page   9

Vegetable, condensed, prepared: 10 oz /
Campbell   10

Vegetable, condensed, prepared: 8 oz /
  Manischewitz   7.7

Vegetable, condensed, prepared: 1 cup /
  Town House   9.3

Vegetable, mix, prepared: 6 fl oz / **Lipton**
  Cup-A-Soup   7

Vegetable, mix, prepared: 6 oz serving /
  Wyler's   4

Chili beef

  Condensed, prepared: 10 oz / **Campbell**   24

  Condensed, prepared: 1 cup / **Town House** 21.2

  Ready to serve: ½ can / **Campbell**
    Chunky 9¾ oz   32

  Ready to serve, individual service size:
    1 can / **Campbell** Chunky 11 oz   37

Chowder

  Clam, ready to serve: 8 fl oz / **Progresso** 16

  Clam, Manhattan, ready to serve: ½ can /
    Campbell Chunky 9½ oz   23

  Clam, Manhattan, condensed, prepared:
    10 oz / **Campbell**   15

  Clam, Manhattan, condensed, prepared:
    1 cup / **Snow's**   7.8

  Clam, Manhattan, condensed, prepared:
    7 oz / **Snow's**   11

  Clam, Manhattan, ready to serve: ½ can /
    Crosse & Blackwell   9

  Clam, New England, condensed, prepared:
    10 oz / **Campbell**   13

  Clam, New England, condensed, made
    w milk: 10 oz / **Campbell**   20

  Clam, New England, condensed, prepared:
    7 oz / **Snow's**   13

  Clam, New England, condensed, prepared:
    1 cup / **Snow's**   16.9

GRAMS

Clam, New England, semi-condensed, prepared: 1 can / **Campbell** Soup for One 11⅝ oz	16
Clam, New England, ready to serve: ½ can / **Crosse & Blackwell**	14
Corn, condensed, prepared: 1 cup / **Snow's**	20
Fish, condensed, prepared: 1 cup / **Snow's**	11.9
Seafood, New England, condensed, prepared: 1 cup / **Snow's**	12.7
Consommé, beef, condensed, prepared: 10 oz / **Campbell**	4
Consommé Madrilene, clear, ready to serve: ½ can / **Crosse & Blackwell**	4
Consommé Madrilene, red, ready to serve: ½ can / **Crosse & Blackwell**	5
Crab, ready to serve: ½ can / **Crosse & Blackwell**	8
Escarole, in chicken broth, ready to serve: 1 cup / **Progresso**	1
Gazpacho, ready to serve: ½ can / **Crosse & Blackwell**	1
Lentil, condensed, prepared: 8 oz / **Manischewitz**	29.4
Lentil, ready to serve: 1 cup / **Progresso**	22
Lentil w ham, ready to serve: ½ can / **Crosse & Blackwell**	13
Meatball Alphabet, condensed, prepared: 10 oz / **Campbell**	16
Minestrone	
Condensed, prepared: 1 cup / **Ann Page**	13
Condensed, prepared: 10 oz / **Campbell**	15
Condensed, prepared: 1 can / **Town House**	34
Ready to serve: ½ can / **Campbell** Chunky 9½ oz	25
Ready to serve: ½ can / **Crosse & Blackwell**	18

GRAMS

Mushroom
    Condensed, prepared: 10 oz / **Campbell**   11
    Mix, prepared: 1 env / **Souptime**   9
    Mix, prepared: 6 oz serving / **Wyler's**   7
    Barley, condensed, prepared: 8 oz /
      Manischewitz   12.2
    Bisque, ready to serve: ½ can /
      Crosse & Blackwell   8
    Cream of, condensed, prepared: 1 cup /
      Ann Page   12
    Cream of, condensed, prepared: 10 oz /
      Campbell   11
    Cream of, condensed, prepared: 1 cup /
      Town House   10.4
    Cream of, semi-condensed, prepared: 1 can /
      Campbell Soup for One 11¼ oz   12
    Cream of, mix, prepared: 6 fl oz / **Lipton**
      Cup-A-Soup   11
    Cream of, low sodium, ready to serve,
      individual service size: 1 can /
      Campbell 7¼ oz   10
Noodle
    Mix, prepared: 6 fl oz / **Lipton**
      Cup-A-Soup Giggle   8
    Mix, prepared: 6 fl oz / **Lipton**
      Cup-A-Soup Ring   9
    Mix, prepared: 8 fl oz / **Lipton**
      Giggle Noodle   12
    Mix, prepared: 8 fl oz / **Lipton**
      Ring-O-Noodle   9
    w beef flavor, mix, prepared: 6 fl oz /
      Lipton Cup-A-Soup   6
    w chicken, condensed, prepared: 10 oz /
      Campbell Curley   12
    w chicken broth, mix: ⅕ env / **Ann Page**   6
    w chicken broth, mix, prepared: 8 fl oz /
      Lipton Noodle   8

w ground beef, condensed, prepared: 10 oz / **Campbell**	14
Onion	
Condensed, prepared: 10 oz / **Campbell**	9
Mix: 1/5 env / **Ann Page**	4
Mix, prepared: 8 fl oz / **Lipton**	6
Mix, prepared: 8 fl oz / **Lipton** Beefy	4
Mix, prepared: 6 fl oz / **Lipton** Cup-A-Soup	5
Mix, prepared: 6 oz serving / **Wyler's**	5
Cream of, condensed, prepared: 10 oz / **Campbell**	20
French, condensed, prepared: 1 can / **Town House**	30
French, mix, prepared: 1 env / **Souptime**	4
Mushroom, mix, prepared: 8 fl oz / **Lipton**	5
Oriental style, mix, prepared: 8 oz / **Lipton** Lite-Lunch	31
Oyster stew, condensed, prepared: 10 oz / **Campbell**	5
Oyster stew, condensed, prepared w milk: 10 oz / **Campbell**	12
Pea, green	
Condensed, prepared: 10 oz / **Campbell**	29
Mix, prepared: 8 fl oz / **Lipton**	22
Mix, prepared: 6 fl oz / **Lipton** Cup-A-Soup	20
Mix, prepared: 1 env / **Souptime**	14
Low sodium, ready to serve, individual service size: 1 can / **Campbell** 7½ oz	24
Pea, split	
Condensed, prepared: 8 oz / **Manischewitz**	22.4
w ham, condensed, prepared: 1 cup / **Ann Page**	27
w ham, condensed, prepared: 1 cup / **Town House**	23
w ham, ready to serve: ½ can / **Campbell** Chunky 9½ oz	30

w ham and bacon, condensed, prepared: 10 oz / **Campbell**	30
Pepper Pot, condensed, prepared: 10 oz / **Campbell**	12
Potato, cream of, condensed, prepared: 10 oz / **Campbell**	14
Potato, cream of, condensed, prepared w milk: 10 oz / **Campbell**	17
Potato, cream of, condensed, prepared: 1 can / **Town House**	32
Potato w leeks, mix, prepared: 6 oz serving / **Wyler's**	9
Scotch broth, condensed, prepared: 10 oz / **Campbell**	11
Shrimp, cream of, condensed, prepared: 10 oz / **Campbell**	10
Shrimp, cream of, condensed, prepared w milk: 10 oz / **Campbell**	17
Shrimp, cream, ready to serve: ½ can / **Crosse & Blackwell**	7
Sirloin burger, ready to serve: ½ can / **Campbell** Chunky 9½ oz	21
Sirloin burger, ready to serve, individual service size: 1 can / **Campbell** Chunky 10¾ oz	24
Steak & potato, ready to serve: ½ can / **Campbell** Chunky 9½ oz	23
Stockpot, vegetable, mix, prepared: 8 oz / **Lipton** Lite-Lunch	31
Stockpot, vegetable-beef, condensed, prepared: 10 oz / **Campbell**	13
Tomato	
Condensed, prepared: 1 cup / **Ann Page**	13
Condensed, prepared: 10 oz / **Campbell**	20
Condensed, prepared w milk: 10 oz / **Campbell**	27
Condensed, prepared: 8 oz / **Manischewitz**	9.6

Condensed, prepared: 1 cup / **Town House**	18.3
Mix, prepared: 6 fl oz / **Lipton** Cup-A-Soup	13
Mix, prepared: 1 env / **Souptime**	13
Ready to serve: 8 fl oz / **Progresso**	23
Beef, condensed, prepared: 10 oz / **Campbell** Noodle-O's	24
Bisque, condensed, prepared: 10 oz / **Campbell**	27
Low sodium, ready to serve, individual service size: 1 can / **Campbell** 7¼ oz	22
Rice, condensed, prepared: 1 cup / **Ann Page**	16
Rice, condensed, prepared: 10 oz / **Campbell** Old Fashioned	26
Rice, condensed, prepared: 8 oz / **Manischewitz**	12.8
Rice, condensed, prepared: 1 can / **Town House**	48
Royale, semi-condensed, prepared: 1 can / **Campbell** Soup for One	33

Turkey

Ready to serve: ½ can / **Campbell** Chunky 9¼ oz	17
Noodle, condensed, prepared: 1 cup / **Ann Page**	9
Noodle, condensed, prepared: 10 oz / **Campbell**	10
Noodle, condensed, prepared: 1 cup / **Town House**	10
Noodle, low sodium, ready to serve, individual service size: 1 can / **Campbell** 7¼ oz	7
Vegetable, condensed, prepared: 1 cup / **Ann Page**	8
Vegetable, condensed, prepared: 10 oz / **Campbell**	10

Vegetable

Canned, ready to serve: ½ can / **Campbell** Chunky 9½ oz	22
Canned, ready to serve, individual service size: 1 can / **Campbell** Chunky 10¾ oz	25
Condensed, prepared: 1 cup / **Ann Page** Vegetarian	12
Condensed, prepared: 10 oz / **Campbell**	17
Condensed, prepared: 10 oz / **Campbell** Old Fashioned	11
Condensed, prepared: 10 oz / **Campbell** Vegetarian	16
Condensed, prepared: 8 oz / **Manischewitz**	10.1
Condensed, prepared: 1 cup / **Town House** Vegetarian	14.2
Semi-condensed, prepared: 1 can / **Campbell** Old World Soup for One	18
Mix, prepared: 8 fl oz / **Lipton** Country	13
Mix, prepared: 8 fl oz / **Lipton** Italian	19
Mix, prepared: 6 oz serving / **Wyler's**	9.3
Beef, condensed, prepared: 1 cup / **Ann Page**	10
Beef, condensed, prepared: 10 oz / **Campbell**	10
Beef, condensed, prepared: 1 cup / **Town House**	9.6
Beef, mix, prepared: 8 fl oz / **Lipton**	9
Beef, mix, prepared: 6 fl oz / **Lipton** Cup-A-Soup	9
Beef, ready to serve: ½ can / **Campbell** Chunky 9½ oz	19
Beef, low sodium, ready to serve: 1 can / **Campbell** 7¼ oz	8
Beef w shells, mix, prepared: 8 fl oz / **Lipton**	18
w beef stock, condensed, prepared: 1 cup / **Ann Page**	10

GRAMS

w beef stock, condensed, prepared: 1 cup / **Town House**	13.4
Cream of, mix, prepared: 1 env / **Souptime**	9
Low sodium, ready to serve, individual service size: 1 can / **Campbell** 7¼ oz	15
w noodles, condensed, prepared: 10 oz / **Campbell** Noodle-O's	13
Spring, mix, prepared: 6 fl oz / **Lipton** Cup-A-Soup	7
Vichyssoise, ready to serve: ½ can / **Crosse & Blackwell**	5

Spaghetti and Spaghetti Dishes

GRAMS

Spaghetti, plain, enriched, cooked firm, "al dente": 1 cup	39.1
Spaghetti, plain, enriched, cooked, tender stage: 1 cup	32.2
Spaghetti, in tomato sauce, canned	
Buitoni Twists / ½ can	29
w beef: 7½ oz can / **Hormel Short Orders**	25.7
w cheese: 7⅜ oz / **Franco-American**	33
w cheese sauce: 7⅜ oz / **Franco-American** "SpaghettiOs"	31
w frankfurters: 7⅜ oz / **Franco-American** "SpaghettiOs"	26
w meat sauce: 7¾ oz / **Franco-American**	26
w meatballs: ½ can / **Buitoni**	26

	GRAMS
w meatballs: ½ can / **Buitoni** Twists	26
w meatballs: 7¼ oz / **Franco-American**	23
w little meatballs: 7⅜ oz / **Franco-American** "SpaghettiOs"	24
w meatballs: 7½ oz can / **Hormel Short Orders**	22.9
w meatballs: 1 cup / **Libby's**	32
Spaghetti w sauce, frozen	
Banquet / 3 oz	31.3
Morton Casserole / 1 pkg	31
Stouffer's / 1 pkg (14 oz)	62
w meatballs: 32 oz / **Banquet** Buffet Supper	129.1
w meatballs: 9 oz / **Green Giant** Boil-in-Bag Entrees	30
Spaghetti and sauce, mixes	
Prepared: 1 pouch / **Betty Crocker** Mug-O-Lunch	30
Prepared: 1 cup / **Kraft** American Style	42
Prepared: 1 cup / **Kraft** Tangy Italian Style	39

Spreads

	GRAMS
1 oz = about ¼ cup	
Anchovy paste: 1 tbsp / **Crosse & Blackwell**	1
Chicken, canned: 1 oz / **Swanson**	1
Chicken: 1 oz / **Underwood**	1.1
Chicken salad: 1½ oz / **Carnation** Spreadables	2.6
Corned beef: 1 oz / **Underwood**	trace

GRAMS

Ham
 Deviled: 1 oz / **Hormel**   0
 Deviled, canned: 1½ tbsp / **Libby's**   .2
 Deviled: 1 oz / **Underwood**   trace
 Salad: 1½ oz / **Carnation** Spreadables   3.4
Liverwurst: 1 oz / **Underwood**   1.1
Peanut butter: 1 tbsp unless noted
 Ann Page Krunchy   4
 Ann Page Smooth   3.5
 Ann Page Regular   3.5
 Home Brands Natural   3
 Home Brands Real   2
 Kitchen King Crunchy   4
 Kitchen King Smooth   4
 Peter Pan Crunchy   3
 Peter Pan, low sodium   2.5
 Peter Pan Smooth   3
 Planters Creamy   3
 Planters Crunchy   3
 Skippy Creamy Smooth   2
 Skippy Old Fashioned Super Chunk   1.7
 Skippy Super Chunk   1.9
 Smucker's Crunchy   4
 Smucker's Natural   3
 Smucker's Smooth   3
 Sultana Krunchy   4
 and jelly: 1 oz / **Smucker's** Goober Grape   14
Potted meat: 1½ tbsp / **Libby's**   .2
Roast Beef: 1 oz / **Underwood**   .3
Sandwich spread: 1 tbsp unless noted
 Best Foods Spred   2.3
 Hellmann's   2.3
 Kraft   3
 Mrs. Filbert's   3
 Nu Made   4
 Oscar Mayer / 1 oz   3.5
Spam, deviled: 1 oz / **Hormel**   0

GRAMS

Tuna salad: 1½ oz / **Carnation** Spreadables	3.2
Turkey salad: 1½ oz / **Carnation** Spreadables	3

Sugar and Sweeteners

GRAMS

Honey, strained or extracted: 1 tbsp	17.3
Honey, strained or extracted: 1 cup	279
Sugar	
Brown, not packed: 1 cup	139.8
Brown, packed: 1 cup	212.1
Maple: 1 oz	25.5
Powdered, unsifted: 1 cup	119.4
Powdered, unsifted: 1 tbsp	8
Powdered, sifted: 1 cup	99.5
White, granulated: 1 cup	199
White, granulated: 1 tbsp	11.9
White, granulated: 1 tsp	4
Sugar substitute, granulated: 1 packet / **Weight Watchers** Sweet'ner	1
Sweetener, artificial: 1 tsp / **Sprinkle Sweet**	.5
Sweetener, artificial: ⅛ tsp / **Sweet*10**	0

Syrups

	GRAMS
1 tbsp	
Pancake, waffle	
Aunt Jemima	13.5
Cary's Diet	1.5
Diet Delight	4.2
Golden Griddle	13.5
Karo	14.9
Karo Imitation Maple	14.6
Log Cabin Buttered	12.7
Log Cabin Country Kitchen	13.1
Log Cabin Maple-Honey	14
Mrs. Butterworth's	13
Tillie Lewis	4
Corn, dark / **Karo**	15
Corn, light / **Karo**	14.9
Maple, pure / **Cary's**	15.7
Maple blend / **Log Cabin**	12.2
Molasses, cane, dark (third extraction)	11
Molasses, cane, light (first extraction)	13
Sorghum	14

Tea

	GRAMS
Bags, prepared: 1 cup / **Tender Leaf**	0
Iced tea	
Canned: 8 fl oz / **No-Cal**	0
Instant: 1 level tsp / **Nestea**	0
Instant, lemon-flavored: 8 fl oz / **Nestea**	0
Instant, lemon-flavored: 1 tsp dry mix /	
A & P Our Own Low Calorie	1
Instant, lemon-flavored, w sugar: 1	
env / **A & P** Our Own	126
Instant, w sugar and lemon: 6 fl oz / **Nestea**	17

Toppings

	GRAMS
1 tbsp unless noted	
Black cherry: 1 tsp / **No-Cal**	0
Black raspberry: 1 tsp / **No-Cal**	0
Butterscotch / **Kraft**	12
Butterscotch / **Smucker's**	17
Caramel / **Smucker's**	17
Caramel, chocolate-flavored / **Kraft**	12
Cherry / **Smucker's**	16

	GRAMS
Chocolate	
Bosco	13.4
Hershey's	11
Kraft	12
No-Cal / 1 tsp	0
Smucker's	14
Tillie Lewis	4
Fudge / **Hershey's**	5
Fudge / **Kraft**	11
Fudge / **Smucker's**	16
Fudge, chocolate-mint / **Smucker's**	16
Fudge, Swiss milk chocolate / **Smucker's**	16
Coffee: 1 tsp / **No-Cal**	0
Cola: 1 tsp / **No-Cal**	0
Grape: 1 tsp / **No-Cal**	0
Marshmallow / **Kraft**	9
Peanut butter caramel / **Smucker's**	15
Pecans in syrup / **Smucker's**	14
Pineapple / **Kraft**	13
Pineapple / **Smucker's**	16
Strawberry / **Kraft**	11
Strawberry: 1 tsp / **No-Cal**	0
Strawberry / **Smucker's**	15
Walnut / **Kraft**	10
Walnuts in syrup / **Smucker's**	14
Whipped, non-dairy, frozen / **Cool Whip**	1
Whipped, mix, prepared / **D-Zerta**	0
Whipped, mix, prepared / **Dream Whip**	1

Vegetables

FRESH

	GRAMS
Amaranth, raw, leaves: 1 lb	29.5
Artichokes (value may range from 8 for freshly harvested artichokes to 44 for stored artichokes), cooked, bud or globe: 1 small	.2
Artichokes (value may range from 10 for freshly harvested artichokes to 53 for stored artichokes), cooked, bud or globe: 1 medium	.2
Artichokes (value may range from 12 for freshly harvested artichokes to 67 for stored artichokes), cooked, bud or globe: 1 large	.3
Asparagus	
Raw: 1 lb	22.7
Raw, cut (1½–2 in): 1 cup	6.8
Cooked, cut (1½–2 in), drained: 1 cup	5.2
Spears, cooked, drained: 1 small	1.4
Spears, cooked, drained: 1 medium	2.2
Spears, cooked, drained: 1 large	3.6
Bamboo shoots, raw, 1-in pieces: 1 lb	23.6
Barley, pearled, light: 1 cup	157.6
Barley, pearled, Pot or Scotch: 1 cup	154.4
Beans	
Great Northern, cooked, drained: 1 cup	38.2
Lima, immature (green), raw: 1 cup	34.3
Lima, immature (green), cooked, drained: 1 cup	33.7

GRAMS

Lima, mature, cooked, drained: 1 cup	48.6
Mung, mature, dry, raw: 1 cup	126.6
Mung, mature, dry, raw: 1 lb	273.5
Mung, sprouted seeds, raw: 1 cup	6.9
Mung, sprouted seeds, cooked, drained: 1 cup	6.5
Pea (navy), cooked, drained: 1 cup	40.3
Pinto, dry, raw: 1 cup	121
Pinto or calico or red Mexican, dry, raw: 1 lb	288.9
Red, dry, cooked: ½ cup	21.4
Red, dry, raw: ½ cup	61.9
Red, kidney, cooked, drained: 1 cup	39.6
Snap, green, raw, cut: 1 cup	7.8
Snap, green, cooked, drained: 1 cup	6.8
Snap, yellow or wax, raw, cut: 1 cup	6.6
Snap, yellow or wax, cooked, drained: 1 cup	5.8
White, dry, raw: 1 lb	278.1
Beets, common, red, raw, peeled, diced: 1 cup	13.4
Beets, common, red, peeled, cooked, drained, whole (2-in diam): 2 beets	7.2
Beets, common, red, peeled, cooked, drained, diced or sliced: 1 cup	12.2
Beet greens, common, edible leaves and stems, raw: 1 lb	20.9
Beet greens, common, edible leaves and stems, cooked, drained: 1 cup	4.8
Broadbeans, raw, immature seeds: 1 lb	80.7
Broadbeans, raw, mature seeds, dry: 1 lb	264
Broccoli	
Stalks, raw: 1 lb	26.8
Cooked, drained: 1 small stalk	6.3
Cooked, drained: 1 medium stalk	8.1
Cooked, drained: 1 large stalk	12.6
Cooked, drained, ½-in pieces: 1 cup	7
Cooked, drained, whole or cut: 1 lb	20.4

GRAMS

Brussels sprouts, cooked: ½ cup	5
Brussels sprouts, raw: 9 med	8.3
Cabbage	
Raw: 1 lb	24.5
Raw, ground: 1 cup	8.1
Raw, shredded coarsely or sliced: 1 cup	3.8
Raw, shredded finely or chopped: 1 cup	4.9
Chinese, raw: 1 lb	20.9
Chinese, raw, 1-in pieces: 1 cup	2.3
Red, raw: 1 lb	31.3
Red, raw, shredded coarsely or sliced: 1 cup	4.8
Red, raw, shredded finely or chopped: 1 cup	6.2
Savoy, raw: 1 lb	20.9
Savoy, raw, shredded coarsely or sliced: 1 cup	3.2
Spoon, raw, 1-in pieces: 1 cup	2
Spoon, cooked, drained, 1-in pieces: 1 cup	4.1
Carrots	
Raw: 1 carrot (2⅛ oz)	7
Raw: 1 lb	44
Raw, grated or shredded: 1 cup	10.7
Raw, strips: 1 oz or 6-8 strips	2.7
Cooked, drained, diced: 1 cup	10.3
Cooked, drained, sliced crosswise: 1 cup	11
Cauliflower	
Raw: 1 head (1.9 lb)	44.7
Raw, flowerbuds, whole: 1 cup	5.2
Raw, flowerbuds, sliced: 1 cup	4.4
Raw, flowerbuds, chopped: 1 cup	6
Cooked, drained: 1 cup	5.1
Celeriac, raw: 4 to 6 roots	8.5
Celery	
Raw: 1 lb	17.7
Raw, large outer stalk (8-in long, 1½-in wide): 1 stalk	1.6
Raw, small inner stalk (5-in long, ¾-in wide): 3 stalks	2

GRAMS

Raw, chopped or diced: 1 cup	4.7
Cooked, diced: 1 cup	4.7
Chard, Swiss, raw: 1 lb	20.9
Chard, Swiss, cooked, drained, leaves: 1 cup	5.8
Chayote, raw: ½ med squash	7.1
Chickpeas or garbanzos, mature seeds, dry, raw: 1 cup	122
Chickpeas or garbanzos, mature seeds, dry, raw: 1 lb	276.7
Chicory, Witloof, raw: 1 head (5–7 in long)	1.7
Chicory, Witloof, raw: 1 lb	14.5
Chicory, Witloof, raw, chopped, ½-in pieces: 1 cup	2.9
Chives, raw, chopped: 1 tbsp	.2
Collards	
Raw, leaves w stems: 1 lb	32.7
Raw, leaves wo stems: 1 lb	34
Cooked, drained, leaves w stems: 1 cup	7.1
Cooked, drained, leaves wo stems: 1 cup	9.7
Corn, sweet, raw, white and yellow, husked: 1 lb	55.1
Corn, sweet, white and yellow, cooked, drained, kernels only: 1 cup	31
Corn, sweet, white and yellow, cooked, drained, on cob: 1 ear (5 x 1¾ in)	16.2
Cowpeas (including blackeye peas)	
Immature, raw: 1 cup blackeye peas	31.6
Immature, cooked, drained: 1 cup blackeye peas	29.9
Mature seeds, dry, cooked, drained: 1 cup	34.5
Young pods w seeds, raw: 1 lb	43.1
Young pods w seeds, cooked, drained: 1 lb	31.8
Cress, garden, raw, trimmed: 5 to 8 sprigs	.5
Cress, garden, raw, trimmed: ½ lb	12.4
Cucumbers	
Raw, unpeeled, whole: 1 small	5.8
Raw, unpeeled, whole: 1 large	10.2

GRAMS

Raw, unpeeled, sliced: 1 cup	3.6
Raw, peeled, whole: 1 small	5.1
Raw, peeled, whole: 1 large	9
Dandelion greens, raw: 1 lb	41.7
Dandelion greens, cooked, drained: 1 cup	6.7
Dock or sorrel, raw: ½ lb	8.9
Eggplant, cooked, drained, diced: 1 cup	8.2
Endive, raw: 1 lb	18.6
Endive, raw, small pieces: 1 cup	2.1
Fennel leaves, raw, trimmed: ½ lb	10.7
Garlic, cloves, raw: 1 clove	.9
Hyacinth-beans, raw, young pods, ½-in pieces: 1 cup	6.6
Hyacinth-beans, raw, mature, dry: 1 lb	276.7
Kale, leaves wo stems, raw: 1 lb	40.8
Kale, cooked, drained: 1 cup	6.7
Kohlrabi, raw, diced: 1 cup	9.2
Kohlrabi, cooked, drained: 1 cup	8.7
Leeks, raw: 3 (5-in long)	11.2
Lentils, mature seeds, dry, whole, raw: 1 cup	114.2
Lentils, mature seeds, cooked, drained: 1 cup	38.6
Lettuce	
Butternut (Boston types and Bibb): 1 head	4.1
Butternut (Boston types and Bibb), chopped or shredded: 1 cup	1.4
Cos or romaine: 1 lb	15.9
Cos or romaine, chopped or shredded: 1 cup	1.9
Crisphead (including Iceberg): 1 wedge (¼ head)	3.9
Crisphead (including Iceberg): 1 head	15.6
Crisphead (including Iceberg), chopped or shredded: 1 cup	1.6
Looseleaf varieties, chopped or shredded: 1 cup	1.9
Mushrooms: 1 lb	20
Mushrooms, sliced, chopped or diced: 1 cup	3.1

	GRAMS
Mustard greens, raw: 1 lb	25.4
Mustard greens, cooked, drained: 1 cup	5.6
Mustard spinach, raw: 1 lb	17.7
Mustard spinach, cooked, drained: 1 cup	5
New Zealand spinach, raw: 1 lb	14.1
New Zealand spinach, cooked, drained: 1 cup	3.8
Okra, crosscut slices, cooked, drained: 1 cup	9.6
Onions	
Raw: 1 lb	39.5
Raw, chopped: 1 cup	14.8
Raw, chopped or minced: 1 tbsp	.9
Raw, sliced: 1 cup	10
Cooked, drained, whole or sliced: 1 cup	13.7
Young green: 2 medium or 6 small	3.2
Young green, chopped: 1 tbsp	.5
Young green, chopped or sliced: 1 cup	8.2
Parsley, raw: 10 sprigs (2½-in long)	.9
Parsley, raw, chopped: 1 tbsp	.3
Parsnips, raw: 1 lb	67.5
Parsnips, cooked, drained: 1 large parsnip	23.8
Parsnips, cooked, drained, diced: 1 cup	23.1
Peas	
Green, immature, raw: 1 cup	20.9
Green, immature, raw: 1 lb	65.3
Cooked, drained: 1 cup	19.4
Mature, dry, split, cooked: 1 cup	41.6
Peppers, chili, green, raw: ½ lb	15
Peppers, chili, red w seeds: ½ lb	39.4
Peppers, chili, red wo seeds: ½ lb	26.2
Pepper, hot, red, wo seeds, dried: 1 tbsp	8
Peppers, sweet	
Green, raw, whole: 1 small (about 5 per lb)	3.5
Green, raw, whole: 1 large (about 2¼ per lb)	7.9
Green, chopped or diced: 1 cup	7.2
Green, cooked, drained: 1 large	6.1
Red, raw, whole: 1 small (about 5 per lb)	5.2

GRAMS

Red, raw, whole: 1 large (about 2¼ per lb)	11.6
Red, chopped or diced: 1 cup	10.7
Pokeberry (poke), shoots, cooked, drained: 1 cup	5.1
Potatoes	
Baked in skin: 1 potato (2⅓ x 4¾ in)	32.8
Boiled in skin: 1 potato (2⅓ x 4¾ in)	38.9
Boiled in skin: 1 potato, round, 2½-in diam	23.3
Boiled in skin, diced or sliced: 1 cup	22.5
Peeled, boiled: 1 potato (2⅓ x 4¾ in)	32.6
Peeled, boiled: 1 potato, round, 2½-in diam	19.6
Peeled, boiled, diced or sliced: 1 cup	22.5
French fried: 10 strips, 2–3½-in long	18
Fried from raw: 1 cup	55.4
Mashed w milk and butter or margarine:	
1 cup	25.8
Pumpkin, pulp: 8 oz	10.3
Purslane leaves and stems, raw: ½ lb	8.6
Radishes, raw, whole: 10 medium	1.6
Radishes, raw, whole: 10 large	2.9
Radishes, raw, sliced: 1 cup	4.1
Rutabagas, raw, cubed: 1 cup	15.4
Rutabagas, cooked, drained, cubed or sliced:	
1 cup	13.9
Shallot bulbs, raw, chopped: 1 tbsp	1.7
Soybeans	
Mature seeds, dry, cooked: 1 cup	19.4
Sprouted seeds, raw: 1 cup	5.6
Sprouted seeds, cooked, drained: 1 cup	4.6
Curd (tofu): 1 piece (2½ x 2¾ x 1 in)	2.9
Spinach, raw: 1 lb	19.5
Spinach, raw, chopped: 1 cup	2.4
Spinach, leaves, cooked, drained: 1 cup	6.5
Squash	
Acorn, baked: ½ squash	24.6
Acorn, baked, mashed: 1 cup	28.7
Butternut, baked, mashed: 1 cup	35.9

GRAMS

Butternut, boiled, mashed: 1 cup	25.5
Crookneck and straightneck, yellow, raw, sliced: 1 cup	5.6
Crookneck and straightneck, yellow, raw: 1 lb	19.5
Crookneck and straightneck, yellow, cooked, sliced: 1 cup	5.6
Crookneck and straightneck, yellow, cooked, mashed: 1 cup	7.4
Hubbard, baked, mashed: 1 cup	24
Hubbard, boiled, mashed: 1 cup	16.9
Hubbard, boiled, diced: 1 cup	16.2
Scallop varieties, white and pale green, raw, sliced: 1 cup	6.6
Scallop varieties, white and pale green, raw: 1 lb	23.1
Summer, all varieties, cooked, sliced: 1 cup	5.6
Summer, all varieties, cooked, cubed or diced: 1 cup	6.5
Summer, all varieties, cooked, mashed: 1 cup	7.4
Winter, all varieties, cooked, baked, mashed: 1 cup	31.6
Winter, all varieties, cooked, boiled, mashed: 1 cup	22.5
Zucchini and Cocozelle, green, raw, sliced: 1 cup	4.7
Zucchini and Cocozelle, green raw: 1 lb	16.3
Zucchini and Cocozelle, green, cooked, sliced: 1 cup	4.5
Zucchini and Cocozelle, green, cooked, mashed: 1 cup	6
Sweet potatoes, baked in skin: 1 potato (5 x 2 in)	37
Sweet potatoes, boiled in skin: 1 potato (5 x 2 in)	39.8
Sweet potatoes, mashed: 1 cup	67.1

GRAMS

Tomatoes, raw: 1 small (3½ oz)	4.3
Tomatoes, raw: 1 large (4¾ oz)	5.8
Tomatoes, boiled: 1 cup	13.3
Turnips, raw: 1 cup	8.6
Turnips, cooked, drained, cubed: 1 cup	7.6
Turnips, mashed: 1 cup	11.3
Turnip greens, raw: 1 lb	22.7
Turnip greens, cooked, drained: 1 cup	5.2
Water chestnut, Chinese, raw: 1 lb	66.4
Watercress, raw, whole: 1 cup	1.1
Watercress, raw, finely chopped: 1 cup	3.8

CANNED AND FROZEN

(⅓ pkg = about ½ cup)

Artichoke hearts, frozen: 3 oz (5 or 6 hearts) / **Birds Eye**	5
Asparagus, canned: 1 cup unless noted	
Cut / **Green Giant**	5
Cut / **Kounty Kist**	5
Cut / **Lindy**	5
Cut / **Stokely-Van Camp**	6
Spears / **Green Giant**	5
Spears / **Le Sueur**	5
Spears: 5 whole / **S and W Nutradiet**	2
Spears / **Town House**	6
Spears and tips / **Del Monte**	6
Spears, tipped / **Del Monte**	7
Whole / **Stokely-Van Camp**	6
White / **Del Monte**	7
Asparagus, frozen	
Cut: 3.3 oz (about ½ cup) / **Birds Eye**	3
Cut, in butter sauce: 1 cup / **Green Giant**	7
Cuts and tips: ½ cup / **Seabrook Farms**	3.5
Cuts and tips, in Hollandaise sauce: ½ cup / **Seabrook Farms**	5

Spears: 3.3 oz (about ½ cup) / **Birds Eye**	3
Spears: 5 spears / **Seabrook Farms**	1.5
Spears, jumbo: 3.3 oz (about ½ cup) / **Birds Eye**	3
Beans, baked: 1 cup	
Pea / **B & M**	51.2
Red kidney / **B & M**	49.6
Yellow eye / **B & M**	50.4
Beans, baked style	
w bacon: 7½ oz can / **Hormel Short Orders**	40
In barbecue sauce: 8 oz / **Campbell**	46
In chili gravy: 8 oz / **Ann Page**	36
w frankfurters: 7½ oz can / **Hormel Short Orders** Beans 'n Wieners	31.4
w frankfurters, in tomato and molasses sauce: 8 oz / **Campbell** Beans & Franks	40
w ham: 7½ oz can / **Hormel Short Orders**	37.1
In molasses and brown sugar sauce: 8 oz / **Campbell Old Fashioned**	49
w pork and molasses: 8 oz / **Ann Page** Boston Style	50
w pork, in molasses sauce: 1 cup / **Libby's**	49
w pork and tomato sauce: 8 oz / **Ann Page**	42
w pork, in tomato sauce: 8 oz / **Campbell**	44
w pork, in tomato sauce: 1 cup / **Libby's**	49
In tomato sauce: 8 oz / **Ann Page** Vegetarian	44
In tomato sauce: 1 cup / **Libby's** Vegetarian	51
In tomato sauce: 8 oz / **Morton House**	45
Beans, black turtle, canned: 1 cup / **Progresso**	37
Beans, fava, canned: 1 cup / **Progresso**	31
Beans, green, canned: 1 cup unless noted	
Cut / **Del Monte**	8
Cut / **Green Giant**	6
Cut / **Kounty Kist**	7

GRAMS

Cut / **Libby's** Blue Lake	8
Cut / **Lindy**	7
Cut: ½ cup / **S and W Nutradiet**	2.8
Cut / **Stokely-Van Camp**	8
French / **Del Monte**	7
French / **Green Giant**	6
French / **Kounty Kist**	7
French / **Libby's** Blue Lake	8
French / **Lindy**	7
Italian / **Del Monte**	11
Seasoned / **Del Monte**	8
Sliced / **Stokely-Van Camp**	8
Whole / **Del Monte**	6
Whole / **Green Giant**	6
Whole / **Kounty Kist**	7
Whole / **Libby's** Blue Lake	8
Whole / **Lindy**	7
Whole / **Stokely-Van Camp**	7
Whole, tiny / **Del Monte**	7
Beans, green, frozen	
Cut: 3 oz (about ½ cup) / **Birds Eye**	5
Cut: 1 cup / **Kounty Kist** Poly Bag	6
Cut: ½ cup / **Seabrook Farms**	4
Cut, in butter sauce: 1 cup / **Green Giant**	7
Cut, in mushroom sauce: ½ cup / **Seabrook Farms**	6.5
French: 3 oz (about ½ cup) / **Birds Eye**	6
French: ½ cup / **Seabrook Farms**	4.5
French, in butter sauce: 1 cup / **Green Giant**	7
French w sliced mushrooms: 3 oz (about ½ cup) / **Birds Eye** Combinations	6
French w toasted almonds: 3 oz (about ½ cup) / **Birds Eye** Combinations	8
Italian: 3 oz (about ½ cup) / **Birds Eye**	6
w onions and bacon bits: 1 cup / **Green Giant**	9
and pearl onions: 3 oz (about ½ cup) / **Birds Eye** Combinations	6

GRAMS

and spaetzle w sauce: 3.3 oz (about ½ cup) / **Birds Eye** International	10
Whole: 3 oz (about ½ cup) / **Birds Eye**	5
Beans, kidney, red: 8 oz / **Ann Page**	40
Beans, kidney, red, canned: 1 cup / **Progresso**	33
Beans, kidney, white, canned: 1 cup / **Progresso** Cannellini	32
Beans, lima	
Baby, canned: 8 oz / **Sultana**	36
Baby, frozen: 3.3 oz (about ½ cup) / **Birds Eye**	22
Baby, frozen: 1 cup / **Green Giant** Poly Bag	28
Baby, frozen: 1 cup / **Kounty Kist** Poly Bag	35
Baby, frozen: ½ cup / **Seabrook Farms**	18
Baby, in butter sauce, frozen: 1 cup / **Green Giant**	32
Canned: 1 cup / **Del Monte**	29
Canned: 1 cup / **Libby's**	30
Canned: 1 cup / **Stokely-Van Camp**	33
Canned, seasoned: 1 cup / **Del Monte**	29
Fordhook, frozen: 3.3 oz (about ½ cup) / **Birds Eye**	18
Fordhook, frozen: ½ cup / **Seabrook Farms**	16
Tiny, frozen: 3.3 oz (about ½ cup) / **Birds Eye**	20
Beans, pinto, canned: 1 cup / **Progresso**	31
Beans, red, canned: 8 oz / **Ann Page**	40
Beans, Roman, canned: 1 cup / **Progresso**	36
Beans, salad, canned: 1 cup / **Green Giant** 3 Bean	42
Beans, Shellie, canned: 1 cup / **Stokely-Van Camp**	15
Beans, wax or yellow: 1 cup unless noted	
Cut, canned / **Del Monte**	7
Cut, canned / **Libby's**	9
Cut, canned / **Stokely-Van Camp**	8
Cut, frozen: 3 oz (about ½ cup) / **Birds Eye**	4

GRAMS

Cut, frozen: ½ cup / **Seabrook Farms** — 4
French cut, canned / **Del Monte** — 7
Sliced, canned / **Stokely-Van Camp** — 7
Beets, canned: 1 cup unless noted
Cut / **Del Monte** — 15
Cut / **Libby's** — 16
Cut / **Stokely-Van Camp** — 19
Diced / **Libby's** — 16
Diced / **Stokely-Van Camp** — 15
Harvard / **Stokely-Van Camp** — 36
Harvard, diced / **Libby's** — 40
Pickled, crinkle cut / **Del Monte** — 36
Pickled, sliced / **Libby's** — 37
Pickled, sliced / **Stokely-Van Camp** — 45
Pickled, sliced / **Town House** — 34
Pickled, whole / **Libby's** — 37
Pickled, whole / **Stokely-Van Camp** — 46
Shoestring / **Libby's** — 12
Sliced / **Del Monte** — 15
Sliced / **Libby's** — 16
Sliced: ½ cup / **S and W Nutradiet** — 6
Sliced / **Stokely-Van Camp** — 18
Whole / **Del Monte** — 15
Whole / **Libby's** — 16
Whole / **Stokely-Van Camp** — 20
Broccoli, frozen
Au gratin: ½ pkg / **Stouffer's** — 9
w cauliflower and carrots, in cheese sauce:
　1 cup / **Green Giant** — 17
w cheese sauce: 3.3 oz (about ½ cup) /
　Birds Eye Combinations — 7
In cheese sauce: 1 cup / **Green Giant** — 13
In cheese sauce: 1 cup / **Green Giant**
　Bake n' Serve — 17
Chopped: 3.3 oz (about ½ cup) / **Birds Eye** — 4
Chopped: ½ cup / **Seabrook Farms** — 4
Cut: 1 cup / **Green Giant** Poly Bag — 5

GRAMS

Cut: 1 cup / **Kounty Kist** Poly Bag	5
Spears: 3.3 oz (about ½ cup) / **Birds Eye**	4
Spears: ⅓ pkg / **Seabrook Farms**	3.5
Spears, baby: 3.3 oz (about ½ cup) / **Birds Eye**	4
Spears, in butter sauce: 1 cup / **Green Giant**	8
Brussels sprouts, frozen	
Birds Eye / 3.3 oz (about ½ cup)	5
Green Giant Poly Bag / 1 cup	8
Kounty Kist Poly Bag / 1 cup	8
Seabrook Farms / ½ cup	6
Baby: 3.3 oz (about ½ cup) / **Birds Eye**	6
In butter sauce: 1 cup / **Green Giant**	10
Halves, in cheese sauce: 1 cup / **Green Giant**	19
Butterbeans, canned: 8 oz / **Sultana**	31
Butterbeans, frozen: ½ cup / **Seabrook Farms**	19.5
Butterbeans, baby, frozen: 3.3 oz (about ½ cup) / **Birds Eye**	24
Butterbeans, speckled, frozen: 1 cup / **Green Giant** Boil-in-Bag Southern Recipe	34
Butterbeans w ham, canned: 1 cup / **Libby's**	34
Carrots: 1 cup unless noted	
Cut, canned: ½ cup / **S and W Nutradiet**	5
Diced, canned / **Del Monte**	15
Diced, canned / **Libby's**	9
Diced, canned / **Stokely-Van Camp**	12
Sliced, canned / **Del Monte**	15
Sliced, canned / **Libby's**	9
Sliced, canned / **Stokely-Van Camp**	10
w brown sugar glaze, frozen: 3.3 oz (about ½ cup) / **Birds Eye** Combinations	15
In butter sauce, frozen / **Green Giant** Nuggets	12
Cauliflower, frozen	
Birds Eye / 3.3 oz (about ½ cup)	4
Green Giant Poly Bag / 1 cup	4
Kounty Kist Poly Bag / 1 cup	4

GRAMS

Seabrook Farms / ½ cup	3.5
w cheese sauce: 3.3 oz (about ½ cup) /	
Birds Eye Combinations	8
In cheese sauce: 1 cup / **Green Giant**	13
In cheese sauce: 1 cup / **Green Giant**	
Bake n' Serve	17
Chick-peas, canned: 1 cup / **Progresso**	32
Collard greens, chopped, frozen: 3.3 oz	
(about ½ cup) / **Birds Eye**	4
Collard greens, frozen: ½ cup / **Seabrook Farms**	4
Corn, golden, canned: 1 cup unless noted	
Cream style / **Del Monte**	46
Cream style / **Green Giant**	45
Cream style / **Kounty Kist**	50
Cream style / **Libby's**	42
Cream style / **Lindy**	50
Cream style: ½ cup / **S and W Nutradiet**	17
Cream style / **Stokely-Van Camp**	47
Liquid pack / **Del Monte** Family Style	37
Liquid pack / **Green Giant**	33
Liquid pack / **Kounty Kist**	38
Liquid pack / **Le Sueur**	35
Liquid pack / **Libby's**	37
Liquid pack / **Lindy**	38
Liquid pack: ½ cup / **S and W Nutradiet**	10
Liquid pack / **Stokely-Van Camp**	39
Vacuum pack / **Del Monte**	43
Vacuum pack / **Green Giant** Niblets	30
Vacuum pack / **Kounty Kist**	35
Vacuum pack / **Lindy**	35
Vacuum pack / **Stokely-Van Camp**	53
w peppers / **Del Monte** Corn 'n Peppers	40
w peppers / **Green Giant** Mexicorn	30
Corn, golden, frozen	
In butter sauce: 1 cup / **Green Giant** Niblets	30
On cob: 1 ear / **Birds Eye**	28
On cob: 1 ear / **Birds Eye** Little Ears	16

	GRAMS
On cob: 1 ear / **Green Giant**	33
On cob: 1 ear / **Green Giant** Nibbler	18
Cream style: 1 cup / **Green Giant**	40
w peppers, in butter sauce: 1 cup / **Green Giant** Mexican	30
Souffle: ⅓ pkg / **Stouffer's**	19
Whole kernel: 3.3 oz (about ½ cup) / **Birds Eye**	18
Whole kernel: 1 cup / **Green Giant** Poly Bag	26
Whole kernel: 1 cup / **Kounty Kist** Poly Bag	28
Whole kernel: 3 oz / **Ore-Ida**	20
Whole kernel: ½ cup / **Seabrook Farms**	16.5
Corn, white: 1 cup	
Canned / **Stokely-Van Camp**	49
Cream style, canned / **Del Monte**	42
Cream style, canned / **Stokely-Van Camp**	49
Whole kernel, canned / **Del Monte**	33
Whole kernel, vacuum pack, canned / **Green Giant**	30
Whole kernel, frozen / **Green Giant** Poly Bag	26
Whole kernel, frozen / **Kounty Kist** Poly Bag	28
Whole kernel, in butter sauce, frozen / **Green Giant**	30
Eggplant Parmesan, frozen: 5½ oz / **Mrs. Paul's**	21
Eggplant slices, fried, frozen: 3 oz / **Mrs. Paul's**	22
Eggplant sticks, fried, frozen: 3½ oz / **Mrs. Paul's**	27
Green peppers, stuffed, frozen: 1 pkg / **Stouffer's**	18
Green peppers, stuffed, frozen: 13 oz / **Weight Watchers**	29
Kale, chopped, frozen: 3.3 oz (about ½ cup) / **Birds Eye**	5
Kale, chopped, frozen: ½ cup / **Seabrook Farms**	5

GRAMS

Kale, leaf, frozen: ½ cup / **Seabrook Farms**   5
Mixed, canned: 1 cup
    Del Monte   16
    Libby's Garden Vegetables   17
    Stokely-Van Camp   17
    Town House   18
Mixed, frozen
    Birds Eye / 3.3 oz (about ½ cup)   11
    Green Giant Poly Bag / 1 cup   16
    Kounty Kist Poly Bag / 1 cup   16
    Seabrook Farms / ½ cup   10.5
    California blend: 1 cup / **Kounty Kist**
      Poly Bag   5
    Cantonese style: 3.3 oz (about ½ cup) /
      Birds Eye Stir-Fry   10
    Chinese: 1 pkg / **La Choy**   11
    Chinese style: 1 cup / **Green Giant**
      Boil-in-Bag Oriental Combination   20
    Chinese style w sauce: 3.3 oz (about
      ½ cup) / **Birds Eye** International   5
    Chinese style w seasonings: 3.3 oz (about
      ½ cup) / **Birds Eye** Stir-Fry   7
    Danish style w sauce: 3.3 oz (about ½ cup) /
      Birds Eye International   9
    Hawaiian style: 1 cup / **Green Giant**
      Boil-in-Bag Oriental Combination   33
    Hawaiian style w sauce: 3.3 oz (about ½
      cup) / **Birds Eye** International   12
    Italian style w sauce: 3.3 oz (about ½ cup) /
      Birds Eye International   8
    Japanese: 1 pkg / **La Choy**   12
    Japanese style: 1 cup / **Green Giant**
      Boil-in-Bag Oriental Combination   22
    Japanese style w sauce: 3.3 oz (about ½
      cup) / **Birds Eye** International   9
    Japanese style w seasonings: 3.3 oz (about
      ½ cup) / **Birds Eye** Stir-Fry   6

Jubilee: 3.3 oz (about ½ cup) / **Birds Eye**
Combinations   17

Mandarin style w seasonings: 3.3 oz (about
½ cup) / **Birds Eye** Stir-Fry   6

New England style: 3.3 oz (about ½ cup) /
Birds Eye Americana Recipe   11

New Orleans creole style: 3.3 oz (about ½
cup) / **Birds Eye** Americana Recipe   13

Parisian style w sauce: 3.3 oz (about ½
cup) / **Birds Eye** International   7

Pennsylvania Dutch style: 3.3 oz (about
½ cup) / **Birds Eye** Americana Recipe   7

San Francisco style: 3.3 oz (about ½
cup) / **Birds Eye** Americana Recipe   6

Wisconsin country style: 3.3 oz (about
½ cup) / **Birds Eye** Americana Recipe   6

In butter sauce: 1 cup / **Green Giant**   17

In onion sauce: 2.6 oz / **Birds Eye**   12

Mushrooms

Canned: 4 oz / **Dole**   2

Pieces and stems, canned: 1 oz /
Green Giant   1

Sliced, canned: 1 oz / **Green Giant**   1

Whole, canned: 1 oz / **Green Giant**   1

In butter sauce, frozen: 2 oz / **Green Giant**   2

Mustard greens, chopped, frozen: 3.3 oz (about
½ cup) / **Birds Eye**   3

Mustard greens, chopped, frozen: ½ cup /
Seabrook Farms   3.5

Mustard greens, leaf, frozen: ½ cup /
Seabrook Farms   3.5

Okra

Cut, frozen: 3.3 oz (about ½ cup) /
Birds Eye   5

Cut, frozen: ½ cup / **Seabrook Farms**   6

Gumbo, frozen: 1 cup / **Green Giant**
Boil-in-Bag Southern Recipe   12

GRAMS

Whole, frozen: 3.3 oz (about ½ cup) / **Birds Eye**	7
Whole, frozen: ½ cup / **Seabrook Farms**	6
Onions, boiled, canned: 4 oz / **O & C**	8
Onions, in cream sauce, canned: 1 oz / **O & C**	17
Onions, frozen	
Chopped: 1 oz / **Birds Eye**	2
Chopped: 2 oz / **Ore-Ida**	4
Small, whole: 3.3 oz (about ½ cup) / **Birds Eye**	10
In cheese flavor sauce: 1 cup / **Green Giant**	14
In cream sauce: 3 oz (about ½ cup) / **Birds Eye**	11
In cream sauce: ½ cup / **Seabrook Farms**	5.5
Onion rings, fried, canned: 1 oz / **O & C**	10
Onion rings, fried, frozen: 2½ oz / **Mrs. Paul's**	21
Onion rings, fried, frozen: 2 oz / **Ore-Ida** Onion Ringers	17
Peas, black-eye	
Canned: 1 cup / **Progresso**	29
Canned w pork: 8 oz / **Sultana**	36
Frozen: 3.3 oz (about ½ cup) / **Birds Eye**	21
Frozen: 1 cup / **Green Giant** Boil-in-Bag Southern Recipe	32
Frozen: ½ cup / **Seabrook Farms**	18
Peas, green, canned: 1 cup unless noted	
Early / **April Showers**	22
Early / **Del Monte**	20
Early / **Kounty Kist**	27
Early / **Lindy**	27
Early / **Minnesota Valley**	19
Early / **Stokely-Van Camp**	25
Early, small / **Le Sueur**	19
Early w onions / **Green Giant**	22
Seasoned / **Del Monte**	25
Sweet / **Green Giant**	17
Sweet / **Kounty Kist**	22

GRAMS

Sweet / **Le Sueur**	17
Sweet / **Libby's**	23
Sweet / **Lindy**	22
Sweet: ½ cup / **S and W Nutradiet**	6
Sweet / **Stokely-Van Camp**	24
Sweet, small / **Green Giant** Sweetlets	17
Sweet, tiny / **Del Monte**	18
Sweet w onions / **Green Giant**	17
and carrots / **Del Monte**	19
and carrots / **Libby's**	20
and carrots: ½ cup / **S and W Nutradiet**	5.8
and carrots / **Stokely-Van Camp**	22

Peas, green, frozen

Early: 3.3 oz (about ½ cup) / **Birds Eye**	11
Early: 1 cup / **Kounty Kist** Poly Bag	20
Early: 1 cup / **Green Giant** Poly Bag	16
Early: ½ cup / **Seabrook Farms**	12.5
Early, in butter sauce: 1 cup / **Le Sueur**	20
Sweet: 1 cup / **Green Giant** Poly Bag	16
Sweet: ½ cup / **Seabrook Farms**	9
Sweet, in butter sauce: 1 cup / **Green Giant**	18
Tiny: 3.3 oz (about ½ cup) / **Birds Eye**	9
and carrots: 3.3 oz (about ½ cup) / **Birds Eye**	9
and carrots: 1 cup / **Kounty Kist** Poly Bag	13
and carrots: ½ cup / **Seabrook Farms**	7.5
and cauliflower w cream sauce: 3.3 oz (about ½ cup) / **Birds Eye** Combinations	12
w cream sauce: 2.6 oz / **Birds Eye** Combinations	14
Creamed w bread crumb topping: 1 cup / **Green Giant** Bake n' Serve	33
In onion sauce: ½ cup / **Seabrook Farms**	10
w onions and carrots, in butter sauce: 1 cup / **Le Sueur**	20
w pea pods and water chestnuts, in sauce: 1 cup / **Le Sueur**	20

and pearl onions: 3.3 oz (about ½ cup) / **Birds Eye** Combinations	12
and potatoes w cream sauce: 2.6 oz / **Birds Eye** Combinations	15
w sliced mushrooms: 3.3 oz (about ½ cup) / **Birds Eye** Combinations	11

Potatoes, canned

Au gratin w bacon: 7½ oz can / **Hormel Short Orders**	20
New: 1 cup / **Del Monte**	19
Scalloped w ham: 7½ oz can / **Hormel Short Orders**	20
Whole: 1 cup / **Stokely-Van Camp**	22

Potatoes, frozen

Au gratin: 1 cup / **Green Giant** Bake n' Serve	32
Au gratin: ⅓ pkg / **Stouffer's**	13
Diced, in sour cream sauce: 1 cup / **Green Giant** Boil-in-Bag	36
French-fried: 2.8 oz / **Birds Eye** Cottage Fries	17
French-fried: 3 oz (about ½ cup) / **Birds Eye** Crinkle Cuts	18
French-fried: 3 oz (about ½ cup) / **Birds Eye** Deep Gold Crinkle Cuts	25
French-fried: 3 oz (about ½ cup) / **Birds Eye** French Fries	17
French-fried: 3.3 oz (about ½ cup) / **Birds Eye** Shoestrings	20
French-fried: 3 oz (about ½ cup) / **Birds Eye** Steak Fries	18
French-fried: 3 oz / **Ore-Ida** Cottage Fries	22
French-fried: 3 oz / **Ore-Ida** Country Style Dinner Fries	18
French-fried: 3 oz / **Ore-Ida** Crispers	26
French-fried: 3 oz / **Ore-Ida** Golden Crinkles	21

GRAMS

French-fried: 3 oz / **Ore-Ida** Golden Fries	22
French-fried: 3 oz / **Ore-Ida** Pixie Crinkles	25
French-fried: 3 oz / **Ore-Ida** Self Sizzling Crinkles	23
French-fried: 3 oz / **Ore-Ida** Self Sizzling Fries	24
French-fried: 3 oz / **Ore-Ida** Self Sizzling Shoestrings	26
French-fried: 3 oz / **Ore-Ida** Shoestrings	25
Fried: 3 oz (about ½ cup) / **Birds Eye** Deep Gold	24
Fried: 2.5 oz / **Birds Eye** Tasti Fries	17
Fried: 2.5 oz / **Birds Eye** Tasti Puffs	19
Fried: 3.2 oz / **Birds Eye** Tiny Taters	22
Hash browns: 4 oz / **Birds Eye**	17
Hash browns: 4 oz / **Birds Eye** O'Brien	14
Hash browns: 3 oz / **Ore-Ida** Southern Style	16
Hash browns w butter sauce: 3 oz / **Ore-Ida** Southern Style	15
Hash browns w butter sauce and onions: 3 oz / **Ore-Ida** Southern Style	17
Hash browns, shredded: 3 oz (about ½ cup) / **Birds Eye**	13
Hash browns, shredded: 3 oz / **Ore-Ida**	12
O'Brien: 3 oz / **Ore-Ida**	14
Parsley: ½ cup / **Seabrook Farms**	14.5
Scalloped: ⅓ pkg / **Stouffer's**	14
Shoestring, in butter sauce: 1 cup / **Green Giant** Boil-in-Bag	37
Slices, in butter sauce: 1 cup / **Green Giant** Boil-in-Bag	27
Stuffed w cheese-flavored topping: 5 oz / **Green Giant** Oven Bake	30
Stuffed w sour cream and chives: 5 oz / **Green Giant** Oven Bake	30

and sweet peas, in bacon cream sauce:
  1 cup / **Green Giant** Boil-in-Bag   31
Tater Tots: 3 oz / **Ore-Ida**   20
Tater Tots w bacon flavor: 3 oz / **Ore-Ida** 21
Tater Tots w onions: 3 oz / **Ore-Ida**   21
Vermicelli: 1 cup / **Green Giant**
  Bake n' Serve   42
Whole, boiled: ½ cup / **Seabrook Farms**   16.5
Whole, peeled: 3.2 oz (about ½ cup) /
  Birds Eye   13
Whole, small, peeled: 3 oz / **Ore-Ida**   16
Potatoes, mix, prepared: ½ cup unless noted
  Au gratin / **Betty Crocker**   20
  Au gratin / **French's** Big Tate   28
  Creamed / **Betty Crocker**   20
  Hash browns / **French's** Big Tate   22
  Hash browns w onions / **Betty Crocker**   22
  Julienne / **Betty Crocker**   17
  Mashed / **French's**   16
  Mashed / **French's** Big Tate   16
  Mashed / **Hungry Jack** (4 serving container) 18
  Mashed / **Hungry Jack** (12, 24, 40 serving
    container)   16
  Mashed / **Magic Valley**   16
  Pancakes: three 3-in cakes / **French's**
    Big Tate   17
  Potato Buds / **Betty Crocker**   15
  Scalloped / **Betty Crocker**   20
  Scalloped / **French's** Big Tate   30
  w sour cream and chives / **Betty Crocker**
    Sour Cream 'n Chive   18
Potatoes, sweet, frozen
  Candied: 4 oz / **Mrs. Paul's**   44
  Candied w apples: 4 oz / **Mrs. Paul's**   37
  Candied, orange: 4 oz / **Mrs. Paul's**   44
  Glazed: 1 cup / **Green Giant** Boil-in-Bag
    Southern Recipe   65

GRAMS

Pumpkin, canned: 1 cup / **Del Monte**	18
Pumpkin, canned: 1 cup / **Libby's** Solid Pack	20
Pumpkin, canned: 1 cup / **Stokely-Van Camp**	19
Sauerkraut, canned: 1 cup	
Del Monte	11
Libby's	10
Bavarian style / **Stokely-Van Camp**	14
Chopped / **Stokely-Van Camp**	9
Shredded / **Stokely-Van Camp**	9
Soup greens, in jar: 1 jar / **Durkee**	43
Spinach, canned: 1 cup / **Del Monte**	7
Spinach, canned: 1 cup / **Libby's**	7
Spinach, frozen	
In butter sauce: 1 cup / **Green Giant**	6
Chopped: 3.3 oz (about ½ cup) / **Birds Eye**	3
Chopped: ½ cup / **Seabrook Farms**	4
Creamed: 3 oz (about ½ cup) / **Birds Eye** Combinations	6
Creamed: 1 cup / **Green Giant**	21
Creamed: ½ cup / **Seabrook Farms**	6.5
Leaf: 3.3 oz (about ½ cup) / **Birds Eye**	3
Leaf: ½ cup / **Seabrook Farms**	4
Souffle: 1 cup / **Green Giant** Bake 'n Serve	27
Souffle: ⅓ pkg / **Stouffer's**	12
Squash, cooked, frozen: 4 oz / **Birds Eye**	11
Squash, cooked, frozen: ½ cup / **Seabrook Farms**	11
Squash, summer, in cheese sauce, frozen: 1 cup / **Green Giant** Boil-in-Bag	16
Squash, summer, sliced, frozen: 3.3 oz (about ½ cup) / **Birds Eye**	3
Stew, vegetable, canned: 7½ oz / **Dinty Moore**	18
Stew, vegetable, frozen: 3 oz / **Ore-Ida**	13
Succotash	
Canned: 1 cup / **Stokely-Van Camp**	35
Frozen: 3.3 oz (about ½ cup) / **Birds Eye**	17
Frozen: ½ cup / **Seabrook Farms**	19.5

GRAMS

w cream style corn, canned: 1 cup / **Libby's** 45
w whole kernel corn, canned: 1 cup /
    Libby's 35
Tomato paste, canned
    Contadina / 6 oz 35
    Del Monte / 6 oz 34
    Hunt's / 3 oz 15
    Town House / ⅔ cup 35
Tomato puree, canned: 1 cup / **Contadina** 27
Tomatoes, canned: 1 cup unless noted
    Stewed / **Contadina** 18
    Stewed / **Del Monte** 16
    Stewed: 4 oz / **Hunt's** 8
    Stewed / **Libby's** 15
    Stewed / **Stokely-Van Camp** 15
    Stewed / **Town House** 18
    Wedges / **Del Monte** 14
    Whole / **Del Monte** 10
    Whole: 4 oz / **Hunt's** 5
    Whole / **Libby's** 10
    Whole: ½ cup / **S and W Nutradiet** 4.1
    Whole / **Stokely-Van Camp** 10
    Whole / **Town House** 11
Turnip greens
    Chopped, canned: 1 cup /
        Stokely-Van Camp 7
    Chopped, frozen: 3.3 oz (about ½ cup) /
        Birds Eye 2
    Chopped, frozen: ½ cup / **Seabrook Farms** 3.5
    Chopped w diced turnips, frozen: 3.3 oz
        (about ½ cup) / **Birds Eye** 3
    Leaf, frozen: ½ cup / **Seabrook Farms** 3.5
Zucchini, frozen: 3.3 oz (about ½ cup) /
    Birds Eye 3
Zucchini sticks, in light batter: 3 oz /
    Mrs. Paul's 23

GRAMS

Zucchini, in tomato sauce, canned: 1 cup /
   Del Monte   16

Vegetable Juices

GRAMS

6 oz glass unless noted

Sauerkraut, canned / **Libby's**	4
Tomato	
Bottled / **Welch's**	7.5
Canned / **Campbell**	8
Canned / **Del Monte**	8
Canned / **Libby's**	8
Canned / **S and W Nutradiet**	4.2
Canned / **Sacramento Plus**	7
Canned: 4 fl oz / **Seneca**	5.7
Canned: 1 cup / **Stokely-Van Camp**	9
Canned / **Town House**	8
Tomato cocktail, canned / **Ortega Snap-E-Tom**	6.8
Tomato-flavored cocktail, bottled or canned / **Mott's "Beefamato"**	15
Tomato-flavored cocktail, bottled or canned / **Mott's "Clamato"**	19
Tomato-flavored cocktail, bottled or canned / **Mott's "Nutrimato"**	17
Vegetable cocktail, canned	
S and W Nutradiet	4.2
Town House	8
"V-8"	8
"V-8" Spicy Hot	8
Low sodium / **"V-8"**	8

Wines and Distilled Spirits

GRAMS

All straight liquors—gin, rum, vodka, whiskey,
bourbon, brandy, tequila, etc: any
amount, all brands   trace

4 fl oz

Altar, red / **Gold Seal**	11.8
Altar, red / **Henri Marchant**	11.8
Bordeaux	
Red / **B & G** Margaux	.5
Red / **B & G** Prince Noir	.5
Red / **B & G** St. Emilion	.9
White / **B & G** Graves	.8
White / **B & G** Haut Sauternes	11.6
White / **B & G** Prince Blanc	.8
White / **B & G** Sauternes	10.1
Burgundy	
Red / **B & G** Beaujolais St. Louis	.1
Red / **Gold Seal**	.9
Red / **Gold Seal** Natural	.9
Red / **Henri Marchant**	.9
Red / **Henri Marchant** Natural	.9
Red / **B & G** Nuits St. George	.7
Red / **B & G** Pommard	.5
Red / **Taylor**	4.4
Sparkling / **Gold Seal**	4.7
Sparkling / **Henri Marchant**	4.7
Sparkling / **Taylor**	5.6

GRAMS

White / **B & G** Chablis	.1
White / **B & G** Pouilly Fuisse	.4
White / **B & G** Puligny Montrachet	.4
White / **Gold Seal**	.9
White / **Henri Marchant**	.9
Catawba	
Pink / **Gold Seal**	11.8
Pink / **Henri Marchant**	11.8
Pink / **Manischewitz**	13
Pink / **Taylor**	12.1
Red / **Gold Seal**	11.2
Red / **Henri Marchant**	11.2
White / **Gold Seal**	11.8
White / **Henri Marchant**	11.8
Chablis	
Gold Seal	2.1
Gold Seal Nature	1.5
Henri Marchant	2.1
Henri Marchant Nature	1.5
Taylor	4.4
Rose / **Gold Seal**	4.4
Rose / **Henri Marchant**	4.4
Champagne	
Gold Seal Blanc de Blancs	1.8
Gold Seal Brut	2.1
Gold Seal Extra Dry	4.4
Henri Marchant Blanc de Blancs	1.8
Henri Marchant Brut	2.1
Henri Marchant Extra Dry	4.4
Mumm's Cordon Rouge Brut	1.9
Mumm's Extra Dry	7.4
Taylor Brut	4.4
Taylor Dry	5.3
Pink / **Gold Seal**	4.7
Pink / **Henri Marchant**	4.7
Pink / **Taylor**	6.5

GRAMS

Claret / **Taylor**	3.2
Cold Duck / **Gold Seal**	4.7
Cold Duck / **Henri Marchant**	4.7
Cold Duck / **Taylor**	8.9
Concord	
Cream red / **Manischewitz**	22
Cream white / **Manischewitz**	13
Dry / **Manischewitz**	1
Medium Dry / **Manischewitz**	11
Red / **Gold Seal**	11.8
Red / **Henri Marchant**	11.8
Labrusca	
Gold Seal	11.8
Henri Marchant	11.8
Red / **Henri Marchant**	8.6
White / **Henri Marchant**	7.4
Lake Country	
Taylor Gold	7.3
Pink / **Taylor**	6.5
Red / **Taylor**	6.5
White / **Taylor**	5.6
Madeira / **Gold Seal**	6.5
Madeira / **Henri Marchant**	6.5
Malaga / **Manischewitz** American Extra Dry	26
Moselle / **Julius Kayser's** Graacher Himmelreich	3.3
Moselle / **Julius Kayser's** Piesporter Reisling	2.3
Moselle / **Julius Kayser's** Zeller Schwarze Katz	4
Niagara, cream white / **Manischewitz**	13
Pinot / **Gold Seal** Chardonnay	.9
Pinot / **Henri Marchant** Chardonnay	.9
Port	
Gold Seal	12.1
Henri Marchant	12.1
Taylor	17.9
Ruby / **Gold Seal**	12.1
Ruby / **Henri Marchant**	12.1

GRAMS

Tawny / **Gold Seal**	12.1
Tawny / **Henri Marchant**	12.1
Tawny / **Taylor**	16.2
Pouilly Fume / **B & G**	.1
Rhine	
Gold Seal	2.4
Henri Marchant	2.4
Julius Kayser's Liebfraumilch Glockenspiel	2.4
Julius Kayser's Niersteiner	1.2
Taylor	4.1
Rhone / **B & G** Chateauneuf du Pape	.7
Riesling / **Gold Seal** Johannisberg	2.7
Riesling / **Henri Marchant** Johannisberg	2.7
Rose / **Gold Seal** Vin	4.4
Rose / **Henri Marchant** Vin	4.4
Rose / **Taylor**	5.3
Sancerre / **B & G**	.4
Sangria / **Taylor**	14.6
Sauterne	
Gold Seal Dry	3.8
Gold Seal Haut Altar	6.8
Henri Marchant Dry	3.8
Henri Marchant Haut Altar	6.8
Taylor	6.5
Sherry	
Gold Seal	7.4
Henri Marchant	7.4
Taylor	12.1
Cocktail / **Gold Seal**	2.4
Cocktail / **Henri Marchant**	2.4
Cocktail / **Taylor**	6.1
Cream / **Gold Seal**	13.6
Cream / **Henri Marchant**	13.6
Cream / **Taylor**	17.9
Vermouth, dry / **Taylor**	4.1
Vermouth, sweet / **Noilly Prat**	16.1
Vermouth, sweet / **Taylor**	16.7

Y east

	GRAMS
Bakers: 1 oz	3.1
Brewer's, debittered: 1 tbsp	3.1
Brewer's, debittered: 1 oz	10.9
Dry, active: ¼ oz pkg / **Fleischmann's**	3
Dry, active, in jar: ¼ oz / **Fleischmann's**	3
Fresh, active: .6 oz pkg / **Fleischmann's**	2
Household: .5 oz / **Fleischmann's**	2
Torula: 1 oz	10.5

Yogurt

	GRAMS
1 cup unless noted (8 oz = ⅞ to 9/10 cup)	
All flavors: 8 oz container / **Dannon**	32
All flavors w fruit: 8 oz container / **Dannon**	49
All fruit flavors / **Lucerne** Lowfat	46
Apple, spiced / **Borden** Swiss Style	45.3
Apricot / **Borden** Swiss Style	45.3
Apricot / **Sealtest Light n' Lively** Lowfat	47
Apricot / **Viva** Swiss Style Lowfat	47
Black cherry / **Sealtest Light n' Lively** Lowfat	45

GRAMS

Black cherry / **Viva** Swiss Style Lowfat	47
Blackberry / **Viva** Swiss Style Lowfat	47
Blueberry	
Borden Swiss Style	45.3
Europa / 6 oz container	37
Meadow Gold Western Sundae Style Lowfat	49
Sealtest Light n' Lively Lowfat	47
Viva Swiss Style Lowfat	47
Blueberry-vanilla / **Sealtest Light n' Lively** Lowfat	45
Boysenberry / **Borden** Swiss Style	45.3
Boysenberry / **Meadow Gold** Western Sundae Style Lowfat	49
Boysenberry / **Viva** Swiss Style Lowfat	47
Cherry / **Borden** Swiss Style	45.3
Cherry: 6 oz container / **Europa**	37
Cherry-vanilla / **Borden** Swiss Style	45.3
Coffee / **Borden** Swiss Style	45.3
Cranberry-orange / **Borden** Swiss Style	45.3
Fruit salad / **Viva** Swiss Style Lowfat	47
Lemon / **Sealtest Light n' Lively** Lowfat	45
Lemon / **Viva** Swiss Style Lowfat	47
Lemon-lime / **Viva** Swiss Style Lowfat	49
Lemon-lime-flavored / **Sealtest Light n' Lively** Lowfat	45
Lime / **Borden** Swiss Style	45.3
Orange, mandarin / **Borden** Swiss Style	45.3
Orange, mandarin / **Meadow Gold** Western Sundae Style Lowfat	47
Orange, mandarin / **Sealtest Light n' Lively** Lowfat	45
Orange, mandarin / **Viva** Swiss Style Lowfat	44
Peach	
Borden	51.4
Europa / 6 oz container	37
Meadow Gold Western Sundae Style Lowfat	47
Sealtest Light n' Lively Lowfat	48
Viva Swiss Style Lowfat	44

GRAMS

Peach Melba / **Sealtest Light n' Lively** Lowfat	48
Pear / **Borden** Swiss Style	45.3
Pineapple / **Meadow Gold** Western Sundae Style Lowfat	49
Pineapple / **Sealtest Light n' Lively** Lowfat	50
Pineapple-coconut / **Viva** Swiss Style Lowfat	47
Pineapple-orange / **Viva** Swiss Style Lowfat	47
Plain	
Borden Lite-Line Lowfat	18
Borden Swiss Style	19.4
Dannon / 8 oz container	17
Europa / 6 oz container	11
Lucerne Lowfat	17
Sealtest Light n' Lively Lowfat	19
Prune / **Borden** Swiss Style	45.3
Prune: 8 oz / **Light n' Lively**	50.8
Raspberry	
Borden	52.9
Europa / 6 oz container	37
Meadow Gold Western Sundae Style Lowfat	49
Sealtest Light n' Lively Lowfat	42
Viva Swiss Style Lowfat	47
Red cherry / **Viva** Swiss Style Lowfat	47
Strawberry	
Borden	50
Europa / 6 oz container	37
Meadow Gold Western Sundae Style Lowfat	49
Sealtest Light n' Lively Lowfat	46
Viva Swiss Style Lowfat	47
Strawberry-banana / **Sealtest Light n' Lively** Lowfat	55
Strawberry fruit cup / **Sealtest Light n' Lively** Lowfat	48
Vanilla / **Borden**	30.9
Vanilla: 8 oz / **Light n' Lively**	32.7

FROZEN

	GRAMS
Danny Flip / 5 fl oz	37
Danny In-A-Cup / 8 fl oz	20
Danny Parfait / 4 fl oz	35
Danny Sampler / 3 fl oz	14
Danny-Yo / 3½ fl oz	21
Fruit: 8 fl oz / **Danny** In-A-Cup	42
Peach: ½ cup / **Sealtest**	23
Red raspberry: ½ cup / **Sealtest**	23
Vanilla: ½ cup / **Sealtest**	23
Bars	
Carob-coated: 1 bar / **Danny** On-A-Stick	13
Chocolate- coated: 1 bar / **Danny** On-A-Stick	13
Uncoated: 1 bar / **Danny** On-A-Stick	13
Yosicle / 2½ fl oz	17

FAST FOODS

Fast Foods

ARBY'S

	GRAMS
Roast Beef Sandwich	32
Beef and Cheese Sandwich	36
Super Roast Beef Sandwich	61
Junior Roast Beef Sandwich	21
Swiss King Sandwich	55
Ham 'N Cheese Sandwich	33
Turkey Sandwich	36
Turkey Deluxe Sandwich	46
Club Sandwich	43

ARTHUR TREACHER'S

Fish—two pieces	25
Chicken—two pieces	17
Shrimp—7 pieces	27
Chips	35
Krunch Pup	12
Cole Slaw	11
Lemon Luvs	35
Chowder	11
Fish Sandwich	40
Chicken Sandwich	44

BURGER CHEF

Hamburger	24
Cheeseburger	24

GRAMS

Double Cheeseburger	24
Big Shef	35
Super Shef	39
Skipper's Treat	47
French Fries	25
Shakes	47
Mariner Platter	85
Rancher Platter	44

BURGER KING

Whopper	51
Double Beef Whopper	54
Whopper w Cheese	54
Double Beef Whopper w Cheese	55
Whopper Junior	31
Whopper Junior w Cheese	32
Whopper Jr. w Double Meat	32
Whopper Jr. Double Meat Pattie w Cheese	33
Hamburger	30
Hamburger w Cheese	31
Double Meat Hamburger	32
Double Meat Hamburger w Cheese	33
Steak Sandwich	64
Whaler	54
Whaler w Cheese	55
Onion Rings—Large	36
Onion Rings—Regular	24
French Fries—Large Bag	42
French Fries—Regular Bag	28
Chocolate Milkshake	62
Vanilla Milkshake	55
Apple Pie	32

CARL'S JR.

Famous Star Hamburger	35
Super Star Hamburger	44

	GRAMS
Old Time Star Hamburger	42
Happy Star Hamburger	31
Steak Sandwich	65
California Roast Beef Sandwich	43
Fish Fillet Sandwich	59
Original Hot Dog	28
Chili Dog	34
Chili Cheese Dog	36
American Cheese	1
11 oz Regular Salad w Condiments	26
2 oz Blue Cheese Dressing	0
2 oz Thousand Island Dressing	5
2 oz Lo-Cal Italian Dressing	1
French Fries	33
Onion Rings	35
Apple Turnover	44
Carrot Cake	46
20 oz Shake	59
20 oz Soft Drink	48

CHURCH'S FRIED CHICKEN

1 average piece, boned, dark	6
1 average piece, boned, white	10

DAIRY QUEEN / BRAZIER

Snacks and Desserts

Cone—Small	18
Cone—Regular	35
Cone—Large	52
Chocolate Dipped Cone—Small	20
Chocolate Dipped Cone—Regular	40
Chocolate Dipped Cone—Large	58
Chocolate Sundae—Small	30
Chocolate Sundae—Regular	51
Chocolate Sundae—Large	71

GRAMS

Chocolate Malt—Small	51
Chocolate Malt—Regular	89
Chocolate Malt—Large	125
Float	59
Banana Split	91
Parfait	81
"Fiesta" Sundae	84
Freeze	89
"Mr. Misty" Freeze	87
"Mr. Misty" Float	85
"Dilly" Bar	22
"DQ" Sandwich	24
"Mr. Misty" Kiss	17

Fast Foods

Hamburger	29
Cheeseburger	30
Big "Brazier"	36
Big "Brazier" w Cheese	38
Big "Brazier" w Lettuce and Tomato	36
Super "Brazier" / The "Half-Pounder"	35
Hot Dog	23
Hot Dog w Chili	25
Hot Dog w Cheese	24
Fish Sandwich	41
Fish Sandwich w Cheese	39
French Fries	25
French Fries—Large	40
Onion Rings	33

HARDEE'S

Hamburger	21
Cheeseburger	32
Huskie	41
Big Twin	29
French Fries—Small	28

	GRAMS
French Fries—Large	44
Apple Turnover	37
Milkshake	63
Roast Beef Sandwich	44
Fish Sandwich	42
Hot Dog	26

KENTUCKY FRIED CHICKEN

Chicken Dinner:
3 pieces chicken w mashed potatoes
and gravy, cole slaw, and roll

Original Recipe Dinner	56
Extra Crispy Dinner	63

Individual pieces, Original Recipe:

Wing	4
Drumstick	2
Keel	6
Rib	8
Thigh	12

LONG JOHN SILVER'S SEAFOOD SHOPPES

Fish w Batter	
(2 piece order)	24
Fish w Batter	
(3 piece order)	36
Treasure Chest	
(1 piece fish & 3 peg legs)	27
Chicken Planks	
(4 piece order)	35
Peg Legs w Batter	
(5 piece order)	30
Ocean Scallops	
(6 piece order)	27
Shrimp w Batter	
(6 piece avg order)	31
Breaded Oysters	58

Breaded Clams	46
S.O.S. Super Ocean Sandwich	49
Fryes	32
Cole Slaw	16
Corn on the Cob	29
Hush Puppies	20

MCDONALD'S

Hamburger	30
Cheeseburger	31
Quarter Pounder	33
Quarter Pounder w Cheese	34
Big Mac	39
Filet-O-Fish	34
Egg McMuffin	26
Hot Cakes w Butter and Syrup	89
Scrambled Eggs	2
Pork Sausage	0
English Muffin (Buttered)	28
French Fries	26
Apple Pie	31
Cherry Pie	33
McDonaldland Cookies	45
Chocolate Shake	60
Vanilla Shake	52
Strawberry Shake	57

PIZZA HUT

Serving size: one half of a 10-inch pizza (3 slices)

Thin 'N Crispy Pizza

Beef	51
Pork	51
Cheese	54
Pepperoni	45
Supreme	51

GRAMS

Thick 'N Chewy Pizza
Beef	73
Pork	71
Cheese	71
Pepperoni	68
Supreme	74

STEAK N SHAKE

Steakburger	33.3
Steakburger w Cheese	33.7
Super Steakburger	33.3
Super Steakburger w Cheese	33.7
Triple Steakburger	33.3
Triple Steakburger w Cheese	34.1
Low Calorie Platter	3.3
Baked Ham Sandwich	36.5
Toasted Cheese Sandwich	23.5
Ham & Egg Sandwich	33.3
Egg Sandwich	33.4
Lettuce & Tomato	.8
French Fries	27.7
Chili & Oyster Crackers (⅔ oz)	36.9
Chili Mac and 4 Saltines	34.5
Chili—3 Ways & 4 Saltines	44.6
Baked Beans	26.9
Lettuce & Tomato Salad (1 oz, 1000 Island dressing)	6.9
Chef Salad	6.1
Cottage Cheese (½ cup)	2.9
Apple Danish	35.2
Strawberry Sundae	29.3
Hot Fudge Nut Sundae	50.9
Brownie Fudge Sundae	80.6
Apple Pie	60.6
Cherry Pie	47.9
Apple Pie a la Mode	75.9
Cherry Pie a la Mode	63.2

GRAMS

Cheese Cake	60.9
Cheese Cake w Strawberries	65.1
Brownie	39.1
Vanilla Ice Cream (1½ scoops)	22.9
Vanilla Shake	58.4
Strawberry Shake	61.5
Chocolate Shake	57.1
Orange Freeze	62.8
Lemon Freeze	68.5
Coca-Cola Float	75.7
Orange Float	73.9
Lemon Float	81.8
Root Beer Float	78
Orange Drink	21.6
Lemon Drink	22.3
Orange Juice	24.5
Coffee	0
Hot Tea	.8
Iced Tea	2
Milk	11
Root Beer	29.5
Dr. Pepper	35.7
Hot Chocolate	129.3

TACO BELL

Bean Burrito	48
Beef Burrito	37
Beefy Tostada	21
Bellbeefer	23
Bellbeefer w Cheese	23
Burrito Supreme	43
Combination Burrito	43
Enchirito	42
Pintos 'N Cheese	21
Taco	14
Tostada	25

GRAMS

WHITE CASTLE

French Fries	27
Cheeseburger	18
Hamburger	18
Fish (wo tartar sauce)	20

Index

ABOUT THE AUTHOR

JEAN CARPER is a free-lance writer, specializing in consumer and health subjects. She has written numerous articles for national magazines (*Reader's Digest, Consumer Reports, Saturday Review, Today's Health*) in the medical field, including articles on food. She is the author of seven other books: *Stay Alive!; Bitter Greetings: The Scandal of the Military Draft; The Dark Side of the Marketplace* (co-written with Senator Warren G. Magnuson); *Not With A Gun; The All-In-One Calorie Counter; The All-In-One Low Fat Gram Counter;* and *Eating May be Hazardous to Your Health.* Ms. Carper writes a syndicated column for *Princeton Features* and is the national consumer reporter for Westinghouse Broadcasting. She is a graduate of Ohio Wesleyan University and lives in Washington, D.C.

How's Your Health?

Bantam publishes a line of informative books, written by top experts to help you toward a healthier and happier life.

SPECIAL
MONEY SAVING
OFFER

Now you can have an up-to-date listing of Bantam's hundreds of titles plus take advantage of our unique and exciting bonus book offer. A special offer which gives you the opportunity to purchase a Bantam book for only 50¢. Here's how!

By ordering any five books at the regular price per order, you can also choose any other single book listed (up to a $4.95 value) for just 50¢. Some restrictions do apply, but for further details why not send for Bantam's listing of titles today!

Just send us your name and address plus 50¢ to defray the postage and handling costs.